Equity in the

Equity in the Classroom

*Essays on Curricular
and Pedagogical Approaches
to Empowering All Students*

Edited by TODD M. MEALY
and HEATHER BENNETT

McFarland & Company, Inc., Publishers
Jefferson, North Carolina

ISBN (print) 978-1-4766-8703-2
ISBN (ebook) 978-1-4766-4658-9

LIBRARY OF CONGRESS AND BRITISH LIBRARY
CATALOGUING DATA ARE AVAILABLE

Library of Congress Control Number 2022046371

Front cover: photograph by Monkey Business Images/Shuttertstock

Printed in the United States of America

*McFarland & Company, Inc., Publishers
Box 611, Jefferson, North Carolina 28640
www.mcfarlandpub.com*

For everyone at the National Institute
for Customizing Education.
—Todd M. Mealy

For the teachers, administrators, and school board
directors committed to disrupting systems of oppression
and empowering student voice and advocacy.
—Heather Bennett

Table of Contents

Introduction

TODD M. MEALY *and* HEATHER BENNETT

Since the inception of free public education, educators have explored ways to make teaching and learning accessible and responsive to all students. But in 1888, after efforts by state and national equal rights leagues to desegregate schools across the country resulted in little changes to curricular and general educational equity, William Howard Day, the first Black school board president in the United States, felt compelled to characterize public schools as the "People's College." The school system "belongs to the people, and is for the benefit of the people," he said. "It borrows its eminence not simply from its curriculum, but from the usefulness with which it is intended to serve the whole people, high or low, rich or poor, in the graded and necessary preparations for American duties ... this is the *people's college*" (Mealy, 2020, p. 9).

Since then, a marginalized group in the education community has questioned traditional practices for framing curricula and pedagogy through values exclusive to the dominant culture. Drawing on the experiences of Black students at a small number of newly integrated schools in the North in the late 19th century, Day identified curricular flaws in the school system that have endured ever since. In theory, he said, schools are supposed to be an academy for all students. In practice, however, schools defaulted to dominant values.

Day's assertion was not an isolated moment in history. In fact, the push for curricular equity has existed as a rich and inspirational movement to rectify the problems of academic inequity and aversion to school systems for many decades. While curricular equity exists as a byproduct of the demand for culturally responsive curricula and pedagogies dating back to Day's era, it was in 1967 when Black college students attending both historically Black colleges and predominantly White institutions embarked on a nationwide campus disruption movement to make the campus experience more inclusive and representative of a diverse nation. The final three years of the Sixties witnessed Black students sitting in or seizing administrative buildings while demanding Black studies programs and reforms to colorblind academic offerings that promoted and celebrated Black culture and history (Rogers/Kendi, 2012). Those efforts suggested that the solutions to the problems of the American education system could be resolved if confronted with a culturally responsive lens. Educators have since argued that culturally responsive pedagogy (Ladson Billings, 1994; Gay, 1994) can mitigate antipathy toward the school system by providing all students with learning opportunities, regardless of their gender, race, ethnicity, class, first language, religion, or ability. The practice now utilizes strategies that integrate diverse assessments, empower students to share personal testimonies tied to the content, and challenge teachers to understand each student's learning needs and styles.

While one is an instructional practice and the other is a philosophical framework, culturally responsive teaching and curricular equity work in their own ways to close gaps in academic achievement, discipline, attendance, programming, hiring, and student and faculty retention. They have been both buttressed and supported by critical pedagogy (Freire, 1970; Giroux, 2011), culturally sustaining pedagogy (Paris and Alim, 2017), equity literacy (Gorski, 2017; Muhammad, 2020) and antiracist or abolitionist pedagogy (Love, 2019). For as much as educators enter the field to mold our nation's future leaders, issues of race, sexuality, class, religion, and cultural arrogance along with both willful and unintentional ignorance have always existed as barriers to doing what is best for *all* of America's students.

Part of the reason for this is that culturally responsive principles, while simple in themselves, can be difficult within the context and universe of a school community, especially when politics and power are so influential in the direction of a school district. The reason for the gulf between the public's and educators' perceptions of what is best for all students is driven by political maneuvering that frames any mention of race, sex, and culture as an attempt to brainwash students into hating America. The most unrelenting attack has been on Critical Race Theory, a legal framework often conflated to be the same thing as culturally responsive pedagogy and curricular equity. To be candid, neither culturally responsive teaching nor curricular equity should be confused with Critical Race Theory (CRT). Founded by legal scholars in the 1980s to reassess personal interests in landmark legislative and judicial civil rights victories along with the ubiquity of racism in American institutions, CRT is a diagnostic approach of seeing race as fixed within power systems (Bell, 1993; Delgado, 1984; Crenshaw, 1991). Yes indeed, this legal framework has evolved into an intellectual lens that helps academics critique society across disciplines. Asian Critical Theory, Gender Studies, Women's Studies, Poverty Studies, Ethnic Studies, and Educational Criticism, which have endured a firestorm of conservative political attacks since the final year of the Trump Administration, have long helped legal scholars and largely higher education instructors problematize the education system in America and abroad. The critical legal theory, with its derivatives, exists to help prognosticators offer solutions to prevailing institutional problems. Critical race theorists strive to move the country toward a more perfect, more democratic, and more inclusive union.

Despite resistance from within and outside the field of education, scholars have pressed for curricular equity to close outcome gaps and to make PK–12 schools, colleges, and universities inclusive and unbiased spaces. The authors of this book offer its readers material to reconsider approaches to ensure fair and just representation in the classroom. Let us be clear: the editors of this volume believe in a heterodox commitment to ideological diversity as much as we believe in diversity within categories such as race, sexuality, class, and ability. When placing the call for contributors, we reached out to liberal and conservative educators alike from both PK–12 and collegiate levels. We wanted this book to become the prototype for balancing diverse perspectives and ideas equitably from primary and secondary teachers to school counselors, from district leadership to school board members, and from college professors to university administrators. We believe in bringing diverse people together to debate personal convictions, to confront one's socialization process, to challenge even the veteran teacher to evolve their praxis so it benefits a protean student demographic, and to create solutions. Students should leave their school different from who they were upon entering. The same holds for educators. Regrettably, not everyone we hoped answered the call for essays.

We are, nevertheless, very excited about our authors. In fact, we are over the moon about the range of our authors (Note: this is the first of a two-volume publication). This book has something for everyone. Elementary teachers will gain tools for utilizing picture books to teach young students positive representations about the varying cultures of their peers. Several of our authors provide culturally responsive pedagogies for secondary and postsecondary instructors. Recognizing that educators commonly label the successful students from those most at-risk of failing, one essay provides mentoring and counseling strategies for those who work tirelessly to prevent voiceless students from going unnoticed. Readers will learn how one teacher uses the applied theater classroom as a space for liberation. Another essay targeting school directors shares case studies in how the Covid-19 pandemic reinforced the need for district-wide equity policies in rural, suburban, and urban districts. Several authors undertook ethnographic and qualitative studies on social justice pedagogies and dis/ability services in higher education. We are also very excited about our essays on culturally responsive teaching in the STEM field.

Table 1.1 Areas Addressed by Essay

Essay	College Educators	6–12 Educators	PK–5 Educators	Counselors	Humanities	STEM	Special Ed	Drama	School Board
O'Neill	X	X			X				
Ross					X	X			
Torres	X	X				X			
Matthews & Banks	X	X				X			
Herard			X	X					
Chesnakas	X	X			X				
Jones & Rolle	X	X	X	X					
Teo	X	X			X				
Akbar et al.									X
Perro & Nelson	X	X	X						
Rutledge & Parker	X			X					
Slanda et al.	X			X			X		
Masterpaul	X	X		X				X	

In particular, Monique S. Ross explains how to make computer sciences more welcoming for Students of Color.

This volume includes a special contribution from journalist Connor Towne O'Neill, bestselling author of *Down Along with That Devil's Bones: A Reckoning with Monuments, Memory, and the Legacy of White Supremacy.* Using Confederate imagery, O'Neill provides educators a syllabus for using context to facilitate discussions on hot-button topics. It is a timely piece for our age.

Overall, this first of two volumes publication aims to chart a new and inclusive direction for curricular equity. Our closing thought is to challenge scholars and educational critics of all ideologies and walks of life to engage with one another. Covid-19 and the racial reckoning of 2020 have enabled new possibilities for our field—despite the ugly political maneuvering of 2021 and 2022. Teachers don't just teach subjects like history. They teach *students* subjects like history. We, educators, should be empathetic for all students. Their emotional and intellectual needs must come first. To get there, students need everyone engaging in this discussion rather than canceling one another and censoring critical philosophical ideas that have proven to be the mode by which our nation improves. It is the only way to make our schools an actual *people's college* that belongs to the students and functions to benefit the students.

REFERENCES

Bell, Derrick. (1993). *Faces at the Bottom of the Well: The Permanence of Racism.* New York: Basic Books.

Crenshaw, Kimberle. (1991). "Mapping the Margins: Intersectionality, Identity Politics, and Violence Against Women of Color." *Stanford Law Review,* 43(6).

Delgado (1984). *Critical Race Theory: An Introduction,* 2nd edition. New York: NYU Press.

Freire, Paulo. (1970). *Pedagogy of the Oppressed.* London: Bloomsbury Academic.

Gay, Geneva. (1994). "Coming of Age Ethnically: Teaching Young Adolescents of Color." *Theory Into Practice,* 33(3), 149–155.

Giroux, Henry A. (2011). *On Critical Pedagogy.* London: Bloomsbury.

Gorski, Paul C. (2017). *Reaching and Teaching Students in Poverty: Strategies for Erasing the Opportunity Gap.* New York: Columbia Teacher's College Press.

Ladson-Billings, Gloria. (1994). *The Dreamkeepers: Successful Teachers of African American children.* San Francisco: Jossey-Bass.

Love, Bettina L. (2019). *We Want to Do More Than Survive: Abolitionist Teaching and the Pursuit of Educational Freedom.* Boston: Beacon Press.

Mealy, Todd M. (2020). *Race Conscious Pedagogy: Disrupting Racism at Majority White Schools.* Jefferson, NC: McFarland.

Muhammad, Gholdy. (2020). *Cultivating Genius: An Equity Framework for Culturally and Historically Responsive Literacy.* New York: Scholastic Teaching Resources.

Paris, Django, and H. Samy Alim. (2017). *Culturally Sustaining Pedagogies: Teaching and Learning for Justice in a Changing World.* New York: Columbia University Teacher's College Press.

Rogers (Kendi), Ibram H. (2012). *Black Campus Movement: Black Students and the Radical Reconstitution of Higher Education, 1965–1972.* New York: Palgrave Macmillan.

In the Context
of "Additional Context"

A Syllabus

Connor Towne O'Neill

The summer of 2020 will be remembered—along with its many calamities, reckonings, and uprisings—as the season of the toppled monument. Nearly 100 Confederate monuments alone have been torn down since the spring of 2020, as protesters descend on them as a means to express their grief and rage over the murders of Breonna Taylor, Ahmaud Arbery, and George Floyd, to name only three people recently killed for being Black in America. Still, more than 1500 public symbols of the Confederacy remain. This is due, in part, to rear-guard actions by legislatures in many states that constrain removal efforts—"historical preservation" their stated rationale. In response, whether stymied by such laws or simply seeking compromise on a polarizing issue, some municipalities have chosen to provide "additional context" to the signage on Confederate monuments. Franklin, Tennessee's, city council recently voted to install markers near their Confederate monument which include information on the role of U.S. Colored Troops in the Civil War as well on the history of the slave market which once operated where the monument now stands. Meanwhile, county commissioners in Jackson, North Carolina, voted to keep their Confederate monument but cover the image of the Confederate flag on the pedestal with the phrase "E Pluribus Unum." Such efforts, though well intentioned, are insufficient and likely ineffective. Yes, we desperately need interventions into Lost Cause and, more broadly, American exceptionalist ideologies. But such interventions would be better suited to the classroom than a plaque on the courthouse square.

This "third way" of additional context in the monument debate is something that has come up often in my reporting on Confederate monuments. I've spent the past six years covering campaigns to remove monuments of the Confederate General Nathan Bedford Forrest, interviewing the activists working to take them down as well as his defenders fighting to keep the monuments up. And there are no shortage of contested symbols. In Forrest's home state of Tennessee alone, more markers are dedicated to him than there are to all three Presidents who hail from the state combined—over thirty in all. The plaque on a Forrest monument is likely to recount only a partial resume of the cavalry leader, reciting his nicknames and *nom de guerre*: Wizard of the Saddle, The First with the Most, The Untutored Genius. What's left out? Well, his titles as slave trader, the Butcher of Fort Pillow, the first Grand Wizard of the Ku Klux Klan. Which is to say: he is one of the most infamous and controversial figures from the Civil War era and the debates over his monuments have been heated affairs.

One of the stories I followed in my reporting was the campaign to change the name of Forrest Hall at Middle Tennessee State University. MTSU is a big school—some 20,000 undergrads. And a diverse one, too: people of color make up nearly a third of the student body. But MTSU is in Murfreesboro, a predominantly white town in a part of the state with a reputation for conservativism and Confederate sympathizing. The school, too, has a long history of wielding Confederate symbols. Over the years, Forrest has appeared everywhere from the top of the school's stationery to a massive bronze medallion displayed on the front of the student center to the school's mascot: a student with a likeness to Forrest patrolling the sidelines of football games on horseback and in full Confederate uniform. "Happiness," as the school yearbook once put it, "is having your own Confederate flag to fly at football games." Perhaps unsurprisingly then, almost immediately upon desegregation, those symbols came under fire from students of color. Hard-fought battles over the decades have brought about the removal of the medallion from the student center and a ride into the sunset for the mascot. By 2015, the last major Confederate symbol on campus was the ROTC building which bore Forrest's name. Following the Charleston Nine murders and inspired by activist Bree Newsome's removal of the Confederate flag from the South Carolina Statehouse, students at MTSU launched a campaign to rename Forrest Hall. It was an honorific the students saw as racist, demeaning, and wholly out of step with a university claiming values of inclusion and diversity. In response, the university did what universities so often do: they started a task force. Their mandate? Take the year, hold forums, hear testimony from stakeholders both on campus and in the wider community, and decide: should MTSU change the name, keep the name, or keep the name with additional context?

I have to admit that, early in the reporting of this story, I was intrigued by the proposed "third way" of additional context. Wouldn't there be some power in truth-telling? Why not put up a plaque detailing the school's decision to name a building for the first Grand Wizard of the Klan in the middle of the civil rights movement? Why not connect some dots between the Civil War, the civil rights movement, and today? Why not break the deafening silence that attends so many discussions of the Civil War or, more broadly, about the ways race in America is used to maintain a deeply unequal society?

Partly I was open to such a move because as I was digging into the so-called "additional context" of Confederate monuments—where they came from, why they were still here, what they said about where the United States was headed—I was coming to feel like, in some pretty fundamental ways, I didn't understand my country. Or rather that I didn't live in a country that I'd so long told myself I lived in. In other words, like a growing number of white Americans, I was belatedly coming to understand how this country's terrifying notions of race had shaped its history, its present, and me. It's been a belated, transformative, and often discomfiting set of realizations.

I mean, I knew those statues were wrong at the outset of my reporting, sure. But gathering the relevant "additional context" about these statues in my research and reporting allowed me to better fathom the depth of that wrong. Such work involved charting not just the harm of slavery—its physical and spiritual torture—but its central, catalytic, role in creating country's modern economy. Likewise, I had to grapple with the lasting injury of the white supremacist ideology used to justify that system, an ideology that long outlived emancipation and morphed into less conspicuous but no less pernicious forms of exclusionary, violent, wealth- and power-hoarding policies, from the Homestead Act to the GI Bill, FHA loans to redlining, state-sanctioned lynchings to the War on Drugs, gerrymandering to school segregation—all enforcing a racial hierarchy that, among countless other inequities, has left the country with a ten-to-one racial wealth gap. Such "additional context" insisted that my writing on Confederate monuments reckon with the terror and pain of America's history. That context likewise insisted that I reckon with the terror and pain of America's present. That context was, in a sense, the gap between what white Americans tell themselves about this country and its lived reality. All to say, I found all this additional context powerful, enlightening, harrowing. And that additional context became the basis of the book I wrote. And yet, despite its power, I started to question the efficacy and appropriateness of including all this context at the site of the monument. What would all that context look like on a plaque? Would it even fit? And could it overcome the honor inherently bestowed by the monument to one of the architects of this violent inequity?

In fact, it was a piece of testimony from MTSU that caused me to question the role of additional context at the site of a monument. During one of the debates, a student admitted that they took a more circuitous route to class each morning to avoid walking past Forrest Hall, a building that honored a man who did not think she was human, a man who had made a great fortune trafficking her ancestors, a man who had fought violently for the right to continue to do so. They were familiar with the necessary "additional context," thank you very much, and needed no reminder of it on their walk to a 9:00 a.m. biology class. So long as the school kept honoring Forrest, they'd be insulted, humiliated, alienated on their campus, by their campus. No plaque—no matter how honest or incisive or condemnatory it was—could change that. No plaque could right that wrong.

It's important to remember that monuments like Forrest Hall aren't history; they enshrine and immortalize a figure from history and pull them into the present. As the student's testimony made clear, monuments cannot be contextualized out of the honor they bestow. It was becoming clear to me that such context, even though it felt like a revelation to me, was remedial to others who knew how that history shaped our present, and who experienced the consequences of people like being so naïve about it all. Forrest's name isn't on the front of the building to be a teachable moment about race and racism. It's there because the all-white leaders of a then all-white school wanted to publicly honor a vicious white supremacist at a moment when all-white power structures were being forcefully challenged by the civil rights movement. If that's how the marker would read, why not just change the name instead? "These statues have no business being there in the first place," Jalane Schmidt, a University of Virginia professor who leads tours of Charlottesville's monuments recently told the *Washington Post*. "You're just putting a Band-Aid on it—a little tiny plaque compared to this huge monument."

And, it turns out, such context might be as ineffective as it is insufficient. As Laurajane Smith discovered in her study of monuments and historical sites, efforts to expand the perspectives of America's past often fall on deaf ears. In her new book *Emotional Heritage* Smith notes that a paltry three percent of people she interviewed had learned something substantial after a visit to a monument or historical site like Monticello, which has recently endeavored to highlight information on Thomas Jefferson's slaveholding. Smith notes how many visitors to historic sites are there because they admire this person and so, as a result, a counternarrative will often fall on deaf ears. A new plaque is no match for confirmation bias, it seems. And as city leaders in Helena, Montana, realized (yes, there was a Confederate monument in Montana), they would need a bigger plaque if they wanted to sufficiently contextualize their monument. "It was too massive an amount of information," a city commissioner said. "Ultimately, people thought language was just inadequate."

Look, I recognize the irony here. On the one hand I've just told you that my entire worldview has been upended by delving into the context of these monuments. (Really, in some perverse way, Nathan Bedford Forrest and his monuments have been my most important teachers of American history.) And yet on the other hand I'm saying that, despite its importance, such context is insufficient and ineffective at the site of the monument. The plaque is simply the wrong messenger for this urgent message. So where, then? Well, at the risk of preaching to the choir, the classroom would be a fine start. The book I ended up writing about Confederate monuments is, essentially, the relevant "additional context" obscured by these monuments as they currently stand. (And, it's worth mentioning, a context likewise obscured by the historical education I received as a student.) So what eleventh-hour revelations had I come to in this reporting project that might be more useful for future students to encounter in their history classes? Here, then, are some sources toward a syllabus of additional context.

Let's Start with the Start of the War

As David Blight notes in his terrific series of Yale lectures on the Civil War, the monetary value of those men, women, and children held in bondage in 1860 was approximately 3.5 billion dollars, which tallies as the "largest single asset in the entire U.S. economy. That was worth more than all railroads, more than all manufacturing, all other assets combined." That year, the Mississippi Valley was home to more millionaires per-capita than anywhere else in the country. Lost Cause apologists like to argue that the practice of slavery was outmoded and inefficient and thus destined to be phased out, rendering an abolitionist conflict excessive and tyrannical. But that is just not so, as the figures attest. It was an extremely profitable, viciously extractive system that the Confederates fought to maintain and expand. "What made the cotton economy boom in the United States, and not in all the other far-flung parts of the world with climates and soil suitable to the crop," writes Matthew Desmond in his incisive essay for the *New York Times'* 1619 Project, "was our nation's unflinching willingness to use violence on nonwhite people and to exert its will on seemingly endless supplies of land and labor." It was this system of low-road, racial capitalism, Desmond argues, "which helped turn a poor, fledgling nation into a financial colossus," and we are still grappling with the consequences of such a system today.

It's important to keep this context—the racial violence and the great sums of extracted wealth—in mind when you read the documents central to the founding of the Confederacy. Jefferson Davis, speaking on the floor of the Senate in 1860, laid out a justification for slavery that would become the rationale for the nascent Confederacy. "The condition of slavery with us is, in a word, Mr. President, nothing but the form of civil government instituted for a class of people not fit to govern themselves." That inferiority was, to Davis and to the Confederacy he would go on to lead, a God-given state. As he put it: "the inferiority stamped upon that race of men by the creator." It's this line that Ibram X. Kendi takes for the title of his astounding, crucial text *Stamped from the Beginning: The Definitive History of Racist Ideas in America.* Educators looking to set the racism embodied in Confederate statues in a broader context would do well to look at Kendi's work. A number of illuminating primary sources are collected by Loewen and Sebesta in their useful anthology *The Confederate and Neo-Confederate Reader: The "Great Truth" about the "Lost Cause."*

A year after Davis' speech, soon-to-be Confederate Vice-President Alexander H. Stephens addressed a crowd in Savannah, Georgia. Stephens picked up on Davis's theme as he laid out the rationale for the recent secession of southern states. Their government, he told the crowd, is built "upon the great truth that the negro is not equal to the white man; that slavery subordination to the superior race is his natural and normal condition. This, our new government, is the first, in the history of the world, based upon this great physical, philosophical, and moral truth." They were committed to a slave system and were justifying it, in no uncertain terms, on their foundational belief in white supremacy. Slavery was, he said, "the proper status of the negro in our form of civilization. This was the immediate cause of the late rupture and present revolution." Just weeks later, Confederate troops would fire on Fort Sumter.

And so the war—in no uncertain terms fought on the Confederacy's claimed right to enslave, reserved on their belief in white supremacy—came. Four years, 10,000 military engagements, and 750,000 deaths later, Lee would surrender to Grant in an Appomattox farmhouse. But the 1700 Confederate symbols and statues we've been reckoning with lately did not appear suddenly once the sun went down on that fateful April day in 1865. The Southern Poverty Law Center's "Whose Heritage? Public Symbols of the Confederacy" data project instead identifies two spikes in Confederate honorifics. The first comes in the early twentieth century, decades after the war and likewise after the undermining of Reconstruction, once ex-confederates and white supremacists had returned to power, implemented Jim Crow policies and set about hoisting statues to their heroes. The second spike, with an emphasis on place names—buildings like MTSU or names of schools themselves—came in the 1950s and 1960s. In other words, with the rise of the civil rights movement. Like I said, these monuments are not about the past.

The flooding of public space with Confederate symbols was a part of a broader ideological project, as Henry Louis Gates emphasizes in *Stony the Road: Reconstruction, White Supremacy, and the Rise of Jim Crow*, to enshrine white Americans as heroic and cast Black Americans as inferior. "The privileging of white culture and white people was directly tied to the denigration of black culture and black people in a mutually reinforcing relationship." *Stony the Road* offers a survey of the racist depictions of Black Americans in post-war American culture—think Sambo caricatures and the portrayal of Black men in D.W. Griffith's *Birth of a Nation*. Such depictions, Gates compellingly argues, enshrined stereotypes of Black Americans as incompetent, corrupt, licentious into the very nerve-endings of white Americans north and south. And why? Gates resists letting an analysis of these images stop at congenital racism. "Why in the world was it necessary to produce tens of thousands, perhaps hundreds of thousands, of these separate and distinct racist images to demean the status of the newly freed slaves," Gates asks. Well, simply put: "Three words: Justifying Jim Crow, or, in three different words, disenfranchising black voters."

Harnessing white Americans' deep and often unconscious sense of Black inferiority as justification for the country's racist policies and racial hierarchy was perhaps what Mary Singleton Slack had in mind when, in 1904, in a speech at a meeting of the United Daughters of the Confederacy, she urged those gathered to build, in addition to the monuments of stone and bronze proliferating across the South, "the greatest of all monuments, a thought monument." For more on the role of the United Daughters of the Confederacy in this ideological battle, see Karen L. Cox's *Dixie's Daughters: The United Daughters of the Confederacy and the Preservation of Confederate Culture*.

The central question of the Civil War era was nothing less than this: can a settler, slave society fully transform itself into a multiracial democracy? The very presence of Confederate monuments offers hundreds of conspicuous reminders that we have not yet achieved such a transformation. If we hope to topple the thought monuments along with all the monuments of stone and bronze, there's work to be done in the classroom. That politicians from Missouri to Texas are working to outlaw the discussion of racism in high school classrooms should only reinforce our commitment to doing so, as their proposed legislation betrays their sense of the power of antiracist interventions. Simply appending "E Pluribus Unum" to a statue symbolizing the deep divisions of our society is not enough. We must teach the next generation of students—of citizens—to understand the roots of our divisions. There is power in honesty; there will be no reconciliation without truth. It's my hope that these sources will help facilitate urgent conversations about equity and race, about the influence of the past on our present, and help us envision a more equitable, honest future.

References

Blight, David W. "The Civil War and Reconstruction Era, 1845–1877." Open Yale Courses. Yale University.

Blight, David W. *Race and Reunion: The Civil War in American Memory.* Harvard University Press, 2001.

Cox, Karen L. *Dixie's Daughters: The United Daughters of the Confederacy and the Preservation of Confederate Culture.* University Press of Florida, 2003.

Davis, Jefferson. "Jefferson Davis' Reply in the Senate to William H. Seward." The Papers of Jefferson Davis. Rice University. https://jeffersondavis.rice.edu/archives/documents/jefferson-davis-reply-senate-william-h-seward

Desmond, Matthew. "In Order to Understand the Brutality of American Capitalism, You Have to Start on the Plantation." *New York Times Magazine,* August 14, 2019. https://www.nytimes.com/interactive/2019/08/14/magazine/slavery-capitalism.html

Gates, Henry Louis. *Stony the Road: Reconstruction, White Supremacy, and the Rise of Jim Crow.* Penguin, 2020.

Kendi, Ibram X. *Stamped from the Beginning.* Nation Books, 2016.

Knoepp, Lilly. "Jackson County Gets First Look at Confederate Monument Changes." *Blue Ridge Public Radio.* April 19, 2021. https://www.bpr.org/post/jackson-county-gets-first-look-confederate-monument-changes#stream/0

Loewen, James W., and Edward H. Sebesta. *The Confederate and Neo-Confederate Reader: The "Great Truth" About the "Lost Cause."* University Press of Mississippi, 2010.

McIntosh, Kriston, Emily Moss, Ryan Nunn, and Jay Shambaugh. "Examining the Black-white Wealth Gap." *Brookings Institute.* February 27, 2020.

Middle Tennessee State University. "Forrest Hall Protest Collection." https://digital.mtsu.edu/digital/collection/p15838coll11

Natanson, Hannah. "There's a New Way to Deal with Confederate Monuments: Signs that Explain Their Racist History." *Washington Post,* September 22, 2019. https://www.washingtonpost.com/history/2019/09/22/theres-new-way-deal-with-confederate-monuments-signs-that-explain-their-racist-history/

Smith, Laurajane. *Emotional Heritage: Visitor Engagement at Museums and Heritage Sites.* Routledge, 2020.

Southern Poverty Law Center. "Whose Heritage? Public Symbols of the Confederacy." Last modified February 23, 2021. https://www.splcenter.org/20190201/whose-heritage-public-symbols-confederacy

Stephens, Alexander H. "Cornerstone Speech." 1861. In *Alexander H. Stephens, In Public and Private: With Letters and Speeches, Before, During, and Since the War,* edited by Henry Cleveland. War College Series, 2015.

Thompson, Erin. "Why Just 'Adding Context' to Controversial Monuments May Not Change Minds." *Smithsonian,* December 20, 2020. https://www.smithsonianmag.com/history/why-just-adding-context-controversial-monument-may-not-change-minds-180976583/

Towards an Inclusive and Equitable Future

The Imperative to Broaden Participation in Computing

Monique S. Ross

Introduction

Computers and the software associated with them are rapidly becoming ubiquitous. It is harder and harder to escape their presence and impact. What was, at one time, a tool for expediting mundane tasks and means of increased accuracy for calculations too complicated for one human, has morphed into the purveyor of ideas, beliefs, and goods (Lim et al., 2017). More importantly, software has become the arbiter of matters related to healthcare coverage, prison sentences, child services, and many other pivotal decisions that impact the lives of many, often to the detriment of those most vulnerable (Dressel & Farid, 2018; Eubanks, 2018). Compounded by the rise in use of such programming advancements like artificial intelligence and machine learning, we also see the movement away from the empathy often found in human engagement in favor of the presumed "impartial" algorithms (Feng & Wu, 2019).

In recent years, there has been a movement growing inside and outside of computing that challenges the infallibility of algorithms and their "unintended consequences" called *algorithmic accountability*. Algorithmic accountability is a line of inquiry that challenges the idea that algorithms are merely artifacts developed in isolation or within a bubble free of bias. Instead, algorithms are political, meaning they have power and authority in human associations (Winner, 1980). By extension, this means that algorithms tend to perpetuate the ills associated with the racist structures pervasive in American culture (Leavy, 2018). These ills range from upholding

15

stereotypes and racist tropes to the continued segregation of communities, and disparity in quality of education, jobs, housing, healthcare, and criminal justice system for people of color. Through close analysis of facial recognition software (Leslie, 2020) and extensive research of recidivism software, we know that the same prejudice, bias, and inequity are interwoven in the technology fabric.

One reason why these algorithms are so biased is because they are largely developed by the demographic group most represented in computing, White men (Lunn et al., 2021). This is not to say that White men are intentionally programming algorithms that support and conserve hegemony but instead that in the absence of diversity, equity, and inclusion in computing, we will continue to experience technology that often does not consider the effects on "other" populations (Lee, 2018). Making the call of broadening participation in computing not simply a supply and demand problem—there are too many jobs and not enough White men, so we need to expand to broader participation (Peckham et al., 2007). Nor is it the argument for broadening participation because "diverse teams equate to higher returns on investment for companies" solution. But instead, the call to *broaden participation* is a *social justice* issue (Herring, 2009). If we continue to have participation of only one demographic in computing, we will continue to see injustice perpetuated in computing algorithms.

The purpose of this essay is to create a sense of urgency around broadening participation as well as bring attention to some evidence-based practices in existence in computing classrooms around the country that could aid in making computing more inclusive. The most powerful, being the adoption of culturally responsive teaching (CRT) practices. This work will build the argument for broadening participation in computing to ensure that all readers have a general understanding of the necessity to create pathways to computing for diverse populations as well as retaining them in computing. Then follow up with an exploration of CRT—beginning with the origins and benefits. Next, CRT will be situated within the context of computer science and other related fields, and close with a call to action to the computing community to do the work for the benefit of all.

What Is the Problem?

In 2016, shortly after the U.S. Presidential election, we saw a rise in popular works and news coverage centered on the age of misinformation. Most notably was the attack on Google's algorithm for prioritizing search results. It was discovered through investigative reporting that

Google (along with other tech giants like Facebook, Twitter, etc.) may have been one of the contributing factors to the rapid spread of misinformation (Bump, 2018; Overby, 2017; Caldwalladr, 2016; Solon & Levin, 2016). When these findings were brought to light, tech companies were quick to point to the data—the data is biased, *not* the algorithm (Hooker, 2021). They seemingly washed their hands of any wrongdoing and continued to operate with business as usual. However, simultaneously, investigative journalists, sociologists, and anthropologists were unveiling algorithm after algorithm that demonstrated blatant or covert implementation of bias, discrimination, and prejudice in the algorithms we use daily (Diakopoulos, 2015; Eubanks, 2018; Epstein & Robertson, 2015).

In the fall of 2016, at the annual Grace Hopper Celebration (the largest women in Tech conference in the world) a scholar by the name of LaTanya Sweeney told a story about engaging with a journalist about her amazing work in computing at Harvard University. During her conversation, she decided to share some of her latest work with the journalist by first executing what seemed to be a perfectly harmless search for the artifact. However, when she searched her name, an advertisement appeared that stated—LaTanya Sweeney Arrested? Suddenly, the conversation changed from her contributions to scholarly works and the body of knowledge to her presumed arrest record. After this incredibly embarrassing interaction, she was inspired to conduct a study on this phenomenon of online advertising. Her work would demonstrate that Google's advertising algorithm was not just flawed but that it was biased and discriminatory in its selection of advertisement based on racially coded names (Sweeney, 2013). While results such as these may seem innocuous, it is symptomatic of a much larger problem.

Sweeney's work is just one of many studies that have surfaced that begin to unveil how complex computing systems often embody the ills of society. Another collection of investigative reports in a book by Eubanks (2018) places a spotlight on the use of software to determine (1) if children should be removed from their homes by child protective services, (2) who should be covered by state-funded healthcare, and (3) how the unhoused electronic registry was exploited by the justice system in Los Angeles. Eubanks' assessment revealed that in Alleghany County, Pennsylvania, an algorithm was developed to predict which children might be future victims of abuse or neglect which demonstrated an inconsistent impact (in the best-case scenario) for poor and working-class families in that area. Likewise, in Indiana automation of welfare eligibility resulted in thousands of people losing benefits (including Medicaid) across the state.

Algorithms similar to these are also used to calculate or predict the likelihood a criminal is to re-offend, often referred to as recidivism. An investigation into a tool called COMPAS (which stands for Correctional Offender Management Profiling for Alternative Sanctions) used in Florida was determined to predict that Black defendants were far more likely than White defendants to be incorrectly judged to be at higher risk of recidivism, while White defendants were more likely than Black defendants to be incorrectly flagged as low risk (Larson, Mattu, Kirchner, Angwin, 2016). Given that these tools are often used in pretrial to determine bond eligibility or rates and at sentencing, these tools have an immense impact on people's lives. Similar perpetuation of existing inequality was determined in a health care risk-prediction algorithm that helped hospitals and insurance companies identify patients eligible for specialized care, resulting in higher costs for some patients. In a study published in *Science*, those patients were oftentimes Black patients (Obermeyer, Powers, Vogeli, Mullainathan, 2019).

Noble (2018) coined the phrase *technological redlining*, through her work that centers the ways that technology "[...] reinforce[s] oppressive social relationships and enact new modes of racial profiling [...]" (Noble, 2018, p. 1). She questions one of the main tenets of algorithms—prioritization and pushes the community to be reflective about who and what we prioritize and at whose behest and to whose detriment. Likewise, Benjamin (2019) re-emphasizes the need for technologists to be deliberate in their examination of technology through a critical lens to acknowledge that emerging technology often reinforces White supremacy and deepens social inequity by ignoring the existing racial hierarchies and thus reproducing and sometimes amplifying them.

This spotlighting of biased algorithms has also brought to light a common theme—they often disproportionately affect communities of color, more specifically Black and Brown communities. In child welfare cases, African American and Native Americans are overrepresented in the system (Huggins-Hoyt, 2014). Likewise, evidence indicates that low-income and ethnic minority patients are more likely to be denied claims for their insurance coverage (Smedley et al., 2003). And when you explore homelessness in America, African Americans make up more than 40 percent of the homeless population. In short, these algorithms replicate and, in some cases, exacerbate an already biased, unjust, and oppressive structure that continues to disadvantage the poor, Black, and Brown.

One Solution

One approach to addressing this bias problem is to examine the composition of representation in this field—computing. A current snapshot of

CRT in CS

As early as 2008, scholars have placed a call to action to the computing education community to investigate, adopt, and put into practice the principles of a culturally relevant/responsive curriculum (Goode, 2008). And some scholars and educators have heeded this call by meeting students where they are with regards to pop-technologies. For example, Guzdial (n.d.) leveraged students' propensity for media (social or otherwise) and thus identified an opportunity to develop a Media Computation course that introduced students to computing concepts through the manipulation of media while also centering social issues. Others have elected to center their computing education on the interests of students by providing socially-motivated examples to increase engagement in the discipline and content (Goode, 2008). Drawing on the scholars in mathematics that explored the impact of culturally situated examples to teach math (hair braiding—African American/Black and beading—Indigenous populations, Eglash et al, 2006), computing educators have begun to determine which cultural references and experiences lend themselves to computing concepts. Eglash et al (2013), continues to call on the computing education community to go beyond the pre-canned, long adopted, but outdated examples for implementing computing principles to be mindful of broader populations in order to: honor Indigenous knowledge, explore vernacular culture, encourage/foster civic engagement, and expand who and what we glorify in hacking culture (Eglash, Gilber, Foster, 2013). Eglash (2013) makes the case that Black and Brown people have been "hacking" in the absence of resources for years with no acknowledgment for how these hacks contribute to and enhance the lives of many.

Principles of CRT are not new to computing. Scholars have even begun to coin this translation from education (more broadly) to a computing context with the establishment of culturally responsive computing (CRC) in the K–12 space (Scott, Sheridan, Clark, 2015). CRC was founded on the principles of CRT; however, scholars in computing have expanded on these foundational principles (discussed above) with aspiration of adopting "culturally responsive pedagogical strategies [that] make technologies and technology education accessible to diverse sociocultural groups using asset building approaches" (Scott, Sheridan, Clark, 2015, p. 413). Scott et al. adapted the principles of CRT of asset building, reflection, and connectedness to better align with the "transformative potential of new technologies" (Scott, Sheridan, Clark, 2015, p. 413). This resulted in the following adapted goals/objectives:

1. All students are capable of digital innovation.
2. The learning context supports the transformational use of technology.

3. Learning about self along various intersecting sociocultural lines allows for technical innovation.

4. Technology should be a vehicle by which students reflect and demonstrate understanding of their intersectional identities (Williams, Baert, Williams, 2017).

5. Barometers for technological success should consider who creates, for whom, and to what ends rather than who endures socially and culturally irrelevant curriculum.

The primary objective being that those that build technology, nor the technology that are developed happen in a "cultural neutral context" and thus the products that emerge are not neutral either. In alignment with this principle, scholars have made deliberate decisions to underemphasize the importance of the language and syntax—to avoid privileging those that have prior experience with computing. This approach instead emphasizes the importance of algorithmic thinking and/or computational thinking. It also focuses on the deliberate integration of exercises that target population can relate to, for example the Avengers sample question to teach graph theory using the Washington Metropolitan Area Transit Authority (WMATA) that was integrated into an introductory programming course designed at Howard University (Mejías, Jean-Pierre, Burge, Washington, 2018). The target audience being younger students in that Metropolitan area. It leveraged their knowledge of Avengers and their experiences with the D.C. metro. Similarly, Miller (2014) developed modules that coupled the complexity of machine learning (ML), more specifically natural language processing (NLP) and the ever popular hip-hop to help African American students discover the linguistic power in their culture. Likewise, scholars focusing on engaging with American Indian girls, leveraged the culturally relevant textiles to create a bridge between their identity as American Indian girls and technology (Searle & Kafai, 2015; Kafai, Searle, Martinez, Brayboy, 2014).

Consideration for CRT or CRC has not only served to break down barriers to understanding complex concepts, but it created an environment that was counter to traditional feelings of being "othered" or not belonging in the sphere of computing (Codding, Mouza, Rolón-Dow, Pollock, 2019). Students were encouraged to bring their whole selves into the classroom, embrace their language, their traditions, and their understanding of the world around them into computing.

Negatives/Challenges

Modifications, such as those discussed in prior CRC work, require some awareness about the population of the students an instructor wishes to engage. It does take work to connect the social with the technical and requires a commitment to integrating these seemingly disparate topics. In addition, the connections need to be interwoven in order to have an impact. Students (high school) can often discern the inauthenticity of a brute adaptation (Davis, Lachney, Zatz, Babbitt, Eglash, 2019), and as such, the integration must be thoughtful.

From Principle to Practice

Now that we know that lack of diversity in computing is problematic and that representation in computing is a longstanding problem, we can begin to address some of the issues. One issue is a matter of engagement through inclusion; inclusion through culturally relevant computing. How do we translate the principles of CRT and CRC from K–12 and the sparse examples in high education to a broader audience?

One is to dismantle the notion that we must do it all at once. Instead, the call to action here is to identify the low-hanging fruit and commit to more adaptation over time.

Simple Adaptations:

1. Construct an environment that acknowledges and celebrates the contributions from ALL innovators and theorists (Bradley, Long & Mejía, 2016; McGee, in press; Provenzo et al., 2011; Long, 2020 JEE editorial; Mejías, Jean-Pierre, Burge, Washington, 2018). This includes wall art and other artifacts in the classroom that should represent inventors from diverse racial, ethnic, and gender backgrounds.
   a. Low hanging fruit
2. Become familiar with the communities in which students reside (or have come from) in order to draw on local and culturally relevant examples. Think about the Howard University computing course that designed an assignment around the transit system that all students had to engage with. It was practical, social, and did not require privileged knowledge to understand. Or, for more depth, consider the example of hip-hop drawn on by Miller that drew on students' "funds of knowledge" (personal background knowledge) to solve complex problems.
   a. Requires the time and space to get to know the population more intimately

3.   An alternative approach might be to allow students to pick their project. That is, create opportunities for students to deepen their understanding of the CS content on applications or projects relevant to them (the student) and not always predetermined by the instructor.

    a.   This requires a level of vulnerability on behalf of the instructor. You will not know the answers to questions you let students develop. You may have to struggle a little with them.

    b.   The added bonus is that such practices help to foster a space for students to develop and build personal relationships with computer science concepts and applications (Goode, Chapman, Margolis, 2012)

4.   Honor the fact that very few students have access to computing before college. And thus, our presumption of these students should not be focused on what they do not have but instead uncover what they do (e.g., community cultural wealth, funds of knowledge, and other assets). Likewise, what can they achieve with these long-ignored assets they bring into the classroom and ultimately to computing and tech.

    a.   This is, by far, the hardest and yet more necessary objective/goal—asset framing vs. deficit framing. Reminding ourselves that these students have assets to share in computing; in fact, I would go as far as to say we need them and what they have to share to right the course of computing.

While the CRT purists would argue that surface-level adaptations like changing the "ambient cues" present in the environment is not going far enough, I think those of us resident in computing departments would argue it is a start (Cheryan et al., 2009). A good start is a deliberate and distributed action to keep moving towards a computing curriculum that honors those in the classrooms and exposes those that do not have a shared identity to be exposed to diverse cultural experiences and diverse means of solving complex problems.

Conclusion

Computers are ubiquitous and their algorithms are permeating every facet of our day-to-day lives. Likewise, in the absence of diversity, the outcomes of these algorithms have demonstrated that they can (when unchecked) have harmful effects on historically vulnerable populations—women, Black people, Latiné people, Indigenous people, and the poor. To combat these effects, we MUST engage more diverse populations in computing by creating a truly inclusive environment in which they can thrive. Culturally relevant teaching is a movement towards liberation and freedom (Holly, 2020 JEE Editorial) with a final destination of empowerment (cite empowerment work from AISL grant); empowerment of all people.

GLOSSARY

algorithmic accountability: Algorithmic Accountability examines the process of assigning responsibility for harm when algorithmic decision-making results in discriminatory and inequitable outcomes. https://datasociety.net/library/algorithmic-accountability-a-primer/

algorithmic thinking: is a derivative of computer science and coding. This approach automates the problem-solving process by creating a series of systematic logical steps that process a **defined** set of inputs and produce a defined set of outputs based on these. https://equip.learning.com/computational-thinking-algorithmic-thinking-design-thinking

computational thinking: Computational thinking is a set of skills and processes that enable students to navigate complex problems. https://equip.learning.com/computational-thinking-algorithmic-thinking-design-thinking

critical race theory (CRT): an intellectual movement and loosely organized framework of legal analysis based on the premise that race is not a natural, biologically grounded feature of physically distinct subgroups of human beings but a socially constructed (culturally invented) category that is used to oppress and exploit people of color. https://www.britannica.com/topic/critical-race-theory

culturally responsive computing (CRC): in particular, helps youth examine the relationship between technology, identities, cultures, and communities. https://ncwit.org/blog/news-on-the-radar-1-27-21/

culturally responsive teaching (CRT): is a pedagogy that recognizes the importance of including students' cultural references in all aspects of learning. https://www.brown.edu/academics/education-alliance/teaching-diverse-learners/strategies-0/culturally-responsive-teaching-0

funds of knowledge: describe the historical accumulation of abilities, bodies of knowledge, assets, and cultural ways of interacting. https://www.k12.wa.us/student-success/access-opportunity-education/migrant-and-bilingual-education/funds-knowledge-and-home-visits-toolkit/funds-knowledge

technological redlining: is the perpetuation of racial, cultural, and economic inequities in technologies. https://atnd.medium.com/technological-redlining-how-algorithms-are-dividing-the-country-6939dcc88659

REFERENCES

Bump, P. (2018, March 22). All the ways Trump's campaign was aided by Facebook, ranked by importance. *Washington Post.* https://www.washingtonpost.com/news/politics/wp/2018/03/22/all-the-ways-trumps-campaign-was-aided-by-facebook-ranked-by-importance/.

Caldwalladr, C. (2016, December 4). Google, democracy and the truth about internet search. *The Guardian.* https://www.theguardian.com/technology/2016/dec/04/google-democracy-truth-internet-search-facebook.

Cheryan, S., Plaut, V.C., Davies, P.G., & Steele, C.M. (2009). Ambient belonging: How stereotypical cues impact gender participation in computer science. *Journal of Personality and Social Psychology, 97*(6), 1045.

Codding, D., Mouza, C., Rolón-Dow, C., Pollock, L. (2019). Positionality and belonging: Analyzing an informally situated and culturally responsive computer science program. *Proceedings of 8th annual conference on maker education.*

Cuny, J., Aspray, W. (2001). *Recruitment and retention of women graduate students in computer science and engineering.* The Computer Research Association Committee on the Status of Women in Computing Research.

Davis, J., Lachney, M., Zatz, Z., Babbitt, W., Eglash, R. (2019). A cultural computing curriculum. *SIGCSE.*

Diakopoulos, N. (2015). Algorithmic accountability. *Digital Journalism, 811,* 1–18. http://doi.org/10.1080/21670811.2014.976411.

Eglash, R., Bennett, A., O'Donnell, C., Jennings, S., Cintorino, M. (2006). Culturally situated design tools: Ethnocomputing from field site to classroom. *American Anthropologist, 108*(2), 347–362.

Eglash, R., Gilbert, J., Foster, E. (2013). Broadening participation toward culturally responsive computing education: Improving academic success and social development by merging computational thinking with cultural practices. *Communications of the ACM, 56*(7), 33–36.

Eubanks, V. (2018). *Automating inequality: How high-tech tools profile, police, and punish the poor.* St. Martin's Press.

Favero, T.G., & Van Hoomissen, J.D. (2019). Leveraging undergraduate research to identify culturally relevant examples in the anatomy and physiology curriculum. *Advances in physiology education, 43*(4), 561–566.

Feng, A., & Wu, S. (2019). *The myth of the impartial machine.* Parametric Press, 1(Science +Society). Retrieved from: https://parametric.press/issue-01/the-myth-of-the-impartial-machine/.

Fincher, S., & Robins, A. (2019). *The Cambridge handbook of computing education research.* Cambridge University Press.

Forte, A., & Guzdial, M. (n.d.). *Computers for communication, not calculation: Media as a motivation and context for learning.* [Paper, Georgia Institute of Technology]. http://citeseerx.ist.psu.edu/viewdoc/download?doi=10.1.1.477.5785&rep=rep1&type=pdf.

Gay, G. (2018). *Culturally responsive teaching: Theory, research, and practice.* Teacher's College Press.

Goode, J. (2008). *Increasing diversity in K–12 computer science: Strategies from the field.* Special Interest Group in Computer Science Education, Portland, Oregon.

Goode, J., Chapman, G., & Margolis, J. (2012). Beyond curriculum: The exploring computer science program. *ACM Inroads, 3*(2), 47–53.

Google Inc. & Gallup Inc. (2015). Images of computer science: Perceptions among students, parents, and educators in U.S. Results From the 2015–2016 *Google-Gallup Study of Computer Science in U.S. K–12 Schools.*

Google Inc. & Gallup Inc. (2017a, August). Computer science learning: Closing the gap: Rural and small town school districts. Results fom the 2015–2016 *Google-Gallup Study of Computer Science in U.S. K–12 Schools* (Issue Brief No. 4). https://goo.gl/hYxqC.

Google Inc. & Gallup Inc. (2017b, December). Encouraging students toward computer science learning. Results From the 2015–2016 *Google-Gallup Study of Computer Science in U.S. K–12 Schools* (Issue Brief No. 5). https://goo.gl/iM5g3A.

Hammond, Z. (2014). *Culturally responsive teaching and the brain: Promoting authentic engagement and rigor among culturally and linguistically diverse students.* SAGE Publications.

Herring, C. (2009). Does diversity pay? Race, gender, and the business case for diversity. *American sociological review, 74*(2), 208–224.

Holly, J.S., Jr. (2020). A critical autoethnography of a black man teaching engineering to black boys. *Journal of African American Males in Education (JAAME), 11*(2), 25–42.

Byrd, C.M. (2016). Does culturally relevant teaching work? An examination from student perspectives. *Sage Open, 6*(3), 2158244016660744.

Hooker, S. (2021). Moving beyond "algorithmic bias is a data problem." *Patterns, 2*(4). https://doi.org/10.1016/j.patter.2021.100241.

Karai, Y., Searle, K., Martinea, C., & Brayboy, B. (2014). Ethnocomputing with electronic textiles: Culturally responsive open design to broaden participation in computing in American Indian youth and communities. *SIGCSE.*

Ladson-Billings, G. (1994). *The Dreamkeepers.* San Francisco: Jossey-Bass.

Ladson-Billings, G. (1995a). But that's just good teaching! The case for culturally relevant pedagogy. *Theory into practice, 34*(3), 159–165.

Ladson-Billings, G. (1995b). Toward a theory of culturally relevant pedagogy. *American educational research journal, 32*(3), 465–491.

Larson, J., Mattu, S., Kirchner, L., & Angwin, J. (2016). How we analyzed the COMPAS recidivism algorithm. *ProPublica.* https://www.propublica.org/article/how-we-analyzed-the-compas-recidivism-algorithm.

Leavy, S. (2018). Gender bias in artificial intelligence: The need for diversity and gender theory in machine learning. *Proceedings of the 1st international workshop on gender equality in software engineering,* 14–16.

Lee, N.T. (2018). Detecting racial bias in algorithms and machine learning. *Journal of Information, Communication and Ethics in Society, 16*(3).

Leslie, D. (2020). Understanding bias in facial recognition technologies. *arXiv:2010.07023.*

Lunn, S., Zahedi, L., Ross, M., & Ohland, M. (2021). Exploration of intersectionality and computer science demographics: Understanding the phenomena related to historical Shifts. *ACM Transactions on Computing Education, 21*(2), 1–30. https://dl.acm.org/doi/10.1145/3445985.

Margolis, J., Estrella, R., Jellison Holme, J., & Nao, K. (2018). *Stuck in the shallow end: Education, race, and computing.* MIT Press.

Mejias, M., Jean-Pierre, K., Burge, L., & Washingtin, G. (2018). Culturally relevant CS pedagogy—Theory and practice. *2018 Research on Equity and Sustained Participation in Engineering, Computing, and Technology (RESPECT).*

Mensah, F.M. (2011). A case for culturally relevant teaching in science education and lessons learned for teacher education. *The Journal of Negro Education, 80*(3), 296–309.

Miller, O. (2014). It's deeper than rap, toward culturally responsive CS. *ACM XRDS, 20* (4).

Milner, H.R. (2011). Culturally relevant pedagogy in a diverse urban classroom. *The Urban Review, 43*(1), 66–89.

Noble, S. (2018). *Algorithms of oppression: How search engines reinforce racism.* NYU Press. doi:10.2307/j.ctt1pwt9w5.

Obermeyer, Z., Powers, B., Vogeli, C., & Mullainathan, S. (2019). Dissecting racial bias in algorithm used to manage health of populations. *Science, 366*(6464), 447–453. DOI: 10.1126/science.aax2342.

Overby, P. (2017, September 8). Facebook acknowledges Russian ads in 2016 election. Will investigations follow? *NPR.* https://www.npr.org/2017/09/08/549284183/facebook-acknowledges-russian-ads-in-2016-election-will-investigations-follow.

Peckham, J., Harlow, L.L., Stuart, D.A., Silver, B., Mederer, H., & Stephenson, P.D. (2007). Broadening participation in computing: Issues and challenges. *ACM SIGCSE Bulletin, 39*(3), 9–13.

Ross, M., Hazari, Z., Sonnert, G., & Sadler, P. (2020). The intersection of being Black and being a woman: Examining the effect of social computing relationships on computer science career choice. *ACM Transaction on Computing Education, 20*(2), 1–15. https://doi.org/10.1145/3377426.

Scott, K., Sheridan, K., & Clark, K. (2015). Culturally responsive computing: A theory revisited. *Learning, Media and Technology, 40*(4), 412–436. https://doi.org/10.1080/17439884.2014.924966.

Searle, K. & Kafai, Y. (2015). Bridging the identity gap in crafting and computing with electronic textiles. *GenderIT '15.*

Solon, O. & Levin, S. (2016, December 16). How Google's search algorithm spreads false information with a rightwing bias. *The Guardian.* https://www.theguardian.com/technology/2016/dec/16/google-autocomplete-rightwing-bias-algorithm-political-propaganda.

U.S. Census. (2019). *QuickFacts.* https://www.census.gov/quickfacts/fact/table/US/PST045219.

Ware, F. (2006). Warm demander pedagogy: Culturally responsive teaching that supports a culture of achievement for African American students. *Urban Education, 41*(4), 427–456.

Williams, A., Baert, K., & Williams, A. (2017). Culturally responsive social robotics instruction for middle school girls. *HRI'17 Companion.*

Training the Next Generation of Science Activists Using Critical Race Pedagogy

LISETTE E. TORRES

Introduction

Since the beginnings of the Enlightenment, dominant notions of Western/Eurocentric science were developed by and shared with the public. Laypeople who were affluent, educated, White men, initially drove the scientific enterprise in Europe, and it was not until the late 18th and early 19th centuries where we saw the first scientific laboratories "in which scientists 'worked' rather than pursued their interests" (Gregory & Miller, 1998, p. 21). Scientists, such as chemist Michael Faraday, gave public lectures where they shared their work with the White working class and the elite. Their aim was to "bring to the masses the joy and moral benefit of knowledge," "to reveal the hand of God in Nature," and to show the world "an organized, ordered system, to keep the working class in their place" (Gregory & Miller, 1998, p. 23). By the 20th century, Western science was an established profession, creating a demarcation between insiders and outsiders—academic science and popular science (Paul, 2004). Science journalists (and later science broadcasters) took up the popularization of science rather than the scientists themselves. By the 1970s, the only professional scientists who engaged with the public to popularize science were a few high profile, White scientists like Carl Sagan, Paul Ehrlich, and Margaret Mead (Gregory & Miller, 1998).

The "public understanding of science" movement, developed in the 1980s, grew out of the concerns of scientists and science educators regarding the scientific literacy of the public (Gregory & Miller, 1998). Taking a deficit model approach to science communication (Smith, 2015), the assumption of many in the movement was that science experts needed to educate the public about the nature of science in order for them to make informed decisions (the "dominant view" of science popularization—Hilgartner, 1990; see also review by Besley & Nisbet, 2011). This sentiment still exists today, as the predominant view among scientists is that the public lacks knowledge about science due to too little STEM (science, technology, engineering, and mathematics) education in K–12, lack of public interest, and poor media coverage, despite the fact that a majority of the public (75 percent) view science positively (Pew Research Center, 2015) and that "experts" have the ability to shape media coverage of biomedical and scientific issues (Kruvand, 2012). Consequently, the focus of science communication has been the simple transmission of facts and figures rather than the quality of the communication (Bucchi, 2013; Brownell, Price, & Steinman, 2013) and the development of a "culture of public engagement" (Bucchi, 2013, p. 905).

However, as further research is conducted within the sub-disciplines of science education, science communication, and public understanding of science, scholars are coming to realize that (1) publics are diverse and emergent (Fraser, 1990; Michael, 2009; Stilgoe, Lock, & Wilsdon, 2014); (2) the dominant view of science popularization is oversimplified and political (Hilgartner, 1990; Myers, 2003; Paul, 2004); and (3) the goal may not be a complete understanding of science but a building of trust with the public (Gregory & Miller, 1998). In addition, to have effective science communication and research for the public good, scholars will also have to (re)consider the way discourse communities "shape not only the discourse, but also, the members of a discourse community" (Provençal, 2011, p. 103; Myers, 2003).

There is now a shift from the "public understanding of science" to "public engagement with science" (Kouper, 2010; Bauer & Jensen, 2011), and with this relatively new movement comes a (re)evaluation of the responsibilities associated with being a scientist. Historically, scientists have spoken on social issues above and beyond their "expertise" (i.e., public intellectuals)—individually (such as Albert Einstein and J. Robert Oppenheimer—Gregory & Miller, 1998) and collectively (such as the 1970s socialist science movement magazines *Science for the People* in the U.S. and *Science for People* in the U.K.—Bell, 2013). More recently, there has been an increase in the number of scientists who have reconnected with the history of political activism in STEM and have become more involved in the sociopolitical arena by establishing their own groups, such as the revitalized Science for the People, Free Radicals, Particles for Justice, Data for Black Lives, and WokeSTEM. They have also engaged in a variety of actions, including the most recent #ShutDownSTEM /

#ShutDownAcademia / #Strike4BlackLives (*https://www.shutdownstem. com/*) that occurred on June 10, 2020, where scientists committed to stepping away from STEM activities to recharge, learn the history of anti–Black violence, and generate their own plan for confronting anti–Black racism (Chen, 2020). This reemergence of science activism combined with the "public engagement with science" movement provides a new opportunity for scientists to work with and for the public to address today's pressing social and environmental issues.

Similarly, with the perpetual use of biological concepts of race in genomics research (Yudell, Roberts, DeSalle, & Tischkoff, 2016), climate deniers, environmental racism (e.g., Flint, Michigan, water crisis), and racial health disparities illuminated by the recent Covid-19 pandemic, the sociocultural context of STEM, as well as the role of scientists as public intellectuals and activists and how they engage with the public, needs to be (re)examined. Wingfield (2020), Barber et al. (2020), and Schell et al. (2020) argue that scientists need to recognize that structural racism exists in STEM and call for institutions to foster diverse excellence. They call for structural, transformational change.

In a similar vein, in an interview with *The Chronicle of Higher Education* about his involvement in revealing the inaction of city officials to address the lead contamination of Flint's water supply, Marc Edwards, a professor of civil engineering at Virginia Tech, shared,

> I am very concerned about the culture of academia in this country and the perverse incentives that are given to young faculty. The pressures to get funding are just extraordinary. We're all on this hedonistic treadmill—pursuing funding, pursuing fame, pursuing h-index—and the idea of *science as a public good* [emphasis added] is being lost [Kolowich, 2016, para. 7].

If science truly is a public good, then we need even more scientists than the aforementioned groups to speak out, not just for themselves, but for marginalized and oppressed communities. We need them to use science in service to the people without expectations of financial gain or public recognition. Now more than ever, we need scientists to dialogue and work with multiple publics (Fraser, 1990) to address the needs of the 21st century. A place to start is through educating the next generation of scientists.

This essay is a reflection on my experience with designing and implementing two first-year undergraduate courses—one on science communication, public engagement, and activism, and the other on the book *Hidden Figures* by Margot Lee Shetterly. Through the courses, I attempted to get students to critically reflect on the untold history of science activism, representation within science, and the role of scientists in society, with an intentional emphasis on scientists of color and marginalized communities.

I share my learnings here in regards to how we can train future scientists as public intellectuals and activists using Critical Race Pedagogy (CRP). I also include the challenges of being a woman of color engaging CRP in a predominantly White classroom on a historically White campus.

My Positionality and Approach as a Critical Race Pedagogue

Before I describe the courses in full, I must be clear about my positionality and relationship to STEM. I identify as a disabled Puerto Rican momma-scholar-activist with a critical, transdisciplinary lens. I am also a woman of color who left her doctoral program in the sciences after being confronted with the reality that the scientific community tends to be unwelcoming and unwilling to serve those who do not fit the White male norm. Some of my experiences with gendered racism in science have been documented elsewhere in a counter-story (Torres, 2016) I wrote for the edited book *Envisioning critical race praxis in higher education through counter-storytelling* (Croom & Marsh, 2016); using critical race theory, I recount and analyze the moments that led me to my decision to leave the sciences. I will not share that story here, but my racialized and gendered experiences in STEM have shaped my scholarship and pedagogical approach.

I am a scientist, social justice educator, and "intellectual activist" (Collins, 2013) with an intimate knowledge of STEM culture and higher education. I believe that we—scientists, science educators, and science communicators—would do our students a disservice if we did not teach them about the history of science and train them to not only produce scientific knowledge, but to be able to work with and for the public, an amorphous and complex entity that is actually comprised of multiple stakeholders (or multiple publics) whose interactions are full of power dynamics that differentially empower some, while marginalizing others (Frazer, 1990). There is currently a burgeoning field called inclusive science communication that "aims to address the shortcomings in how researchers and communicators define and engage public audiences in STEMM topics" (Canfield et al., 2020, p. 2). It is important for our students to know this work.

Part of my scholarly identity is a dedication to CRiT walking, defined as "a constructivist and metaphorical tool that offers education scholars and practitioners a framework to use genre driven writing, autobiography, auto-ethnography, social justice principles, and radical perspectives to analyze, re-interpret, deconstruct, and reform educational settings"

(Hughes & Giles, 2010, p. 41). It is "an effort to connect CRT [Critical Race Theory] as a theoretical construct to a livable, observable, teachable process of critical consciousness, knowing and doing" (Hughes & Giles, 2010, p. 42). Originating from critical legal studies of the 1970s (Delgado & Stefancic, 2001), CRT has expanded to other disciplines, including education. There are at least five premises that inform the work of CRT within education: (1) the centrality of race, racism, intersectionality and other forms of oppression, (2) the importance of challenging the dominant ideology (e.g., meritocracy, objectivity, colorblindness, equal opportunity), (3) a commitment to social justice, (4) the significance of experiential knowledge, and (5) the use of interdisciplinary methods to ground research in a historical and contemporary context (Solórzano & Delgado Bernal 2001; Solórzano & Yosso, 2001). CRiT walking is essentially putting these tenets into "social justice action-community action" (Hughes & Giles, 2010, p. 43), including teaching.

One way to practice CRiT walking is by using Critical Race Pedagogy (CRP) (Lynn, 1999) in the classroom. This involves centering the lived experiences of Black, Indigenous, and People of Color (BIPOC), fostering dialogue, "engaging in daily self-affirmation exercises," and contesting master narratives and hegemony (Lynn, 2019, p. 619). It is being aware of negotiations of power (Jennings & Lynn, 2005) in and outside the classroom as well as acknowledging interlocking systems of oppression ("matrix of domination"—Hill Collins, 2004). Educators must also engage in reflexivity, including exploring "one's 'place' within a stratified society … to illuminate oppressive structures in society" (Jennings & Lynn, 2005, p. 27). The ultimate goal is not necessarily the mastery of the course material, but justice and liberation for students and communities of color.

Seminar Course Descriptions and Context

I worked at a predominantly White, liberal arts institution in the Midwest where, over the past ten years, we revised our curriculum to give undergraduate students a more interdisciplinary and experiential learning experience. Now, students are exposed to a variety of disciplines and topics, with writing, speaking, and critical thinking skills intentionally scaffolded throughout their four years on campus. They are introduced to the expectations of the curriculum and institutional culture during their first-year seminar, which is a requirement for all incoming students. Each student is given a list of seminar options before the start of the fall, where they rank, in order of preference, the courses they would be willing to take to fulfill the requirement. All seminars, no matter the topic, are required to incorporate activities to assist students with the transition to campus and a research paper. In addition, seminar instructors serve as the new students' advisers until they declare a major by the end of the academic year.

Though I was not obligated to teach in my role as a staff member when I was employed at the university, I elected to teach the first-year seminar every other year. Each time, I designed the seminar around a new topic, though all of them were related to my research and advocacy interests. The first AWS course I created was based on what is now called inclusive science communication (Canfield et al., 2020). It was entitled *Science for the People—Communication, Engagement, and Activism in Science*, and it was my attempt to understand the history and future of science communication and public engagement. I designed the seminar to look at how the involvement of scientists with the public has changed and attempted to address the following questions: Who is the public? What is science communication and public engagement? Who benefits from this interaction? Why is it important for scientists to engage with the public? What are the potential challenges? Do scientists have a special obligation to society? By addressing these questions, I hoped that my students and I would have a better understanding of the complex relationship between the scientific community and the rest of society as well as reflect on the emancipatory possibilities of science.

The specific course objectives were as follows:

- Become familiar with and critically examine the history and purpose of science communication and public engagement
- Engage in service learning to experience science communication and public engagement firsthand
- Develop a better understanding of the connection between science and society
- Appreciate and begin to think about science as a tool for liberation
- Respect and work with multiple ways of knowing
- Reflect on their social responsibility as science learners/knowers
- Become familiar with campus resources
- Reflect on the importance of well-being for themselves and those who work for social justice

My personal goal, however, was to inspire students to think critically about the role of scientists in society and to consider engaging in positive social transformation, using science as one of many tools for change. I was lucky to have a student instructor to help me try to reach this goal; she identified as a cisgendered, straight White woman majoring in Biology. Out of fifteen students, most were White, middle-class Midwesterners who were interested in pursuing majors and careers in science; half of the students were women. I had three domestic students of color, one international student, and one White student from a working-class background. I note the racial composition of both courses in this work because it is significant to my pedagogical approach (CRP) and my thoughts on how to train the next generation of scientists to work with and for marginalized communities.

Two years later, given my research on racialized gender justice and the release and popularity of the movie *Hidden Figures*, I designed an AWS seminar entitled *Hidden Figures, Untold Herstories: Equity & Inclusion for Women of Color in Science*. The course was an introduction to the exploration of how science, as a social organization and epistemology, (historically and currently) impacts women of color and what this means for science fields as a whole. We examined the underrepresentation of women of color in science disciplines by taking a critical look at the social (e.g., one-on-one interactions inside and outside of the science classroom/lab, collaborations, mentoring, science conferences, etc.) and cultural (e.g., clothing and appearance, language and discourse, spoken and unspoken expectations, interests, practices, behavior, etc.) aspects of science. In addition, we discussed the intersection of race/ethnicity and gender in science, as well as feminist critiques of science, to brainstorm ways in which we can simultaneously work toward transforming science fields to be more equitable and inclusive of people from all backgrounds. We thought critically about the power and privilege of knowledge production, particularly focusing on the privilege associated with being identified as a "legitimate" scientist.

For this seminar, I was once again lucky to have an experienced upper-level student as my student instructor. He identified as a queer, cisgendered Black man and was knowledgeable about intersectionality. He helped me with the following course objectives:

- Become familiar with and critically examine the history of power, privilege, equity, and inclusion within science
- Engage in service learning to make connections between the course material and science equity work
- Develop a better understanding of the connection between science and society
- Appreciate and begin to think about science as a tool for liberation
- Respect and work with multiple ways of knowing
- Reflect on their social responsibility as science learners/knowers
- Become familiar with campus resources
- Reflect on the importance of well-being for themselves and those who work for social justice

There were nineteen students, only four of whom were men. The racial composition of the class was eleven White students, two Latinxs, three Black students, and three multiracial students. This demographic change I think is important, as it shifted classroom dynamics and allowed for sensitive issues to be addressed, as I describe in my section on "Lessons Learned."

CRP in a STEM-Related Seminar

For both *Science for the People* and *Hidden Figures* Archway seminars, I was intentional about informing my students at the beginning of the course of my positionality as a disabled Boricua committed to CRiT walking. As a believer in radical honesty (Williams, 2016), I was clear about how I wanted them to become comfortable with the uncomfortable, as we discussed and unpacked power, privilege, and oppression in STEM. Together, we dealt with coming to understand that "we exist within society as subjective entities whose identities are negotiated through multiple lenses that privilege certain race, class, gender and sexual 'norms.'" (Jennings & Lynn, 2005, p. 26). I explained the purpose and learning objectives of the course and, throughout the semester, I articulated my rationale for selected activities and readings, making sure to center BIPOC perspectives and experiences.

My approach for the *Science for the People* course was a little subtler than it was for *Hidden Figures*, as it was my first time teaching an AWS course. However, in both seminars, I engaged students in activities that illuminated and discussed power, privilege, and oppression. I challenged them to think about who benefits from science and science communication as well as who is considered a science knower. For example, I split students into teams to play an identification game related to representation in STEM. They were asked to run up to the whiteboard and list as many White male scientists as possible in thirty seconds, followed by White female scientists, Black male scientists, and Black female scientists. They were shocked when they found it increasingly difficult to name people, and we spent time discussing why that was and how to address it.

I intentionally incorporated different ways of knowing and being. I invited students to do a breathing meditation with me for the first five minutes of every class period. They found this to be the best part of their day, as it allowed them to transition from their busy campus lives to a new, focused learning space. I had them write haikus and draw mind maps and images based on their readings. In addition, they were expected to do six hours of service learning and a reflective photojournal with local organizations related to the course topic. For example, students in the *Science for the People* AWS seminar had to work with organizations doing science communication (e.g., science museum, environmental non-profit, health department, afterschool programs), while students in the *Hidden Figures* course were required to specifically work with the YWCA's Smart Girls Club. Lastly, I ended each course with a collage assignment that asked students to work in groups to demonstrate their learning throughout the semester through text and visual imagery. I provided them with most of the materials they would need, including poster board, construction paper, paint, scissors, and glue sticks. I also gave them time in class to work on their collages. Though most students claimed that they were "not artists," they created wonderful, thoughtful pieces.

The most important aspect of CRP is modeling reflexivity and empathy. Bryan Dewsbury (2019) describes what he calls "Deep teaching" as "the constant, critical reflection practitioners apply to their awareness of self and student, as well as the degree to which this reflection informs the practice of an equitable pedagogy" (p. 5). This Deep teaching allows us to critically think about the quality of our classroom environment and communication. This careful consideration makes us more empathetic as we build deeper relationships with our students and work to comprehend their cultural backgrounds and perspectives. Dewsbury (2019) notes, "Empathy toward students has a macro and a micro level. On a macro level, it is important to understand the historical and social contexts that inform the students' presence in the classroom" (p. 9). At a micro level, instructors need to "place a clear focus on the ways in which they validate students' identities, encourage growth mindset and provide opportunities for students to engage their social realities in the classroom" (Dewsbury, 2019, p. 12).

I kept a notebook where I reflected on what happened each day in class and on things to improve upon. Since my students were also my advisees, I would note things that I noticed about my interactions with them, things they told me, and anything I considered important to remember, including potential warning signs on how they are doing academically and socially. Similar to Dewsbury (2019), I used my reflections to inform my "*aggressive early intervention* approach," where I assumed that any struggles I noticed were due to the fact that they were first-year students adjusting to their transition to college. Then, I would discuss my concerns with them one-on-one after class or during our advising meetings. Foregrounding support and empathy, I would strategize with them how to improve, teach them new study skills, connect them with potential mentors, and recommend on campus resources.

Accomplishments

I am confident that a majority of my students in both courses appreci-ated their learning experience. My course evaluations were extremely pos-itive, and one student commented, "I was surprised by the huge impact that scientists have on the world." Students valued the content, in-class activities, and most of the assignments. To my knowledge, the students felt heard and included since I tried my best to create an inclusive classroom "where all voices, regardless of background have equal opportunity to contribute to and shape the community dialogue" (Dewsbury, 2019, p. 5).

Out of sixteen students enrolled in my *Science for the People* semi-nar and twenty-two students in my *Hidden Figures* course, approximately 50 percent and 47 percent of my students declared a STEM major within their first year, respectively, and a majority of them have since gradu-ated with STEM degrees and have continued on to professional schools (e.g., medical school, physical therapy school). In regard to the students of color who were in my classes, my international student graduated with a STEM degree, completed a Master's degree, and will be applying to med-ical school. Out of eight students of color in my *Hidden Figures* seminar, three women of color are on track to graduate with STEM degrees. Four women of color from that course are active on campus in addressing issues of social justice, though all of my students of color continue to express "an equity ethic that reflects collectivist values" (McGee & Bentley, 2017, p. 17).

I am most proud of being able to mentor a young Black man who was in my *Science for the People* course. I noticed early on that he was tired in my class and was not doing the readings. During one of our advising meet-ings, he opened up to me that he was having trouble sleeping and that he was struggling being on a predominately White campus. He also had dif-ficulties reading due to his lack of sleep. I encouraged him to go to the health center, but I also met with him on a weekly basis to try to help him with his reading and study strategies. Every time I spoke to him, he would be down on himself about his academic performance, believing that he was inherently incapable of success. I coached him through it while vali-dating his feelings and experiences. I told him I believed in him even if he did not believe in himself.

This young man continued to visit with me a few times every semes-ter, even after he was no longer my advisee. We would talk about his prog-ress, challenges, and social life. I would also share my struggles, as I was a doctoral candidate at the time trying to balance dissertation writing, a full-time job, and caring for young children at home. In a small way, these conversations kept him motivated. He graduated and is now a phys-ical education teacher.

Challenges and Lessons Learned

Like most instructors working with first-year undergraduates, I encountered a few stumbling blocks in both courses as the students transitioned to campus life and adjusted to college expectations. It was initially difficult to stimulate classroom conversations, especially since the students were not used to the sheer amount of reading for each week. Despite several of them considering STEM careers, they also had a surprisingly weak understanding of the history and nature of science. It was also challenging to coordinate service learning without assistance and a structured plan. Some of the students did not have cars on campus and almost all of them were overcommitted. Rather than focusing on these relatively common difficulties, I want to critically reflect on my experience of using CRP in a White classroom, since I am hyperaware of being a Brown body navigating a space not created for me (Anderson, 2015).

Gendered Color-Evasiveness and White Resistance

It is not easy to be a disabled woman of color engaging in CRP in a predominantly White classroom on a historically White campus. There were a few moments where I had to deal with White fragility (DiAngelo, 2011) in relation to our conversations about power, privilege, and oppression in STEM. I was also cautious about providing students with hopeful ways to move forward by trying to get them to think about how they can use their privileges to help others. I was especially careful to avoid spotlighting students of color; I did not want them to feel the burden of having to represent their entire racialized community, a weight I know all too well.

There are a couple of clear instances that reminded me that my intersectional identities were unusual in higher education and new to my White students. In my *Science for the People* AWS seminar, a month into the semester, several of the men in my class neglected to do the readings and decided to continually have side conversations during our class discussions. Every time I would pose a question to class, this particular group of men would whisper to each other or ignore what I was saying. They were not taking me seriously because I was a woman of color, as I had seen them give more respect to the White male faculty on campus. One day, I finally had enough and played into the "hot-blooded Latina" stereotype by stopping in the middle of class and stating that I would teach when they were ready to learn. I then collected my items, told them I would see them next class period, and walked out of the room. For the rest of the semester, the side conversations ended.

The second challenge presented itself in my *Hidden Figures* course. Apparently, unbeknownst to me, one of the young White men was muttering racist comments during class to his peers next to him. Each time we talked about the marginalization of women of color in STEM, he would lean over to a classmate and say something offensive. The comments were usually made to two other White men in the class, which I assume was because he thought that they felt the same. He was mistaken. The two young men approached me after class, along with one of the White women and two women of color. They shared with me the things he had been saying and confessed that the comments made them extremely uncomfortable and offended. I thanked them for their candor and promised I would speak to the young man without divulging any names.

I immediately contacted a colleague of mine on our bias response team to ask her to join me in talking to the student. I did not want to run the risk of a "he-said-she-said" situation and felt more comfortable with someone else being with me. She agreed, and I emailed the student to schedule a face-to-face meeting. When we met, he was very quiet. I explained to him that his peers approached me about his comments and behavior and wanted me to talk to him. I expressed to him that I was concerned not only as a woman of color and as his instructor, but also as his advisor. He wanted to be a science educator, and I told him that I would be doing him and future children of color a disservice if I did not address his racist views. He just nodded. To this day, I still do not know if I ever got to him.

Both racialized gendered classroom experiences were clear examples of color-evasiveness (Annamma, Jackson, & Morrison, 2016) and resistance to decentering Whiteness and maleness. It appeared that the students who were the most uncomfortable and avoidant of conversations about privilege, power, and oppression were White men. This was clearly evident by the group of men having side conversations in my *Science for the People* course. Given that I was their first woman of color instructor, they presumed that I was incompetent or unqualified and felt it was acceptable to disrespect me. In describing his theorization of the perceptions of the Black community to "white space," Anderson (2015) writes,

> In the general scheme of the white space, it matters little whether such acute disrespect is intended or unintended. The injury most often has the same effect: deflation and a sense of marginalization … the person [of color] is reminded of her provisional status, that she has much to prove in order to really belong in the white space [p. 15].

Despite the fact that I have years of experience in higher education and multiple degrees, some of the young White men in the course initially did not consider me a legitimate educator and knowledge-holder. I was not the White, male "expert" they were expecting. Meanwhile, my students of color were excited by my presence and, contrary to those in Alemán and Gaytán, (2017) who were reluctant to confront dominant ideologies, they openly embraced my CRP and were willing to engage in difficult conversations about race and intersectionality in STEM.

Structural Issues Beyond My Control

Being a Critical Race Pedagogue is both liberating and discouraging. While I was able to navigate the White classroom, center the lived experiences of BIPOC in science, and disrupt master narratives around who can be a science knower, communicator, and educator, I was also very aware of other structural issues that were impacting my students that were beyond my control. For example, one of my female students from a working-class background ultimately decided to stop attending class halfway through the semester due to financial burdens. Her mother was hospitalized for cancer treatment, and she would drive an unreliable car to and from the hospital to be with her. The young woman also had her own medical impairments she was managing. Even with financial aid, things were just too much for her to continue.

Another female student had to leave campus due to a decline in her mental health. As a young college student not accustomed to the freedom of adulthood, she had stopped taking her medication. Despite advice from campus staff and encouragement to make regular appointments with the counseling center, she refused assistance. Her behavior in the classroom became disruptive and, at one point, she put herself in harm's way.

In both cases, I could see events unfolding and felt powerless to do anything. I could not gift my student the money she needed to complete her degree, and I did not have the power to decrease the price of books, tuition, room, and board. I also did not have the advanced training to address issues of mental health. Similarly, with the exception of our counseling center, our campus was generally not prepared to help students with particular mental health needs. My critical lens allowed me to see these structural challenges, but I was incapable of solving them.

Considerations for the Future

My self-designed undergraduate seminar courses—*Science for the People* and *Hidden Figures*—show promise for beginning to train STEM students as public intellectuals and activists. I exposed them to the untold history of science activism, challenged them to communicate their work to different audiences (i.e., publics), and engaged them in dialogue about power and privilege. We talked about the value of representation, relationship-building, advocacy, and community engagement. I also had them consider different ways of knowing and being and how they shape the kinds of questions we ask and methodological approaches we take as scientists. The fact that many of my students declared STEM or STEM-adjacent majors signifies to me that I was successful in humanizing science.

In thinking about how CRP can be similarly incorporated into established science curricula in higher education, the biggest challenges will be confronting the inertia of White STEM faculty who (1) are unfamiliar with critical pedagogies and the history of oppression of BIPOC folks by science, (2) believe that science is value-neutral and objective, (3) are unwilling to acknowledge current inequities in STEM, and (4) have been socialized to believe that they have the power to determine who can and cannot be a science knower. We also need to eliminate "the false dichotomy of 'excellence or diversity'" (Barber et al., 2020, p. 1441). Due to the influence of the neoliberal focus on efficiency and production in higher education, many STEM faculty members do not feel they have the time or energy to make curricular or pedagogical changes while still covering the content they do currently. What is needed is a prioritization of skills and ethical reasoning over certain content, a problem that I and colleagues (Dr. Cynthia Bauerle, Dr. Laura Bottomley, Dr. Carrie Hall, and Dr. Daniel Howard) are trying to address through the development of an Ethical Reasoning Instrument (ERI) (https://serc.carleton.edu/stemfutures/product/ethical_reasoning_instrument.html) for faculty members in the life sciences and engineering. Faculty need to ask themselves—Do we need individuals who have memorized scientific concepts and theories or do we need individuals who can adapt their skills to fluctuating circumstances and can make ethical decisions grounded in social justice?

Conclusion

Given the dire health disparities exposed by Covid-19, the murdering of Black bodies (particularly, the deaths of Arbery, Taylor, Floyd, and Brooks), the Black Lives Matter Movement protests, and the increased concern with public intellectualism in higher education (e.g., Gasman, 2016), I believe this essay is a timely contribution to help science educators think about how we train students to engage in the messiness that is science communication, public engagement, and activism. It adds to literature regarding culturally relevant pedagogy (Ladson-Billings, 1995) and culturally responsive teaching (Gay, 2010), and it illustrates the importance of confronting White privilege in STEM education (Grindstaff & Mascarenhas, 2019). I join Barber et al. (2020) when they state, "We urge the Academy to combat systemic racism in STEM and catalyze transformational change" (p. 1440). However, as Schell et al. (2020) reminds us, "The road to anti-racism in academia is a long, arduous, uphill climb that will require institutional and personal reconciliation, resolve, discomfort and humility. It is both necessary and urgent to promote inclusive excellence and transformative scholarship" (p. 1). A multi-pronged approach, starting with an antiracist/anti-oppressive classroom pedagogy like CRP, is a beginning.

REFERENCES

Alemán, S.M., & Gaytán, S. (2017). "It doesn't speak to me": Understanding student of color resistance to critical race pedagogy. *International Journal of Qualitative Studies in Education*, *30*(2), 128–146. doi: 10.1080/09518398.2016.1242801.

Anderson, E. (2015). "The White space." *Sociology of Race and Ethnicity*, *1*(1), 10–21. doi: 10.1177/2332649214561306.

Annamma, S.A., Jackson, D.D., & Morrison, D. (2016). Conceptualizing color-evasiveness: using dis/ability critical race theory to expand a color-blind racial ideology in education and society. *Race Ethnicity and Education*, *20*(2), 147–162. doi: 10.1080/136133 24.2016.1248837.

Barber, P.H., Hayes, T.B., Johnson, T.L., Márquez-Magaña, L., and 10,234 signatories. (2020). Systemic racism in higher education. *Science*, *369*(6510), 1440–1441. doi: 10.1126/ science.abd7140.

Bauer, M.W., & Jensen, P. (2011). The mobilization of scientists for public engagement. *Public Understanding of Science*, *20*(1), 3–11. doi:10.1177/0963662510394457.

Bell, A. (2013 July 18). Beneath the white coat: The radical science movement. *The Guardian*. http://www.theguardian.com/science/political-science/2013/jul/18/beneath-white-coat-radical-science-movement.

Besley, J.C., & Nisbet, M. (2011). How scientists view the public, the media and the political process. *Public Understanding of Science*, *22*(6), 644–659. doi:10.1177/0963662511418743.

Brownell, S.E., Price, J.V., & Steinman, L. (2013). Science communication to the general public: Why we need to teach undergraduate and graduate students this skill as part of their formal scientific training. *The Journal of Undergraduate Neuroscience Education*, *12*(1), E6-E10.

Bucchi, M. (2013). Style in science communication. *Public Understanding of Science*, *22*(8), 904–915. doi: 10.1177/0963662513498202.

Canfield, K.N., Menezes, S., Matsuda, S.B., Moore, A., Mosley Austin, A.N., Dewsbury, B.M., Feliú-Mójer, M.I., McDuffie, K.W.B., Moore, K., Reich, C.A., Smith, H.M., & Taylor, C. (2020). Science communication demands a critical approach that centers inclusion, equity, and intersectionality. *Frontiers in Communication*, *5*(2), 1–8. https://doi.org/10.3389/fcomm.2020.00002.

Chen, S. (2020, June 9). Researchers around the world prepare to #ShutDownSTEM and "Strike for Black Lives." *Science Magazine*. doi: 10.1126/science.abd2504.

Collins, P.H. (2013). *On intellectual activism*. Temple University Press.

Delgado, R., & Stefancic, J. (2001). *Critical race theory: An introduction*. NYU Press.

Dewsbury, B.M. (2019). Deep teaching in a college STEM classroom. *Cultural Studies of Science Education*, *15*(2020), 169–191. https://doi.org/10.1007/s11422-018-9891-z.

DiAngelo, R. (2011). White fragility. *The International Journal of Critical Pedagogy*, *3*(3), 54–70.

Fraser, N. (1990). Rethinking the public sphere: A contribution to the critique of actually existing democracy. *Social Text, 25/26,* 56–80.

Gasman, M. (2016). *Academics going public: How to write and speak beyond academe.* Routledge.

Gay, G. (2010). *Culturally responsive teaching: Theory, theory, and practice* (2nd edition). Teachers College Press.

Gregory, J., & Miller, S. (1998). *Science in public: Communication, culture, and credibility.* Basic Books.

Grindstaff, K., & Mascarenhas, M. (2019). "No one wants to believe it": Manifestations of white privilege in a STEM-focused college. *Multicultural Perspectives, 21*(2) 102–111. doi: 10.1080/15210960.2019.1572487.

Hilgartner, S. (1990). The dominant view of popularization: Conceptual problems, political uses. *Social Studies of Science, 20*(3), 519–539.

Hill Collins, P. (2004). Toward a new vision: Race, class, and gender as categories of analysis and connection. In L. Heldke & P.O. O'Connor (Eds.), *Oppression, privilege, and resistance* (pp. 529–543). Boston, MA: McGraw-Hill.

Hughes, R., & Giles, M. (2010). CRiT walking in higher education: Activating critical race theory in the academy. *Race, Ethnicity and Education, 13*(1), 41–57.

Kolowich, S. (2016, February 2). The water next time: Professor who helped expose crisis in Flint says public science is broken. *The Chronicle of Higher Education.* http://chronicle.com/article/The-Water-Next-Time-Professor/235136.

Kouper, I. (2010). Science blogs and public engagement with science: Practices, challenges, and opportunities. *Journal of Science Communication, 9*(1), 1–10.

Kruvand, M. (2012). "Dr. Soundbite": The making of an expert source in science and medical stories. *Science Communication, 34*(5), 566–591. doi:10.1177/1075547011434991.

Ladson-Billings, G. (1995). Toward a theory of culturally relevant pedagogy. *American Educational Research Journal, 32*(3), 465–491.

McGee, E., & Bentley, L. (2017). The equity ethic: Black and Latinx college students reengineering their STEM careers toward justice. *American Journal of Education, 124,* 1–36.

Michael, M. (2009). Publics performing publics: Of PiGs, PiPs and politics. *Public Understanding of Science, 18*(5), 617–631. doi: 10.1177/096366250508098581.

Myers, G. (2003). Discourse studies of scientific popularization: Questioning the boundaries. *Discourse Studies, 5*(2), 265–279.

Paul, D. (2004). Spreading chaos: The role of popularizations in the diffusion of scientific ideas. *Written Communication, 21*(1), 32–68. doi: 10.1177/0741088303261035.

Pew Research Center. (2015). *Public and scientists' views on science and society.* http://www.pewinternet.org/2015/01/29/public-and-scientists-views-on-science-and-society/.

Provençal, J. (2011). Extending the reach of research as a public good: Moving beyond the paradox of "zero-sum language games." *Public Understanding of Science, 20*(1), 101–116. doi: 10.1177/0963662509351638.

Schell, C.J., Guy, C., Shelton, D.S., Campbell-Staton, S.C., Sealey, B.A., Lee, D.N., & Harris, N.C. (2020, July 24). Recreating Wakanda by promoting Black excellence in ecology and evolution. *Nature Ecology & Evolution, 2020,* 1–3. https://doi.org/10.1038/41559-020-1266-7.

Smith, A. (2015). "Wow, I didn't know that before; thank you": How scientists use Twitter for public engagement. *Journal of Promotional Communications, 3*(3), 320–339.

Solórzano, D.G., & Delgado Bernal, D. (2001). Examining transformational resistance through a critical race and Latcrit theory framework: Chicana and Chicano students in an urban context. *Urban Education, 36*(3), 308–342. doi: 10.1177/0042085901363002.

Solórzano, D.G., & Yosso, T. (2001). Critical race and LatCrit theory and method: Counter-storytelling Chicana and Chicano graduate school experiences. *International Journal of Qualitative Studies in Education, 14*(4), 471–495.

Stilgoe, J., Lock, S.J., & Wilsdon, J. (2014). Why should we promote public engagement with science? *Public Understanding of Science, 23*(1), 4–15. doi: 10.1177/0963662513518154.

Williams, B. (2016). Radical honesty: Truth-telling as pedagogy for working through shame in academic spaces. In F. Tuitt, C. Haynes, & S. Stewart (Eds.), *Race, equity and the learning environment: The global relevance of critical and inclusive pedagogies in higher education* (pp. 71–82). Stylus.

Wingfield, A.H. (2020). Systemic racism persists in the sciences. *Science, 369*(6502), 351. doi: 10.1126/science.abd8825.

Yudell, M., Roberts, D., DeSalle, R., & Tischkoff, S. (2016). Taking race out of human genetics. *Science, 351*(6273), 564–565. doi: 10.1126/science.aac4951.

Culturally Responsive Teaching Practices in the Mathematics Classroom

Tressa D. Matthews *and* Jennifer D. Banks

National education reforms structured to date fail to address the underlying issue that results in the underachievement of Black students—systematic racism. According to Critical Race Theory (CRT), race and racism are institutionalized aspects of American society (Delgado, 2001; Ladson-Billings & Tate, 1995). According to Darling-Hammond (2004), 70 percent of black children attend school with other people of color. One-third of Blacks and Latinos attend schools where the demographics of the school are more than 90 percent minority. This school structure has created a system of racial isolation. Critical Race Theory further suggests race and racism are social constructions, thus society must also attend to social beliefs and relationships to address underlying causes of underachievement (Ladson-Billings & Tate, 1995). Racism is a reflection of the ideas of a social system that perpetuates a hierarchy among different groups (Bonilla-Silva, 1997). It is any action that promotes preference or inequity as a result of race (Gillborn, 2006). There can also be a culture of racism that is grounded in the societal premise that one group is superior to another (Sue, 2010). This culture of racism permeates throughout society and therefore exists in all institutions including schools (Gillborn, 2006; Sue, 2010).

In a society that is grounded in a culture of racism, every person has an unconscious bias towards different groups. Black students are often the target of racism in school and experience what is known as microaggressions. Microaggressions can be displayed in a variety of ways and are imposed on people of color in various aspects of their lives (Pierce, 1995; Sue, 2010). In schools, students of color can experience a sense of alienation. For Black students, in particular, a lack of understanding of the learning and communication styles of Black students is a common micro-aggression that Black students face (Hale-Benson, 1986; Pierce, 1995; Sue, 2010). Microaggressions can also be experienced through the school's or teacher's failure to acknowledge, or validate the feelings and experiences of Black students. (Allen, 2013; Sue & Constantine, 2007; Sue et al., 2008). Microaggressions can have a significant impact on the psychological and physical well-being of Blacks. For Black children, microaggressions can disengage students from the learning process. In addition, microaggressions can lead to racial mistrust in that Black children may not trust their White teachers (Pierce, 1995; Sue, 2010). Hence, each microaggression has an impact on the classroom environment (Allen, 2013).

For Black students, racial isolation and microaggressions in the mathematics classroom is too often a norm. The mathematics classroom consists of low expectations and instruction that does not promote critical thinking or problem solving for Black students (Ladson-Billings & Tate, 1995; Oakes, 1990; Walker, 2007; Banks, 2016). Therefore, Black students are more likely to participate in remedial mathematics, rather than the college prep mathematics courses their White counterparts are taking (Walker, 2007). Walker (2007) further asserts that within advanced math courses, Black students often experience racial isolation, and tend not to take these courses. This racial isolation can lead to emotional and psychological stress as a result of feeling inadequate, experiencing negative peer influence, and perceiving negative societal perceptions (Sheppard, 2006). Ladson-Billings and Tate (1995) further asserts that Black students have limited access to mathematical technology and less access to strong mathematics teachers. Culturally responsive pedagogy mediates racism, microaggressions, and racial isolation in the math classroom.

Culturally Responsive Pedagogy and Black Students

Various scholars have studied and presented theories or models for understanding the academic performance of Black students. Some such as Hale-Benson (1986) have argued that teachers fail to provide instruction in a manner that is compatible with students' culture and learning styles, particularly with Black students. Instruction that was more aligned to the needs of students would incorporate learning styles and cultural patterns of students. For example, Boykins (2011) argues that instruction that incorporates characteristics of Black culture better meets the needs of Black children. Black culture is influenced greatly by the following characteristics: spirituality, harmony, movement, verve, affect, communalism, oral tradition, expressive individualism, and social time perspective. Instruction that incorporates these characteristics is more attuned to the needs of Black children (Boykins, 2011).

Similarly, Irvine (1990) suggests that there is a lack of cultural synchronization in the classroom that results in missed learning opportunities for Black students. The experiences and privileges of teachers are often different from that of their students. As a result, teachers misunderstand or misinterpret behaviors of children of color, resulting in more disciplinary problems. Moreover, instruction is not aligned to students' interests and lacks meaning to their world. Boykins, Tyler, and Miller (2005) also concur that poor academic performance is a result of cultural divergence between instruction approach and students' learning styles.

Culturally responsive pedagogy (CRP) is a pedagogical approach that empowers students by allowing them to see themselves within the classroom learning environment. CRP develops a positive self-identity and contradicts stereotypes that are portrayed by society (Ladson-Billings, 2009; Gay, 2018, Richard et al., 2007). Ladson-Billings (1995) argues that in culturally relevant pedagogy there is evidence of student learning (academic success), students learn about their culture and at least one other culture (cultural competence), and students have the opportunity to critically analyze and critique injustices (critical consciousness). Culturally sustaining pedagogy builds on this approach and seeks to support students in understanding the culture and linguistic attributes of their communities (Paris, 2012). CRP is instruction that recognizes, values, and honors the various differences that students bring to the classroom (Ladson-Billings, 2009; Gay, 2018). An integral part of CRP is centered on the teacher's ability to engage in critical reflection (Richard et al., 2007). Critical reflection allows teachers to critique their own biases and stereotypical beliefs. In addition, critical reflection allows teachers to examine the impact of their life experiences and privilege on their instructional approach (Howard, 2001).

CRP is an inclusive approach to educating children, encompassing the acknowledgment of external factors that influence children's behaviors and achievements. Ford (2011) describes teachers that engage in culturally responsive pedagogy as those that develop a learning environment that appreciates and understands the cultural and developmental needs of students. These teachers recognize that the needs of children extend beyond the classroom environment and look for ways to accommodate these needs within the learning environment. Culturally responsive math teachers infuse social justice, create a sense of belonging, build student competence, and ensure equity in grading.

Culturally Responsive Pedagogy and Social Justice

Muhammad (2020) builds on the scholarship of culturally responsive and sustaining pedagogies, suggesting that black literacy histories provide a framework for culturally responsive instruction. In the book *Cultivating Genius: An Equity Framework for Culturally and Historically Responsive Literacy,* Muhammad (2020) outlines a four-layered framework for instructional practices, regardless of the content area. This model is referred to as the Historically Responsive Literacy Framework (HRL), and suggests that instruction includes the development of identity, skills, intellect, and criticality. Identity provides a space for students to learn about themselves and others. Skills develop students' academic knowledge, while intellect expands students' understanding. Criticality challenges the learner to analyze the world with a critical lens that challenges the structures and systems that perpetuate oppression. Learning becomes a tool for disrupting power, inequity, and oppression. How might the mathematics classroom look and feel different, if instruction allowed students to learn about their identities? How might the math classroom look different if students were challenged to develop procedural, process, and application knowledge through the lens of social justice?

In Muhammad's (2020) model skills development is the focus for many teachers, and the important aspects of identity, intellectual, and criticality development are left on the sidelines. Similarly, in Ladson-Billings (1995) culturally relevant teaching model, teachers focus on academic success, and lose sight of the important aspects of the development of cultural competence and sociopolitical awareness. Math tasks that are centered in a sociopolitical context have the potential to support teachers in developing lessons that build students' intellect, identity, and criticality within the mathematics instruction.

Various scholars have specifically explored the intersection of cultural, social justice, and criticality in mathematics instruction. Frameworks such as Teaching Mathematics for Social Justice, Ethnomathematics, and Critical mathematics all attempt to conceptualize mathematics through the lens of culture and/or social justice. Among these frameworks there is a consensus that mathematics needs to be taught within a context that is relevant to students. According to Berry, Conway, Lawler, & Staley (2020), teaching mathematics for social justice allows students to understand their cultural and community histories. Moreover, this form of instruction allows students to examine and problem-solve relevant problems that exist within their lives. D'Ambrosio & Rosa (2017) suggests that Ethnomathematics seeks to challenge Western traditional ideas of mathematics, including the notion that mathematics is absolute, and is a knowledge base that only an exclusive group of individuals can comprehend. Moreover, ethnomathematics seeks to expand the students' historical and cultural knowledge of mathematics. Ethnomathematics hopes to create a sense of belonging, respecting one's self and others, as well as, building a collective solidarity and cooperation among students (D'Ambrosio & Rosa, 2017). Critical Mathematics educators argue that students learn to challenge their notions of what it means to be a mathematician. These educators seek first to provide opportunities for students to explore and develop mathematical ideas. Critical Mathematics educators seek to help students develop criticality by examining and problem solving issues that are social, economic, and political (Wager & Stinson, 2012). Gutstein (2006) asserts that mathematics is a tool that students can use to develop their critical consciousness and make sense of the sociopolitical context of their lives. There is a need for teachers to connect mathematics in real and personal ways to students' lives. In order to accomplish the connection, teachers have to understand the sociopolitical context of the community and the students they serve (Gutstein, 2006; Aguirre & Zavala, 2013).

Infusions of social justice lessons or rigorous math tasks within the school's curriculum does not need to be a daunting task. As early as kindergarten, teachers can demonstrate to students the intersection of their culture and math. The book *Rethinking Mathematics: Teaching Social Justice by the Numbers* provides numerous examples of how to integrate content and social justice in a way that empowers the students to use math to view their world differently (Gutstein & Peterson, 2013). Although *Rethinking Mathematics: Teaching Social Justice by the Numbers* is geared towards secondary students, the lessons can be adjusted to better the needs of elementary students. One activity from *Rethinking Mathematics* is Poverty and World Wealth. The activity has students explore the percentage of the world's population on each continent in proportion to the wealth on the continent. Although the lesson is meant for secondary students, the lesson could be adapted for various grade levels. The lesson uses percentages and proportions to show the inequity in wealth per person in the world. The goal is not only to have students apply mathematical knowledge, but also understand the wealth gap in the world. The lesson could also be adapted to look at inequities of wealth in the United States or in a particular region. Infusions of social justice lessons should use real data to spur conversations and raise awareness for current issues. Additionally, Youcubed provides rigorous math tasks that can be easily integrated into any curriculum. Youcubed also has videos and training on ensuring a math classroom focuses on rigor (Youcubed, 2020).

Recently Berry et al. (2020) published a book entitled *High School Mathematics Lessons to Explore, Understand, and Respond to Social*

Justice. This book provides a wide range of lessons that strategically link mathematics standards or concepts with social justice topics. For example, there is a lesson entitled The Mathematics of Transformational Resistance that allows students to use mathematical reasoning to analyze the relationship between social oppression and social justice to examine different types of social resistance. Through this lesson students explore the mathematical concepts of coordinate planes and variables through the context of social resistance. Berry et al. (2020) argues that mathematics is a tool to analyze and challenge our societal systems. Teachers have a responsibility to help students learn and understand mathematics through the context of their world. The book is a helpful resource to support secondary teachers in infusing social justice topics within their mathematics instruction.

It is important to recognize that in order for students to engage in mathematics in meaningful ways, they must feel that they belong in the classroom, and are capable. The following sections focus on students' sense of belonging and student competence in relation to culturally responsive teaching.

Sense of Belonging and Culturally Responsive Teaching

> Teachers turn schoolhouses into school homes, where the 3C's care, concern, and connection are as important as the 3R's—Roberts & Irvine, 2009, p. 143

Research has consistently shown that positive teacher-student relationships influence and impact students' academic success. Finn's (1989) identification-participation model argues that students are prone to disengaging from school if students do not feel connected to school, lack a sense of belonging, or feel undervalued or disrespected. Similarly, Shernoff et al. (2016) suggests that students' commitment to schooling is dependent on students' perception of being cared for and supported by others, particularly by adults. Hall (2014) argues students construct their view about themselves and the world around them at school. Students critique the world and themselves, based on the relationships and interactions they have with their peers and teachers. These educational encounters, as Hall (2014) defines them, can develop a sense of hope or hopelessness, similarly, they can create a sense of empowerment or disempowerment.

Banks (2016) conducted a phenomenological study in Southeastern Michigan exploring the experiences of Black high school students. In this study, 23 Black students in grades 9–12 attending a school in urban (15 students) or suburban districts (8 students) in southeastern Michigan, were interviewed and/or participated in a focus group discussion. The gender demographics of the participants were 48 percent females and 52 percent males. Through a semi-structured interview, participants were asked to share their perception of mathematics and the mathematics classroom. Through this study, Banks (2016) found there is a critical need for students to have a sense of belonging in the mathematics classroom. This sense of belonging for students connects and engages them in mathematics instruction (Banks, 2016).

Teachers' ability to craft a learning environment where students have a sense of belonging and feel cared for is a determining factor for students' engagement in learning and academic success (Goodenow & Grady, 1993; Finn 1992). Attending to students' social, academic and psychological needs is defined as care by Walker (1993). Care and the ability of teachers to create a learning environment where students have a sense of belonging is an essential part of culturally responsive pedagogy (CRP). In order to engage in CRP teachers must know their students from multiple perspectives. This means understanding and valuing students' identities and personalities (Delpit, 2012; Gay, 2002; Ladson-Billings, 2009; Milner, 2009). It requires teachers to learn about students' lives outside of the context of school, including their home life and community. Culturally responsive teachers invest time in learning about students personally and culturally.

Matthews (2020) conducted a study of eleven teachers to explore how teachers motivated and engaged Black students in schools with a high graduation rate for Black students. The phenomenological study found that teachers created a sense of belonging by intentionally engaging students in conversations to learn about each student's life outside of the classroom. The teachers stood at the door to greet students or walked around the classroom and asked students about their day or extracurricular activities. Not only did the teacher ask questions, but they remembered the conversation to later check on the students or connect student interest to the content being taught. Furthermore, building the student-teacher relationship impacted not only the sense of belonging, but also student engagement and motivation (Matthews, 2020). Teachers that are culturally responsive value all aspects of knowledge that children bring to the classroom and use their knowledge as springboards for expanding students' knowledge of the world. Each child is viewed as an asset to the community, and a valuable part of the class community. Perceived deficits that students hold are viewed as opportunities to expand upon their assets (Boykins, 2011; Ladson-Billings, 2009; Gay, 2018). Culturally responsive teachers see the genius in their students and are on a mission to help students achieve their goals.

The classroom is transformed into a place of belonging, safety, and security, when teachers care, hence it is a critical aspect of CRP (Martin, 2012). In this transformation, the classroom becomes a community, where knowledge is valued and shared. Each voice in the classroom is important, the teacher is not the sole bearer of knowledge. Students feel at home within a community of learners. The expectations for all learners are high, and learners are supported in meeting their goals (Howard, 2001). These characteristics of culturally responsive teachers are also referred to as other mothering or warm demanders (Collins, 2000; Vazquez 1988). Case (1997) posits that teachers who are other mothers are invested and committed to the success of their students, and Delpit (2012) adds that other mothers view teaching as their calling.

I Don't Trust You

> A sense of trust, confidence, and psychological safety … allows students to take risks, admit errors, ask for help, and experience failure along the way to high levels of learning—Deplit, 2012, p. 84

According to Buber (1988) relationship development requires a commitment from two individuals, relationships cannot be one sided. Engaging in relationship development can be risky, as each member of the relationship has to share parts of who they are. Bryk & Schneider, 2003, argue that trust in the classroom creates a space where students and teachers are willing to take risks. In the context of the classroom, teachers are charged with the task of creating nurturing and safe learning environments where students are willing to trust and take the risk of developing a relationship with their teacher (Banks, 2016).

Establishing trust is an essential part of creating a classroom environment where students have a sense of belonging. Trust between the teacher and students is a necessity for learning by allowing students to have a willingness to engage in learning (Adams & Forsyth, 2013; Bryk & Schneider, 2002; Hoy & Tschannen-Moran, 1999). If there is a lack of trust between the teacher and students, disruptive behaviors and disengagement result as students attempt to self-protect themselves (Gregory & Ripski, 2008; Klem & Connell, 2004).

Several key themes emerged through Banks' (2016) study, one key theme was the need for Black students to have a sense of belonging and trust within the mathematics classroom. The first need of Maslow's hierarchy of human motivation is the need for physical satisfaction, followed by the need for safety. Black students in this study frequently approached the mathematics classroom with apprehension due to multiple previous negative experiences. Too often the mathematics classroom is not a safe place for Black students, hence students are consistently on the defensive.

Students shared that they either use verbal confrontation or disengagement from learning as a means of protection. Multiple negative experiences with mathematics teachers led to the distrust of teachers and their intentions. Consequently, students avoided asking questions or participating in classroom discussion to avoid being perceived by the teacher and their classmates as not smart (Banks, 2016).

Classroom distrust can result in either teacher or students being suspicious of the other's actions, according to Tschannen-Moran and Hoy (2000). Therefore, a teacher calling on a student to answer a question or engage in a class discussion can be viewed as a personal threat. Bryk and Schneider (2003) asserts that larger confrontations develop as a result of minor misunderstandings, due to a lack of trust. Student engagement and interactions with the teacher and peers provides the opportunity for learning to occur. A lack of trust develops a barrier and impedes learning opportunities. Trust develops over time. In past experiences, students may have learned that the title of teacher does not mean that teachers are to be trusted. In order for trust to develop, students must perceive their teachers to be competent, respectful, have integrity, and genuine care (Bryk and Schneider, 2002).

Another important theme of the Banks' (2016) study was students' perception that mathematics is impersonal and not relevant to their lives. Participants shared that often they do not have the opportunity to engage in conversations. The structure of the daily lesson was consistent for most participants, bell work, lecture, practice, get homework, and dismissal. According to the National Council of Teachers of Mathematics (NCTM), effective mathematics instruction that develops students' understanding, requires that students engage in productive mathematics discussion. Providing students with the opportunity to analyze and compare the responses of their classmates defines productive mathematical discussions. Through these discussions, students are able to develop and extend their current understanding of mathematical concepts (Smith & Stein, 2011).

Teacher's Role in Student Competence

> Too many mathematics classrooms mathematical competence is assigned solely on the basis of quickness and correctness, giving the mistaken impression that only some students are 'good at math'.... Creat[ing] an environment where students' mathematical reasoning goes unexamined and unvalued—Berry, 2020

Sense of competence is a person's confidence in understanding how to effectively complete a given task. Competence is a critical component of motivation and engagement in the math classroom. Teachers' intentional building of a classroom environment which challenges students with appropriate support allows students to feel competent (Shernoff et al., 2016; Wang & Eccles, 2013). Students who lack competence in math may appear to disengage or may be less willing to engage in challenging tasks. Teachers play a critical role in building students' sense of competence which increases student engagement and motivation. When a teacher treats a student as if they are competent, the student also believes they are competent (Ladson-Billings, 2000; Wang & Eccles, 2013). However, Black students often are met with differential treatment which hinders competence (Diemer et al., 2016). Black students sense that teachers have lower expectations and lack confidence in Black students ability (Gay, 2018; Ladson-Billings, 2000; Peixoto et al., 2016). Teachers lack confidence in students which leads to lower student confidence and achievement in math. Support from a teacher provides the structure for the student to view the task as doable. Teacher support of competence supports high expectations and relatedness. As a teacher sets high expectations for students, the teacher relays that the student has the ability to complete the work. Further, the support for competence allows the student to feel cared for and connected to the classroom thereby enhancing relatedness (Peixoto et al., 2016).

A teacher's high expectations build students' sense of competence (Gay, 2018). Low expectations from teachers not only impacts achievement, but also a Black student's chances of graduating from high school and completing a four-year college degree. Black students who experience low expectations from teachers become less engaged and less motivated to learn (Gershenson, Holt, Papageorge, 2016; Wang & Hughley, 2012). White teachers are 12 percent less likely to expect a college degree from Black students and 64 percent of White teachers do not expect quality work from Black students (Gershenson et al., 2016; Mahatmya et al., 2016). Specifically, in the math classroom, White teachers perceive Black students as having less ability in math even when the Black students match the ability of the White students. When grading partially correct or incorrect solutions to math work, White teachers are more likely to grade Black students more harshly (Copur, Cimpian, Lu, 2020). Culturally responsive teachers hold high expectations for mastery of current content and future educational success (Gay, 2018; Mahatymya et al., 2016). Teachers who hold high expectations engage students with rigorous math tasks and Black students successfully complete the tasks (Ladson-Billings, 2000; Pitre, 2014; Wang & Eccles, 2013). Culturally responsive math teachers scaffold rigorous tasks and connect the task to prior knowledge. Activating prior knowledge provides adequate support and connections allowing students to sense the teachers' high expectations. (Chou & Tumminia, 2017; Deci & Ryan 1991; Matthews, 2020, Shernoff et al., 2016). High expectation from teachers increases competence, belonging, and motivation (Cham et al., 2014; Wang & Eccles, 2013).

Myth of meritocracy and deficit mindset often makes teachers reluctant to develop high expectations and use challenging math tasks for Black students. The myth of meritocracy posits that hard work and merit provide opportunities and success (Milner, 2012). However, for many Black students systemic injustices hinder Black students from having opportunities to learn and grow as a student. Teachers often perpetuate the idea that working hard provides opportunities while the same teacher creates barriers for the student to learn (Ladson-Billings 2006; Milner, 2012). The belief that success is earned bleeds into the math classroom and hinders student competence. Often math teachers engage in deficit mindset and fail to provide opportunities for Black students to engage with relevant challenging math tasks (Milner, 2012). Also, the math teacher may view the decision to focus on skills and not deeper conceptual understanding as helping the Black student when in fact the teachers' behavior impedes the learning process (Gay, 2018). The lack of focus on the critical thinking and problem-solving skills necessary to succeed in math hinders development in Black students. The lack of opportunities and access to quality math education leads to lower achievement which fuels the teachers belief in the myth of meritocracy (Milner, 2012).

The teacher demonstrates a belief in the students' competence by providing scaffolds to build on the student's previous knowledge. The connection prepares the student for success as the lesson connects the unknown to a familiar concept. To connect the student's prior knowledge the teacher must know the students, so the carefully crafted lessons provide the necessary support (Pitre, 2014; Shernoff et al., 2016; Wang & Eccles, 2013). One strategy for scaffolding is questioning. Teachers can provide support by asking questions to engage students in the thought process to complete the task. As the teachers question, they are evaluating students' knowledge to assist the student in viewing the task in a way that ensures the student finds success (Gonzolez & DeJanette, 2015; Matthews, 2020). Teachers may ask questions to point a student toward a strategy or connect to a prior lesson. Also, the teacher may provide questions which aid the student in viewing the problem in a new way. When a student arrives at a solution through questioning, the student attributes the work to themselves and not the teacher. When a teacher tells the student how to arrive at the solution, the work belongs to the teacher and the opportunity for growth in student competence vanishes (Gonzolez & DeJanette, 2015). Matthews (2020) found that teachers who create supportive classrooms for Black students use questioning to not only evaluate students' learning, but to assist students in believing in themselves. Questioning not only builds competence but engages students in critical thinking and inquiry.

In conjunction with questioning, teachers may use collaborative groups to increase competence. Collaborative groups give students the opportunity to learn from one another. In the math classroom, students work on a task while the teacher circulates and offers support in the form of questioning. Teachers report that students feel more competent when they work on rigorous tasks collaboratively (Matthews, 2020). A study on a school focused on deeper learning through critical thinking and collaboration found that students had increased engagement and motivation as well as competence. Students felt they could effectively complete the tasks while working in groups. More importantly, using collaborative groups and focusing on critical thinking was effective in building competence in Black students (Agger & Konenka, 2020). Collaboration creates a student-centered learning environment which not only builds the social community, but also motivates students and increases achievement (Talbert, Hofkens, & Wang, 2019; Matthews, 2020).

Intentional frequent positive feedback enhances student competence (Cheon & Reeve, 2015; Reeve, 2006; Weidinger, Steinmayer, Spinanth, 2017). The positive feedback keeps students motivated to engage in challenging tasks (Burns, Martin, & Collie, 2019; Cheon & Reeve, 2015). Math and science teachers in a study on creating supportive classroom environments felt that positive reinforcement was critical for students' sense of competence. Teachers intentionally encouraged students with frequent written and verbal positive feedback (Matthews, 2020). In the culturally responsive math classroom, teachers use verbal and non-verbal positive feedback to support student competence. The feedback provides emotional support to decrease student frustration and hopelessness while increasing confidence in mathematical ability (Peixoto et al., 2016). Teachers' positive feedback requires teachers to assess work and focus the correct mathematical thinking in the student work. The teacher uses the correct thinking to guide the student to find incorrect thinking and learn from mistakes. The positive reinforcement demonstrates belief in students' ability which encourages the student to persevere (Cheon & Reeve, 2015; Reeve, 2006; Weidinger et al., 2017).

Without intervention, sense of competence in math abilities diminish throughout school beginning as early as third grade (Weidinger et al., 2017). Students perceive math as a set of skills which determine success or failure in the subject. The focus on skills rather than conceptual knowledge hinders a sustained sense of competence. Students take the lead from the teacher and the teachers indicate that success in math is revealed by regurgitating skills that lack connection. However, a focus on conceptual knowledge levels the field and can increase competence. Students with perceived failure with math skills in the past need positive reinforcement in the classroom. Teachers can use activities and projects that focus on building conceptual knowledge that requires critical thinking not only to provide vital skills but help the student see beyond a set of skills to remember (Weidinger et al., 2017).

In the current racial climate, teachers desiring to focus on culturally responsive pedagogy should insist on focusing on high expectations and increasing competence. At every grade level, the teacher can choose rigorous math tasks to demonstrate to students that the teacher believes in their ability. Regardless of the student's current level of mathematical understanding, a culturally responsive math teacher uses rigorous tasks with scaffolds. The teacher can guide the students with questioning and positive reinforcement. Additionally, the teacher can use collaborative groups to allow students to support and learn from one another. Teachers moving toward culturally responsive pedagogy do not view a math task as too difficult for their students but rather an opportunity for student learning and growth in critical thinking skills.Culturally responsive teachers fight bias and excuses to provide equity in each rigorous math lesson.

Grading in the Culturally Responsive Math Classroom

> Grading practices must counteract institutional biases
> that have historically rewarded students with privilege
> and punished those without, and also must protect student
> grades from our own implicit biases—Feldman, 2019b

An essential component of a culturally responsive math classroom is equity in grading. Teachers may believe that grading in mathematics is not subjective; however, research supports the reality of teacher bias in grading (Cox, 2011; Feldman, 2019a). The lack of equitable grading practices leads to lack of trust with teachers, lower competence, and lower engagement and motivation (Knight & Cooper, 2019). Especially in the math classroom, students need to understand the process of making, finding, and correcting mistakes. Often grading practices in the classroom lower students' confidence as an emphasis is placed on correct answers when students are practicing (Cox, 2011; Knight & Cooper, 2019). The inequity in grading decreases student motivation and engagement as the pressure for the right answer looms. Also, when students' sense the grades are not equitable, the students begin to lose trust in the teacher (Knight & Cooper,

2019). In the math classroom, culturally responsive teachers should elimi-nate all bias in grading, consider practices to encourage working through mistakes such as standards-based grading, and reflect on grading prac-tices regularly.

Eliminating bias in grading requires teachers to consider the pur-pose of grades. Teachers often have varying views on the purpose of grades such as tracking college readiness, effort, evaluating ability, motivation for students, and other purposes to reflect the norm of what the teacher views as an evaluation of a good student (Olsen & Buchanan, 2019). As grading often is not taught explicitly to pre-service teachers, the teach-ers lack training on the proper view of grading (Feldman, 2019a; Olsen & Buchanan, 2019). Traditional grading systems highlight students' home life, focus on mistakes, and promote a fixed mindset (Feldman, 2017). In essence, grades should reflect mastery of the content (Cox, 2011; Olsen & Buchanan, 2019). Teachers must be careful not to include factors which could include personal bias. When teachers include behavior or participa-tion in a student's grade, the door opens for a teacher to subjectively eval-uate a student's behavior in an effort to control the student. Prior to the teacher building student trust and classroom community, students with past trauma in the classroom may not feel comfortable participating or may act out. Teachers who attach a grade to participation or behavior have provided an opportunity to judge students' behavior without searching for an answer (Feldman, 2019a).

Institutional bias in grading such as accuracy in practice, late deduc-tions, and homework often penalize students for factors outside of their control (Feldman, 2019b; Olsen & Buchanan, 2019). Students accurately completing homework in a timely manner often depends on the students' home life. Requiring accuracy for homework creates inequity in grading as some students have access to parental help or tutors while others may not have a quiet space to complete assignments. Additionally, accuracy in homework penalizes students for misconceptions leading to deflating stu-dent confidence and engagement. Completion of homework proves diffi-cult for students when they do not have access to the proper technology or parental assistance. Instead in the math classroom, homework should be an opportunity to practice the concepts learned in class without pen-alty for having a conducive home environment (Feldman 2017; Feldman, 2019a). Extracting the homework grade also places emphasis on mastery of content, the main purpose of the grade. In turn, students can determine the importance of homework by focusing on learning. Teachers may add after school help sessions to provide a space or students who need assis-tance or a place to complete homework. When teachers provide a space for questions or homework outside of class, the student will feel cared for which increases the student's sense of belonging (Feldman, 2019a; Knight & Cooper, 2019).

Standards-based grading allows for equity in grading. Traditional grades average where a student begins and ends their learning grades. Standards-based grading emphasizes the end result of the students learning (Feldman, 2017; Olsen & Buchanan, 2019). The grade shows whether a student mastered each of the mathematical standards. Once teachers recognize that mastery of content reflects the purpose of the grade, standard-based grading becomes critical (Olsen & Buchanan, 2019). Standards-based grading focuses on assessments. The teacher grades divide the assessments into different grades by standard. The division by standards allows the teacher to recognize student deficiencies and provide individualized support. Teachers allow students more time to master the concepts and allow the student to retake assessments to demonstrate mastery. The intentional design of standards-based grading emphasizes mastery with less emphasis on mastery within a tight timeframe (Cox, 2011; Feldman, 2019a). As part of the focus on assessment, teachers regularly provide formative assessments to offer feedback to students without the pressure of grades. The process of pressure free feedback through formative assessments allows the student to value and learn from mistakes (Hochbein & Pollio, 2016).

Numerous studies have been done on the effects of standards-based grading. Standards-based grading creates an environment that promotes learning and deemphasizes grades (Knight & Cooper, 2019). Students view mistakes as acceptable and opportunities to learn and master math concepts. Standards-based grading supports a growth mindset as students believe they can do better because they understand the teacher provides multiple opportunities for students to demonstrate mastery (Feldman, 2017; Knight & Cooper, 2019). Students willingly try challenging problems as they learn that mistakes provide learning. Sense of belonging increases as the learning environment provides support without judgment. Students are more engaged and ready to learn. Ownership of learning occurs as students know how to improve their grade (Knight & Cooper, 2019).

Standards-based grading provides equity in the classroom. When a teacher uses standards-based grading standardized test scores and grades align (Feldman, 2019a; Hochbein & Pollio, 2016). The lack of emphasis on homework, participation and behavior removes institutional and personal bias. Additionally, teachers that use standards-based grading close the grade gap between Black and White students. Fewer White students receive A's and fewer Black students receive D's or F's in a classroom implementing standards-based grading. Standards-based grading eliminates rewarding students in their grades for adapting to the norms of White culture (Feldman, 2019a; Olsen & Buchanan, 2019). Removing the bias in grading allows Black students to feel the grades reflect mastery and fairness (Feldman, 2019a; Munoz & Guskey, 2015).

Once a teacher has decided to adopt standards-based grading, the teacher should determine the best fit for their classroom, students, and school system. For each lesson, the teacher should decide the skill(s) students should master that correlate to the learning target for the day. Regular formative assessments allow students to self-assess their mastery of the content (Moss, & Brookhart, 2016). There are a variety of resources available to support math teachers in integrating standards-based grading into their math classroom. Marzano's (2010) *Formative Assessment and Standards-Based Grading* details how to implement formative assessments and standards-based grading to increase achievement in the classroom.

Conclusion

> Mathematics educators [must] learn to listen for and to the voices of Black students, using these voices to develop equitable and just schools and classrooms for all students —Stinson, 2013, p. 94

Math is often considered to be culturally neutral, yet it is taught based on white cultural norms such as a focus on individual learning rather than collaborative learning. The myth of meritocracy posits that if you work hard then you will be successful which creates a sense that those who struggle lack work ethic. These beliefs in addition to the systematic practices of remediation, tracking, and inequitable grading hinder Black students' access to higher level mathematics and continue to perpetuate inequity thereby creating opportunity gaps for Black students. Milner (2012) argues that the opportunity gap is framed by teachers' beliefs of color blindness, cultural conflict, myth of meritocracy, or cultural neutral mindset. In the math classroom, the culturally neutral mindset and the myth of meritocracy are often visible and hinder learning.

Culturally responsive practices provide a tool for closing opportunity gaps and creating equitable learning environments. Culturally responsive mathematics teachers embrace the challenge of creating a learning environment where all students feel valued and important. These teachers know the importance of knowing who their students are from a personal, social, and academic perspective. Culturally responsive teachers are masterful at developing positive relationships with students, their families, and the community. The classroom environment in essence becomes a second home. It is a place where students experience community, support, a sense of belonging, and competence. Culturally responsive mathematics teachers use their knowledge of students and the community to contextualize mathematics and provide students with a lens to problematize our world through mathematics. Specifically, the math lessons provide opportunities for students to explore their world through rigorous math tasks. Students can be successful in a classroom where lessons, grading, and treatment are equitable for all students.

REFERENCES

Adams, C.M., & Forsyth, P.B. (2013). Revisiting the trust effect in urban elementary schools. *The Elementary School Journal, 114*(1), 1–21. doi:10.1086/670736.

Agger, C.A., & Koenka, A.C. (2020). Does attending a deeper learning school promote student motivation, engagement, perseverance, and achievement? *Psychology in the Schools, 57*(4), 627–645. doi:10.1002/pits.22347.

Aguirre, J.M., & del Rosario Zavala, M. (2013). Making culturally responsive mathematics teaching explicit: A lesson analysis tool. *Pedagogies: An International Journal, 8*(2), 163–190. https://doi.org/10.1080/1554480x.2013.768518.

Allen, Q. (2013). They think minority means lesser than: Black middle-class sons and fathers resisting microaggressions in the school. *Urban Education, 48*(2).

Banks, J. (2016). *An exploration of the experiences of Black high school students in the mathematics classroom: A qualitative study* (Order No. 10242473). Available from ProQuest Dissertations & Theses Global. (1872353323).

Berry III, R.Q. (2020). *Positioning students as mathematically competent.* National Council of Teachers of Mathematics. https://www.nctm.org/News-and-Calendar/Messages-from-the-President/Archive/Robert-Q_-Berry-III/Positioning-Students-as-Mathematically-Competent/.

Berry, R.Q., Conway, B.M., Lawler, B., & Staley, J.W. (2020). *High school mathematics lessons to explore, understand, and respond to social injustice.* Corwin.

Bonilla-Silva, E. (1997). Rethinking racism: Toward a structural interpretation. *Sociological Review, 62.*

Boykins, A.W. (2011). The talent development model of schooling: Placing students at promise for academic success. *Journal of Education for Students Placed at Risk (JESPAR), 5*, 37–41.

Boykins, A.W., & Noguera, P. (2011). *Creating the opportunity to learn: Moving from research to practice to close the achievement gap.* ASCD.

Boykin, A.W., Tyler, K.M., & Miller, O. (2005). In search of cultural themes and their expressions in the dynamics of classroom life. *Urban Education, 40*(5), 521–549. doi:10.1177/0042085905278179.

Brisson, B.M., Dicke, A., Gaspard, H., Häfner, I., Flunger, B., Nagengast, B., & Trautwein, U. (2017). Short intervention, sustained effects: Promoting students' math competence beliefs, effort, and achievement. *American Educational Research Journal, 54*(6), 1048–1078. doi:10.3102/0002831217716084.

Bryk, A.S., & Schneider, B.L. (2002). *Trust in schools: A core resource for improvement.* Russell Sage Foundation.

Buber, M. (1958). *I and thou.* Scribner.

Case, K.I. (1997). African American other mothering in the urban elementary school. *Urban Review, 29*(1), 25–39. doi:10.1023/A:1024645710209.

Cham, H., Hughes, J.N., West, S.G., & Im, M.H. (2014). Assessment of adolescents' motivation for educational attainment. *Psychological Assessment, 26*(2), 642–659. doi:10.1037/a0036213.

Cheon, S.H., & Reeve, J. (2015). A classroom-based intervention to help teachers decrease students' amotivation. *Contemporary Educational Psychology, 40*, 99–111. doi:10.1016/j.cedpsych.2014.06.004.

Chou, V. & Tumminia, A. (2017). Self-determination theory. In S. Rogelberg (Ed.), *The SAGE encyclopedia of industrial and organizational psychology, 2nd edition* (pp. 1399–1401). SAGE Publications.

Collins, P.H. (2000). *Black feminist thought: Knowledge, consciousness, and the politics of empowerment*. Routledge.

Copur-Gencturk, Y., Cimpian, J.R., Lubienski, S.T., & Thacker, I. (2020). Teachers' bias against the mathematical ability of female, Black, and Hispanic students. *Educational Researcher, 49*(1), 30–43. doi:10.3102/0013189X19890577.

Cox, K.B. (2011). Putting classroom grading on the table: A reform in progress. *American Secondary Education, 40*(1), 67–87.

D'Ambrosio, U., & Rosa, M. (2017). Ethnomathematics and its pedagogical action in mathematics education. *ICME-13 Monographs*, 285–305.

Darling-Hammond, L. (2004). Standards, accountability, and school reform. *Teachers College Record, 106*(6).

Delgado, R., & Stefancic, J. (2001). *Critical race theory: An introduction*. New York University Press.

Delpit, L.D. (2012). *"Multiplication is for White people": Raising expectations for other people's children*. New Press: Distributed by Perseus Distribution.

Diemer, M.A., Marchand, A.D., Mckellar, S.E., & Malanchuk, O. (2016). Promotive and corrosive factors in African American students' math beliefs and achievement. *Journal of Youth and Adolescence, 45*(6), 1208–1225. doi:10.1007/s10964-016-0439-9.

Feldman, J. (2017). Do your grading practices undermine equity initiatives? *Leadership, 47*(2), 8–11.

Feldman, J. (2019). Beyond standards-based grading: Why equity must be part of grading reform. *Phi Delta Kappan, 100*(8), 52–55. doi:10.1177/0031721719846890.

Feldman, J. (2019). Grade expectations. *Harvard Ed. Magazine*. https://www.gse.harvard.edu/news/ed/19/05/grade-expectations.

Finn, J.D. (1989). Withdrawing from school. *Review of Educational Research, 59*(2), 117–142. doi:10.2307/1170412.

Ford, D. (2011). *Reversing underachievement among gifted Black students* (2nd ed.). Prufrock Press.

Gay, G. (2018). *Culturally responsive teaching: Theory, research, and practice* (2nd ed.). Teachers College Press.

Gershenson, S., Holt, S.B., & Papageorge, N.W. (2016). Who believes in me? The effect of student–teacher demographic match on teacher expectations. *Economics of Education Review, 52*, 209–224. doi:10.1016/j.econedurev.2016.03.002.

Gillborn, D. (2006). Public interest and the interests of White people are not the same: Assessment, education policy, and racism. In G. Ladson-Billings & W.F. Tate (Eds.), *Education research in the public interest: Social justice, action, and policy*. Teachers College Press.

Goodenow, C, & Grady, K.E. (1993). The relationship of school belonging and friends' values to academic motivation among urban adolescent students. *Journal of Experimental Education, 62*, 60–71.

Gregory, A., & Ripski, M.B. (2008). Adolescent trust in teachers: Implications for behavior in the high school classroom. *School Psychology Review, 37*(3), 337–353. http://www.nasponline.org/publications/spr/index.aspx?vol=37&issue=3.

Gutstein, E (2006). Reading and writing the world with mathematics: Toward a pedagogy for social justice. Routledge.

Gutstein, E., & Peterson, B. (2013). *Rethinking mathematics: Teaching social justice by the numbers*. Rethinking Schools.

Hale-Benson, J.E. *(1986). Black children: Their roots, culture, and learning styles*. Johns Hopkins University Press.

Hall, C.W. (2014). *Voices of adolescents: A phenomenological study of relational encounters and their significance within the school setting*. (Doctoral dissertation).

Hochbein, C., & Pollio, M. (2016). Making grades more meaningful: Students at 11 high-needs Kentucky high schools experienced stronger correlations between course grades and standardized test scores after their schools switched to standards-based grading practices. *Phi Delta Kappan, 98*(3), 49.

Howard, T.C. (2001). Telling their side of the story: African American students' perceptions of culturally relevant teaching. *The Urban Review, 33*(2), 131–149. doi:10.1023/A:1010393224120.

Hoy, W.K., & Tschannen-Moran, M. (1999). Five faces of trust: An empirical confirmation in urban elementary schools. *Journal of School Leadership, 9,* 184–208.

Irvine, J.J. (1990). *Black students and school failure: Policies, practices, and prescriptions.* Greenwood Press.

Klem, A.M., & Connell, J.P. (2004). Relationships matter: Linking teacher support to student engagement and achievement. *Journal of School Health, 74*(7), 262–273. doi:10.1111/j.1746-1561.2004.tb08283.x.

Knight, M., & Cooper, R. (2019). Taking on a new grading system: The interconnected effects of standards-based grading on teaching, learning, assessment, and student behavior. *NASSP Bulletin, 103*(1), 65–92. doi:10.1177/0192636519826709.

Ladson-Billings, G. (1997). It doesn't add up: African American students' mathematics achievement. *Journal for Research in Mathematics Education, 28*(6), 697. doi:10.2307/749638.

Ladson-Billings, G. (2000). Fighting for our lives: Preparing teachers to teach African American students. *Journal of Teacher Education, 51*(3), 206–214. doi:10.1177/00224871 00051003008.

Ladson-Billings, G. (2009). *The dreamkeepers: Successful teachers of African American children* (2nd ed.). San Francisco, CA: Jossey-Bass Publishers.

Ladson-Billings, G., & Tate, W.F. (1995). Toward a critical race theory of education. *Teacher College Record, 97*(1).

Lampert, M. (2001). *Teaching problems and the problems of teaching.* Yale University Press.

Mahatmya, D., Lohman, B.J., Brown, E.L., & Conway-Turner, J. (2016). The role of race and teachers' cultural awareness in predicting low-income, Black and Hispanic students' perceptions of educational attainment. *Social Psychology of Education, 19*(2), 427–449. doi:10.1007/s11218-016-9334-1.

Martin, D.B. (2012). Learning mathematics while Black. *Educational Foundations, 26*(1–2), 47.

Marzano, R.J. (2010). *Formative assessment and standards-based grading.* Solution Tree.

Matthews, T. (2020). *A phenomenological study that examined the experiences of high school teachers who build supportive classroom environments that encourage African American students to graduate* (Order No. 28150039). Available from ProQuest Dissertations & Theses Global. (2454697401).

McGee, E.O., & Martin, D.B. (2011). "You would not believe what I have to go through to prove my intellectual value!" Stereotype management among academically successful Black mathematics and engineering students. *American Educational Research Journal, 48*(6), 1347–1389. doi:10.3102/0002831211423972.

Milner, H.R. (2012). Beyond a test score: Explaining opportunity gaps in educational practice. *Journal of Black Studies, 43*(6), 693–718. doi:10.1177/0021934712442539.

Moss, C.M., & Brookhart, S.M. (2016). *Learning targets: Helping students aim for understanding in today's lesson.* Hawker Brownlow Education.

Muhammad, G. (2020). *Cultivating genius: An equity framework for culturally and historically responsive literacy.* Scholastic.

Munoz, M.A., & Guskey, T.R. (2015). Standards-based grading and reporting will improve education: Making clear linkages between standards, assessment, grading, and reporting that are concisely reported work for the betterment of ALL students. *Phi Delta Kappan, 96*(7), 64.

Oakes, J., Rand Corporation., & National Science Foundation (U.S.). (1990). *Multiplying inequalities: The effects of race, social class, and tracking on opportunities to learn mathematics and science.* Rand Corp.

Olsen, B., & Buchanan, R. (2019). An investigation of teachers encouraged to reform grading practices in secondary schools. *American Educational Research Journal, 56*(5), 2004–2039. doi:10.3102/0002831219841349.

Paris, D. (2012). Culturally sustaining pedagogy: A needed change in stance, terminology, and practice. *Educational Researcher, 41*(3), 93–97. https://doi.org/10.3102/0013189X12441244.

Peixoto, F., Sanches, C., Mata, L., & Monteiro, V. (2016). "How do you feel about math?": Relationships between competence and value appraisals, achievement emotions and academic achievement. *European Journal of Psychology of Education, 32*(3), 385–405. doi:10.1007/s10212-016-0299-4.

Pierce, C.M. (1995). Stress analogs of racism and sexism: Terrorism, torture, and disaster. In C. Willie, P.P. Rieker, B.M. Kramer & B.S. Brown (Eds.), *Mental health, racism, and sexism* (pp. 277). University of Pittsburgh Press.

Pitre, C.C. (2014). Improving African American student outcomes: Understanding educational achievement and strategies to close opportunity gaps. *Western Journal of Black Studies, 38*(4), 209–217.

Reeve, J. (2006). Teachers as facilitators: What autonomy-supportive teachers do and why their students benefit. *The Elementary School Journal, 106*(3), 225–236. doi:10.1086/501484.

Roberts, M.A., & Irvine, J.J. (2009). African American teachers' caring behaviors: The difference makes a difference. In L.C. Tillman (Ed.), *The Sage handbook of African American education* (pp. 141–152). Sage Publications.

Sheppard, P. (2006). Successful African American mathematics students in academically unacceptable high schools. *Education, 126*.

Shernoff, D.J., Kelly, S., Tonks, S.M., Anderson, B., Cavanagh, R.F., Sinha, S., & Abdi, B. (2016). Student engagement as a function of environmental complexity in high school classrooms. *Learning and Instruction, 43*, 52–60. doi:10.1016/j.learninstruc.2015.12.003.

Smith, M.S., & Stein, M.K. (2018). *5 Practices for orchestrating productive mathematics discussions*. National Council of Teachers of Mathematics/Corwin Mathematics.

Stinson, D. (2013). Negotiating the "White Male Math Myth": African American male students and success in school mathematics. *Journal for Research in Mathematics Education, 44*(1), 69–99. doi:10.5951/jresematheduc.44.1.0069.

Sue, D.W. (2010). *Microaggressions in everyday life: Race, gender, and sexual orientation.* Wiley & Sons.

Sue, D.W., & Constantine, M.G. (2007). Racial microaggressions as instigators of difficult dialogues on race: Implications of student affairs educators and students. *The College Student Affairs Journal, 26*(2).

Sue, D.W., Nadal, K.L., Capodilupo, C.M., Lin, A.I., Torino, G.C., & Rivera, D.P. (2008). Racial microaggressions against Black Americans: Implications for counseling. *Journal of Counseling and Development, 86*(3), 330.

Tschannen-Moran, M., & Hoy, W.K. (2000). A multidisciplinary analysis of the nature, meaning, and measurement of trust. *Review of Educational Research, 70*(4), 547–593.

Vasquez, J.A. (1988). Contexts of learning for minority students. *The Educational Forum, 52*(3), 243–253. doi:10.1080/00131728809335490.

Walker, E.V. (1993). Interpersonal caring in the "good" segregated schooling of Black children: Evidence from the case of Caswell County training school. *The Urban Review, 25*(1), 63–77. doi:10.1007/bf01108046

Walker, E. (2007). Why aren't more minorities taking more advanced mathematics? *Educational Leadership 65*(3), 48–53.

Wang, M., & Eccles, J.S. (2013). School context, achievement motivation, and academic engagement: A longitudinal study of school engagement using a multidimensional perspective. *Learning and Instruction, 28*, 12–23. doi:10.1016/j.learninstruc.2013.04.002

Weidinger, A.F., Steinmayr, R., & Spinath, B. (2018). Changes in the relation between competence beliefs and achievement in math across elementary school years. *Child Development, 89*(2), e138–e156. doi:10.1111/cdev.12806.

Youcubed. (2020, July 20). https://www.youcubed.org/.

Healing Through Stories

*How Picture Books and Storytelling Can Cultivate
Caring Spaces in Early Elementary Classrooms*

DOMINIQUE HERARD

Introduction

Educators are storytellers. If you are a teacher or know one well, then you know that this particular profession can require you to be many things. On the same day, you can transition between being a mathematician, healer, reader, thinker, historian, scientist, first-aid provider, writer, and counselor seamlessly, but educators are definitely storytellers. They are the keepers of the stories that blow like the wind through classrooms, and they have the ability to cultivate spaces where healing can take place. This healing has always been necessary for Students and Educators of Color grappling with the inequities in the institution of school. These inequities became even more apparent in 2020 when schools across America closed with the onset of the Covid-19 pandemic. Healing was needed. Healing *is* needed.

Educators can be the ones to grow communities in which diverse stories are told aloud and shared through books, and those stories can enrich, affirm and amplify the learners who encounter them. Many of us already know the ability stories have to transform minds, speak truth to power, and help us understand our own histories and those of others who are different from us. Knowing our own histories can help us exist as our full selves, having strength of spirit in who we are to ourselves and to the other members of our classroom. Knowing the histories of others can help build compassion and understanding in how those stories connect and can exist together. If stories are in possession of this much power, then classroom environments can and should be the places in which the seeds are planted for those caring spaces to grow.

Cultivating those spaces in which storytelling and care are centered is a challenge. Our educational system is one that rewards conformity, catering a shared vision of "common" goals that can omit certain perspectives. The vision of collective healing can be hard for systematic decision-makers to understand. In turn, this makes it more challenging and draining for the educator to exist as a facilitator of stories. Being a protector of stories makes the educator a kind of artist who facilitates spaces in which liberation exists for young learners. Educators are working in a system that is intentionally designed to inhibit their creative ability to address the full humanity of students in their care, particularly the Black and Brown ones. Storytelling is an art, and educators should be allowed to grow that artistic muscle in how to reframe the narratives that are intentionally fed to us by society, supremacy, and systems and how to do that *well*. A captivating storyteller taps into imaginations and creative consciousness to form their craft, and that also describes education at its best and most beautiful.

It is no easy task to play a system from within. It should not be done in isolation and requires a knowledge of the historical context of our current times and what genius ideas came before that can serve as models for this beautiful work. Stories! According to James Baldwin, "the role of the artist ... is to illuminate the darkness, blaze roads through the vast forest... [and] to make the world a more human dwelling place" (Baldwin, 1985, p. 669). As the artist can critique the world through their craft and form meaningful experiences in relation to society and our human role in it, so can the educator engage in an art that prioritizes the telling of stories. These can be beautiful stories that move to decolonize against systems that were intentionally created to dehumanize and control. Sharing some theories and frameworks that have helped to form my opinions as well as examples of books and storytelling practices, this essay is about creating space for that kind of art, for the stories that will humanize, heal, teach, empower, strengthen, grow, and show love.

The Intentional Language of Imagination and Futuring

As a Black female who has taught in a variety of scholastic settings and as a student who rarely saw herself reflected in any of the myriad of classroom spaces I found myself in, there is an immediate personal recognition for me in how welcoming, comforting, or true educational spaces can feel based on which stories and storytelling practices are valued. Beyond my personal experiences as a student and teacher, many theories and wise words from brilliant minds have and continue to shape the way in which I enter and operate in classroom spaces. These words have also enhanced my growth as a storyteller and the ways in which imaginative practices towards education can support centering healing spaces.

I teach first grade, and imagination has felt like something that should be available in surplus from six and seven-year-olds but is increasingly not as common, particularly in the age of increased remote learning due to the Covid-19 pandemic. This can be seen as districts gravitate towards learning platforms like Seesaw or Google Classroom, for example. These platforms can be used as mediums for dispensing lessons where imagination may be ignored in favor of simplicity. This can be detrimental if specific attention is not paid in how to analyze and critique systemic and personal bias in these platforms and how to continue to make space for stories to be shared. Inequities never rest, and neither should we. Intentional attention to the power of language and creative solutions to promote the thriving of Students of Color are essential in breaking down systems that were set up with as much intention. While more and more imagination for younger minds needs to be specifically cultivated and taught and practiced, so too does the imagination for educators to engage in this work.

The inequitable structure of our educational system and mandates from insensitive school districts serve as inhibitors to the liberation of its learners but also to the growth and freedom of its educators. There is a deep need for imagination to be intentionally cultivated within educators. Too often, more creative pursuits are stifled in favor of standardized practices and skill sets that are standard to whiteness and not inclusive of the histories and cultures of the Global Majority (a term that some use as a variant of People of Color since about 80 percent of the world's population are Indigenous, Black, Asian, or Non-White People of Color). As Dr. Maxine Greene mentions in *Releasing the Imagination: Essays on Education, the Arts, and Social Change*, educators should be allowed to "develop a humane and liberating pedagogy" as they are "more likely to uncover or be able to interpret what we are experiencing if we can at times recapture some of our own lost spontaneity and some awareness of our own backgrounds" (Greene, 1995, p. 52). Teachers need the space to do just that, form their own pedagogies and reclaim educational environments with an artistry and creativity that captures what joy and excellence in learning can be. Teachers need time to use their own backgrounds in conjunction with theoretical frameworks to inform and form their love- and justice-oriented instructional practices as well as antiracist social-emotional learning approaches with students.

The names of Breonna Taylor, Ahmaud Arbery, George Floyd, and other unarmed Black people have unfortunately been burned into our minds because of their senseless murders and lack of consequences for many of the murderers, particularly those in law enforcement. To those of us who have always known and to those who are just learning, the truth is undeniable: critical thinking and recognized humanity of Black folx is essential to bettering our world. Classrooms are a step in that direction, and some might say early elementary classrooms even more specifically.

Educators need space to imagine for themselves and with their colleagues, and they need schedules and structures in place that truly honor and prioritize liberatory education, not just methods that perform honor or care while keeping harmful systems in place. In a different book called *The Dialectic of Freedom*, Dr. Greene is advocating for teachers to investigate the components of their practice, belief, and systems that facilitate learners' path to freedom, as the title suggests. Imagine, she posits, that "education is conceived of as a process of futuring, of releasing persons to become different, of provoking persons to repair lacks and to take action to create themselves" (Greene, 1988, p. 22). Imagine.

And how can that be actualized? Futuring is looking ahead and using all the tools you have obtained as an educator and human, bringing together your identities and strengths, and envisioning a world that invites learners with open arms to come as they are. Futuring is attending to that creative part of yourself that wants to construct a better world, even if you may not be around to see its realization. Futuring is reframing stories so ingrained in our consciousness (that you may not even know how you know them) in favor of a fuller narrative structure for Students of the Global Majority. Futuring is reminiscent of what poet and activist Audre Lorde writes in her essay entitled *The Transformation of Silence into Language and Action*: "[P]rimarily for us all it is necessary to teach by living and speaking those truths which we believe and know beyond understanding … [in] an attempt to break that silence and bridge some of the differences between us, for it is not difference which immobilizes us but silence. And there are so many silences to be broken" (Lorde, 1977, pp. 43–44). Futuring looks like gathering knowledge that grounds history and frameworks that will then lead to breaking those silences in the educational world and inspiring us to act.

The Knowledge Library

I think of this futuring knowledge as being collected in a type of library which is filled with theories and frameworks that I can rely on when issues of inequities are revealed to me. These issues are always there waiting to be unearthed and combatted. The library is also filled with truthful words that can remind myself and others of the necessity to always move towards eradicating the deep-rooted inequities and struggles we face.

Such as:

Abolitionist Education: It is appropriate that the first theory in the alphabetized Knowledge Library is from Dr. Bettina Love because her research and writings center around abolishing the idea of school as we know it. When the Covid-19 pandemic forced nearly all schools in America to close in March 2020, suddenly there was not a need to push the domineering idea of education that was stifling the creativity of educators and students. In schools around the country during this emergency, much standardized testing was cancelled, as it should be permanently. School districts were supplying students with technology that mysteriously appeared out of thin air, technology like Hot Spots or laptops, that could have enhanced learning experiences much earlier. In her book called *We Want to Do More Than Survive: Abolitionist Teaching and the Pursuit of Educational Freedom*, Dr. Love describes abolitionist teaching as being "built on the creativity, imagination, boldness, ingenuity, and rebellious spirit and methods of abolitionists" (Love, 2019, p. 11). She advocates for a collective struggle "not only to reimagine school but to build new schools that we are taught to believe are impossible: schools based on intersectional justice, antiracism, love, healing, and joy" (Love, 2019, p. 11).

As virus rates fluctuated and remote learning was extended throughout many schools, Love's words continued to serve as reminders that going back to the status quo after this time is over should not be an option. The ingenuity that was used to care for children during the earlier days of the pandemic, the flexibility that was afforded to teachers and school districts as the nation grappled with all of the unknowns and poor national leadership around the pandemic, cannot be forgotten as we move towards rethinking what school can-should-will be in whatever learning model it adopts in the next years.

Love's interpretation of imagination is called freedom dreaming "which gives teachers a collective space to methodically tear down the educational survival complex and collectively rebuild a school system that truly loves all children" (Love, 2019, p. 102). Freedom dreaming is not naive to the current context of the United States. Using the Blackprint (an expression some are using instead of blueprint to specifically pay homage to often-ignored contributions of Black thought to our culture) of our ancestors, we can freedom-dream an educational system that 100 percent truly values EACH learner, where educators are not looking for the safe option but radically transforming what we know as school in service of something more complete and just.

Archaeology of Self: A key notion of supporting students in their own identity development and storytelling affirmations is getting it right with yourself. This is the main idea behind the research and work of Dr. Yolanda Sealey-Ruiz. Entitled Archaeology of Self, her research can be described as a deep excavation of personal beliefs and biases that could block pathways to healing and centering the work of racial justice in any space but particularly educational spaces. As Dr. Sealey-Ruiz notes, educators who "develop racial literacy are able to engage in the necessary personal reflection about their racial beliefs and practices, and teach their students to do the same" (Sealey-Ruiz, 2019, Arch of Self). In this era of social media and sensationalized news reporting putting the sufferings and injustices of Black People on display, it feels necessary to create spaces in which educators can care and understand themselves better and allow their students the same respect.

Dr. Sealey-Ruiz's work is an "action-oriented process requiring love, humility, reflection, an understanding of history, and a commitment to working against racial injustice" (Sealey-Ruiz, 2019, Arch of Self). The attention to love is particularly noteworthy, as often conversations around race and antiracist practices can be contentious amongst colleagues. Engaging in this work solidifies an understanding of self even in brave spaces so one is not offended but reflective by someone calling out (or calling in) practices that may be harmful to Children of Color. Rooted in what she calls a critical love of people and culture, this practice aims to create a sustainable way to make action a part of teacher practice, one in which "racial literacy in schools includes the ability to read, write about, discuss and interrupt situations and events that are motivated and upheld by racial inequity and bias" (Sealey-Ruiz, 2019, Arch of Self). Before you get into the hard work of liberating yourself and learners, self-work and spaces in which critical love can be practiced are vital.

Culturally and Historically Responsive Teaching: In Dr. Gholdy Muhammad's book *Cultivating Genius: An Equity Framework for Culturally and Historically Responsive Literacy*, critical thinking, or criticality as she calls it, "helps students assume responsibility for the ways in which they process information—to avoid being passive consumers of knowledge and information" (Muhammad, G. 2020, p. 122). Since it's "an intellect practice of studying the state of humanity," criticality is never outdated, always relevant because it will allow learners as humans to critique what is happening around them whether we are in the midst of times of enslavement, as with the Black literary circles that Muhammad researched for her framework, or in the midst of a global pandemic with a fact-deficient, racist American Presidency (Muhammad, G. 2020, p. 132).

As Dr. Muhammad calls on teachers to be "truth and knowledge seekers," one of many responses to that call is to include young minds in taking part of that journey as well (Muhammad, G. 2020, p. 15). The truth is that Children of Color, particularly Black and Brown children, have been made most vulnerable within our schools and societies. Dr. Muhammad writes that a "productive starting point is to design teaching and learning to the group(s) of student who have been marginalized the most in societies and with schools" (page 11). This idea is common in conversations amongst early elementary educators, as general lesson planning geared towards students who are most "in need of growth" or "struggling" will be able to capture and enhance the learning for all. Dr. Muhammad's research and framework removes the deficit language to focus on the excellence of Black history and experiences. Educators have a responsibility to recognize the excellence of marginalized cultures, which will transform the world for all students and allow for more fulfilled, quality-driven living and learning

Culturally Responsive Teaching: Zaretta Hammond builds a concrete bridge to the landscape of culturally responsive teaching. She talks very clearly about how educators will often use the terms multicultural education, social justice education, and culturally responsive education interchangeably when in fact those all work in tandem to create equitable spaces in schools. Culturally responsive teaching specifically "leverages the science of learning by exploiting (for good) the cultural schema—or funds of knowledge—students come in with to make learning 'sticky.' When we build instructional practices around opportunities to process information in ways that make learning sticky, then students become able to carry more of the cognitive load that leads to doing more rigorous work. We focus on the cognitive development of underserved students and teach them how to be literate, competent readers and writers" (Hammond, 2020).

Hammond's work is a strong call to not minimize equity work in educational spaces by focusing on just one aspect of the areas mentioned in the previous paragraph. Creating a diverse classroom library does not make you antiracist just as centering antiracist consciousness does not necessarily ensure that you are a culturally responsive educator. She specifically highlights how sometimes early elementary educators can think naively about truly transformative instructional practices, really doing multiculturalism instead. Hammond believes the essential work is how "students must comprehend what they're reading, possess advanced decoding skills, have word wealth, and be able to command all of these literacy skills. Our social justice frame should prompt us to ask these questions: *How are students code breakers, how are they text users, how are they text critics, and how are they meaning-makers*? Our culturally responsive pedagogies arm us to build these dispositions and skills in our most vulnerable kids" (Hammond, 2020). With her work, adept educators are learning as many pedagogical areas as possible to support their understanding of responsive interactions and learning styles to enhance instruction for the best possible outcomes.

Decolonization: Cultural theorist Gloria Anzaldúa's work is a tes-
tament to the way in which she refused to silence the parts of herself that
would not be acceptable in our colonized society, intentionally shirking
the binary notions of how to be a certain way. Her transformative way
of living she called a "new mestiza," someone who rejects the notion of
either/or and instead channels an "ability to imagine, enact, and inhabit
spaces that go beyond dichotomies of all kind," living on the borders of
two or more worlds and balancing all of the cultural responsibilities, identities, and understandings (Anzaldúa, 1998). For her, the conversation is
centered on her biculturalism and the tightrope which people are forced
to walk between two or more sides of themselves. Seen as examples of
code-switching, her work continues to inspire the fight against silence and
the rejection of the either/or mentality.

Anzaldúa was also a large proponent of people not always accepting
what they cannot understand. The societal labels which were placed on her
were methods to pigeonhole her existence and her literary discourse, and
the very same can be said of how Black and Brown learners are approached
in educational spaces that are not specifically designed with antiracism
and anti-bias theories in mind. Those same labels can affect student participation and storytelling in all grades. She was torn between being true
to herself as a writer and not alienating those she wanted to influence or
advocate for with her style. The mestiza is a break from these notions. It is
an amalgamation of the parts that create a self and not giving those parts
standard binary labels like Gay/Straight or Black/White or Boy/Girl with
no thought for how identities have nuances and intersections. There are
other methods of finding meaning through creation of your stories (Anzaldúa, 1998). Early elementary learners are turning to all areas of their
environment to make meaning and deconstruct the world around them.
As emerging readers and writers, storytelling is a key feature of how they
conceptualize the world around them and their places in it.

Additionally, Anzaldúa also addressed the need for individuals to take
over their own lives or compose new realities and identities. One of the
words she mentions is *compustura*, which means putting "together frag-
ments to make a garment which you wear ... [one that] represents you, your
identity, and reality in the world" (Anzaldúa, 1998). Essentially, you are
telling your own story, making your own identity, and shaping the identities by which the world can see you. Though the word evokes a poetical
essence, it exemplifies what is not easy for people to portray: the courage it
takes to make your own way, pave a new path, especially if your whole self
has existed in the shadow of a more dominant culture, gender, or race.

Through stories, we are truth-seekers, truth-tellers, and truth-makers.
Those truths were not always easy for Anzaldúa. She shared about the role

of censorship in her life, from institutions wary of her style of bilingualism in her writing or what were deemed as revolutionary ideas. In her work, truth was foremost as a way to break free of what can entrap people. She shared about the tension between her family regarding her sharing stories that were meant to be secret. Those same stories exposed truths, acted as agents for social justice, and offered a chance to call attention to invisible realities.

As each voice is unique, the methods with which teachers help students locate those voices are also unique. As safe as classroom communities can be, what kinds of conversations and emotions happen within them is at the discretion of the way stories are valued in the environment. Unlearning the colonizing, white supremacist values that we have been socialized to believe are superior takes active practice as we move towards collective liberation.

Social Imagination: Throughout the history of the United States of America, imagination has been key to dreaming of different alternatives for the humanity of lives, as evidenced by the myriad of examples of more than four hundred years of resistance against tyranny, inequality, and dehumanization of Non-White people in our country. In such a pervasive system, educational artistry and imagination is essential. Dr. Greene calls this social imagination, a way to "invent visions of what should be and what might be in our deficient society, on the streets where we live, in our schools" (Greene, 1995, p. 5). Only when we connect with this imaginative side and these visions will we be able to "think of humane and liberating classrooms in which every learner is recognized and sustained in her or his struggle to learn how to learn," and educators need to imagine alternatives to this that may seem unachievable so that their classrooms can be places where freedom is achieved to combat "unbureaucratic and uncaring schools" (Greene, 1995, p. 5).

Dr. Maxine Greene asked a beautiful question: "How do we as teachers, cautioned against thinking in terms of predictions and predeterminations, provoke all of students to learn how to learn in a way we and they already know is neither equitable nor fair?" (Greene, 1995, p. 171). Learning how to learn. How is this accomplished in an equitable, inclusive way? How can this be fulfilled in a way that values not just what teachers are taking from schools but also how the teacher-student dynamic can be more transactional with both educators and students co-constructing and driving the learning? How do you give ALL students the freedom, academic tools, social/critical consciousness, and love to continue learning the ways in which they learn? And to do so by rewriting the narratives that privilege some learners over others? Imagination is essential as we dream of a future in which all are free.

mostly reading books with Latinx Characters during a Social Studies unit about Mexico and books with East Asian Characters during a different unit about China. In another revelation during a different year, I recognized that I was reading very few books that centered on authentic, modern portrayals of Indigenous Characters beyond the beginning of the school year, particularly around mid–October. For me, these examples are reminders that the work of centering those within communities that have been marginalized and made more vulnerable by society is a lifestyle choice, one that will constantly ask you to question whether or not you are framing things with a lens against oppression or not.

Truth and Identity in Picture Books

Here are some examples of stories used to create spaces of care for each other and the self. These stories certainly can center more complex conversations that might be avoided in early elementary spaces but need not be focused solely on oppression but also in getting to know yourself and others better.

Book 1: In *Fry Bread: A Native American Family Story* by Kevin Noble Maillard, the story is about a Native American family making a traditional food in many tribes called fry bread. Poetically shared, this book weaves in not only the recipe but also the culture and history of many Indigenous communities. In addition to discussing the varied tribes, languages, and cultures that are present in the Indigenous community, this is also a book that can bring students to sharing and discussing their own cultures and what they and their families do to keep that culture alive just as the family does in the book.

Book 2: In *Between Us and Abuela: A Family Story from the Border* by Mitali Perkins, a pair of siblings are traveling with their mother to visit their grandmother on the border of California and Mexico, literally. A fence that physically divides the countries separates them, but they cannot be divided from sharing presents and love with each other. Past discussions of this text have included talking about how families can live in different places and sharing the types of rituals and ideas we have for missing people that we love.

Book 3: In *The Other Side* by Jacqueline Woodson, a young Black girl and White girl are forbidden by their families to cross a fence that separates their properties from their homes. Instead, they end up sitting on the fence and getting to know each other, realizing they have plenty in common. In this book, prejudice can certainly be a topic but so can the qualities of friendship. For this book, discussions have centered of what qualities we possess as friends as well as the qualities we seek in a friend.

Book 4: In *From the Stars in the Sky to the Fish in the Sea* by Kai Cheng Thom, Miu Lan is a child who transforms into many things and lives in a non-binary, and imaginative space when inquisitive looks and questions from children at school make Miu Lan question who they are. Their mother's words repeat throughout the book: "whatever you dream of, i believe you can be, from the stars in the sky to the fish in the sea." These words offer resolve to show up as their full self. In addition to discussing our own preferred gender pronouns, this can also be used as a way to tell stories about how we make choices that shape how we see ourselves in the world.

Book 5: In *Your Name Is a Song* by Jamilah Thompkins-Bigelow, a young child feels frustrated by her first day of school during which so many people mispronounce her name. Her mother's advice is to treat all names like a song, including her own, and her mom goes into the musicality of various names from different backgrounds as they walk through the city. In addition to talking about the respect in working to correctly pronounce names, the focus for elementary students can be discussing what they love about their names. Do they know how they got their name and what it means? When this book was shared, several of my students did know, and the ones who did not assured me they were going to find out ASAP.

Book 6: In *The Proudest Blue* by Olympic medalist Ibtihaj Muhammad and S.K. Ali, a young girl in awe of her sister's first-day-of school hijab imagines the day she will wear one while remembering lessons from her mother about the importance and meaning of wearing a hijab. Though Islamophobia is illustrated in the book in the form of a young person who makes an offensive remark about her sister's hijab, this is not the center of the story. This story can also exist in conversations about pride. Discussion questions could center around what makes students proud about themselves and proud of the people in their lives, including siblings, neighbors, or even friends. This particular book led to the following exchange:

ME [after finishing the story]: What did you think of the book?
STUDENT: My mom wears one! I loved the story because she looked like my mom does when she wears a hijab.

The same student proceeded to teach other students how to draw pictures of someone wearing a hijab that were then included in many illustrations for the remainder of our year together.

Book 7: In *Milo Imagines the World* by Matt de la Peña, Milo is on a subway ride with his older sibling and spends time sketching the people around him and imagining the lives they lead based on how they look. As one of the subjects of his drawings gets off at the same stop as him and takes an unexpected route (the same one he is on to visit an incarcerated parent), Milo realizes you never really know someone just by looking at them. As a young Black boy, Milo wonders what people see when they look at him. There are many layers to the book about identity, implicit bias, stereotypes, and empathy that can be addressed, and discussions can include some of these questions: What do you see when you look at yourself? What do you think others see when they look at you? Have there been times when you observed and thought things like Milo?

Structured as storytelling sessions, these conversations are made possible by the accessibility of illustrations and words being used in picture books. First graders and other early elementary learners are making sense of the world through stories, the one they hear and the ones they can tell. After reading Jessica Love's *Julian is a Mermaid*, in which a young boy imagines himself with long hair and wearing a skirt and makeup, a young boy in my class proceeded to virtually display some of the dresses he likes to wear. He heard a story, and he told us his. There are many, many more books available that offer entry points into more conversations that are sometimes seen as complex but actually very developmentally appropriate for early elementary students. They can enhance their literary understanding and critical consciousness. Healing spaces will always aim to do both.

Truth and Identity in Storytelling

Storytelling is essential and does not only come in the picture book format for early elementary students. More than ever before, remote learning during a pandemic made me even more reflective of the ways in which students need to come together as a community, particularly when we are not in the same physical spaces. Each of our personalities were on display in rectangles on the computer screen. Making space for telling stories lets learners get to know there are many ways we can all be together including on Zoom. Educators tell stories in how they welcome students, what they line their classroom walls with, how they structure their days, and what voices are given space in their classroom.

One of the storytelling practices I have tried in first grade are story circles, a space in which we listen and respond with care whilst sitting in a circle as if around a campfire. The idea of spending time together in a circle (pre–Covid) is not uncommon in elementary school classrooms and most definitely has roots in many Indigenous cultures. A circle is a representation of wholeness and togetherness. It has direct connections to our learning (e.g., shapes in math, life cycle in science, characters in literacy), but also provides a sense of connectedness with each other. Another one is in the format of talk shows, an interview time where students learn about character perspective and vocabulary by acting as fictional characters from our stories or real life figures from biographies. Both of these spaces offer stories to be told. One values the variety of fiction narratives that can exist beyond "Once upon a time" as the stories we tell are our own but used to connect to literacy pursuits as well. The other allows us to imagine different perspectives in a way that lends itself to creativity and share ideas beyond the Turn and Talk model that is commonly used in elementary classrooms. Circles and interviews allow for curiosity, identity, camaraderie, and vocabulary to flourish and for students to engage in sustainable ways of listening to each other. They both center respect for others, communion with each other, and co-facilitation of our space for being and learning since all members of the community, including me as the teacher, are connected in the same way. Even when some students may need adaptive or flexible seating options, we are still together for that time.

Those practices also pave the way to collaborative forms of storytelling, an academic component that weaves its ways throughout the year's literacy times. As Nancy King puts it, collaborative storytelling can "communicate who we are, what we have experienced, and how we make sense of the world" since they "nourish, inform, comfort, entertain, and teach" (King, 2007, p. 208). We collaborate on stories. Two popular methods are where we each tell a different part of a single story or where we each contribute to a themed anthology. With this, we can learn more about each other, and then educators also have a chance to better understand and improve outcomes for students whose educational interactions have been historically marginalized and plan equitable instruction accordingly.

Conclusion

Educators are storytellers. In addition to telling stories to their students, educators must also reimagine the way stories are presented in their classroom spaces. As Dr. Love writes, teachers interested in abolitionist education must reflect on this:

> why meaningful, long-term, and sustainable change is so hard to achieve in education because of all the forces antithetical to justice, love, and equity—such as racism, sexism, housing discrimination, state-sanctioned violence toward dark people, police brutality, segregation, hate-filled immigration policies, Islamophobia, school closings, the school-to-prison pipeline, and the prison industrial complex [Love, 2019, p. 102].

In this work, there is no quick solution to dismantling a system that is well-designed to perpetuate inequities. Stories can be used to understand the history/perspective needed for building empathy and abolitionist practices.

Stories alone will not heal the inequities mentioned, as well as the multitude of other things that plague our country. Stories alone do not offer a Yes or No and Any Quick Answer to achieving spaces of truly equitable education. During this time of uncertainty not just in our world but also in the educational system, one thing stories can do is accompany us all on the road to revolution. As a type of revolutionary art, stories can begin to disrupt in small ways the grains of sand that pile onto each other in a toxic hourglass. Stories have the power to begin to interrupt the perpetual harm that hate and fear can bring. One story alone cannot change what I do as an educator or support my colleagues in doing, but one story did cause a student to yell "Just like that!" about the women in her family who wear hijabs when listening to *Under My Hijab* by Hena Khan. Another story caused a girl to say, "That's me! That's so me!" after hearing *Don't Touch My Hair* by Sharee Miller.

Every move I make as an educator tries to be in service of contributing ideas to our world that I believe and others believe is possible. This is in the interest of liberation even if we won't get to see its actualization. Stories are pathways to what is possible. Every theory and framework mentioned requires that brand of imagination because it interrupts our current system that is not serving Students of the Global Majority. It is that imagination that is going to radically transform education throughout and beyond the effects of the Covid-19 pandemic. It will allow invested educators, students, families, and community members to push back on a harmful system whilst co-constructing an alternative that is better fit to serve all students. In particular, it will center those the system has been intentionally designed to leave behind and made to feel less worthy of the best intellectual pursuits. Imagination and collective growth is needed to analyze how to take these spaces of care beyond the four walls of a classroom or the imaginary walls of virtual learning.

Let us reach far into the depths of imagination and storytelling to center equitable, humanizing experiences for learners. This translates to any learning model, whether you are on the computer all day, you only see students two or three days in person, or you are in school full-time. The depths of *my* imagination allow me to believe in the potential of the young learners I meet. It allows me to believe in the possibilities and ideas that will encourage them to engage positively with each other. It offers ways to understand the greater communicative purpose of literacy and grow confidently in those skills and the work they produce. It can help us glean some self-awareness and begin to understand how to participate actively in our learning communities. Stories and storytelling spaces can be used in ways that make sense to learners because they are loaded with enough confidence, knowledge, and imagination to know that their many ideas and identities matter as much as they do as humans. Even in first grade.

REFERENCES

Anzaldúa, G. (1998). Toward a new mestiza rhetoric: Gloria Anzaldúa on composition and postcoloniality. Interview by A.A. Lunsford. *Journal of Advanced Composition, 18*(1).

Baldwin, J. (1985). *The price of the ticket: Collected nonfiction, 1948–1985.* Macmillan.

Byers, G. (2018). *I am enough.* (K. Bobo, Illus.). HarperCollins.

De la Peña, M. (2021). *Milo imagines the world.* (C. Robinson, Illus.). Penguin Young Readers.

Greene, M. (1995). *Releasing the imagination: Essays on education, arts, and social change.* Jossey-Bass.

Greene, M. (1988). *The dialectic of freedom.* Teachers College Press.

Hammond, Z. (2020, January 20). *A Conversation about instructional equity, part 1.* Interview by Center for Collaborative Classroom. Collaborative Classroom. https://www.collaborativeclassroom.org/blog/a-conversation-about-instructional-equity-with-zaretta-hammond-part-1/.

Khan, H. (2019). *Under my hijab.* (A. Jaleel, Illus.). Lee & Low Books.

King, N. (2007). Developing imagination, creativity, and literacy through collaborative storymaking: A way of knowing. *Harvard Educational Review, 77*(2).

Love, B.L. (2019). *We want to do more than survive: Abolitionist teaching and the pursuit of educational freedom.* Beacon Press.

Love, J. (2018). *Julián is a mermaid.* (J. Love, Illus.) Candlewick Press.

Lukoff, K. (2019). *When Aidan became a brother.* (K. Juanita, Illus.). Lee & Low Books.

Maillard, K.N. (2019). *Fry bread.* (J. Martinez-Neal, Illus.). Roaring Brook Press.

Miller, S. (2018). *Don't touch my hair.* (S. Miller, Illus.) Little, Brown Books for Young Readers.

Muhammad, G. (2020). *Cultivating genius: An equity model for culturally and historically responsive literacy.* Scholastic Teaching Resources.

Muhammad, I & Ali, S.K. (2020). *The proudest blue.* (H. Aly, Illus.) Andersen Press Limited.

Perkins, M. (2019). *Between us and abuela: A story from the border.* (S. Palacios, Illus.). Farrar, Straus, and Giroux (BYR).

Sealey-Ruiz, Y. (2018). *Arch of self: Towards sustaining racial literacy in teacher education and the academy.* Arch of Self, LLC. https://www.yolandasealeyruiz.com/archaeology-of-self.

Thom, K.C. (2017). *From the stars in the sky to the fish in the sea.* (K.Y. Ching, Illus.). Arsenal Pulp Press.

Thompkins, J. (2021). *Your name is a song.* (L. Uribe, Illus.). Library Ideas, LLC.

Woodson, J. (2001). *The other side.* (E.B. Lewis, Illus.) Putnam's.

Freedom Dreaming Through Culturally and Historically Responsive Literacy

LING-SE CHESNAKAS

Freedom to Be Critical: Cultivating a Language of Resistance

When I was in 10th grade, my English teacher gave our class an assignment to read a story about a small, quiet suburban town, much like the one we lived in, and on the surface everything seemed perfect. White families lived in perfectly manicured yards surrounded by white picket fences. But when you looked deeper, something was not right. The author kept alluding to something sinister about the town, but never outright named it. Many of my white classmates were confused and off-put by the story. They could not figure out what could be wrong with their town. I also could not yet name the sinister forces lurking inside my own town, but I was drawn to the story like a moth to the light. I only later understood what types of illnesses our town and our nation were sick with—a toxic mixture of racism, sexism, classism, homophobia, Islamophobia and ableism. Yet, this mixture was largely invisible to me and my classmates because we breathed it in like air. But as one of only a few biracial Asian Americans in the entire school, I felt something was not right about a public school where I saw no other people of color in my Honors English class.

I also felt in my gut that it was wrong for my white, male 12th grade English teacher, who would correct his students if we called him "Mr. R" instead of "*Doctor* R," to present a unit about comparing the novel *Heart of Darkness* to the movie *Apocalypse Now* without unpacking the racist "White Man's Burden" messages in both texts. I have so many questions now that I wish I had asked Dr. R back then: Why were we learning about

Africans and Asians through the perspective of two white males? Did he and my classmates understand that these stories were perpetuating harmful stereotypes about Africans and Asians needing to be civilized by white men? Or did they only focus on what Dr. R claimed was the "beauty" of Conrad's language and the apparently outstanding cinematography of *Apocalypse Now*? From what I can recall, no one, including myself, questioned or challenged his claims about these "great" pieces of literature.

If I could go back in time to 2001, I would present Dr. R with June Jordan's (1995) essay and speech "Beyond Apocalypse Now" as a counterweight to the colonial forces at play in the texts he chose. Jordan, as she directly addresses her white middle-America audience, is absolutely brilliant in using sarcasm and satire to lay bare the sinister forces lurking within *Heart of Darkness* and *Apocalypse Now*. She flips the colonial script when she says:

> But since I am the Visiting Black Poet at a 99.6 percent white college perhaps my name/my racial identity is in danger. Perhaps I should refuse to learn the name of any of the natives and, instead, efficiently refer to students and faculty, alike, as aborigines or as *bitch* or *son of a bitch,* depending. On the weekend, perhaps I should firebomb the ski slopes or scorch the slumbering wheat fields into cinderland. And rather than peering through eyelash dazzlement as the softly falling snow melts into my eyes, perhaps I should more correctly perceive the snow as yet another insidious subversion by Abominable Atmosphere. Oh, what should I do? [Jordan, 1995, p. 171–172]

The first thing I noticed about this passage is that Jordan uses capital letters to mock what Conrad does in *Heart of Darkness* when he emphasizes important nouns with capital letters, such as "The Director of Companies" or "The Accountant" (Conrad, 2020, p. 1). In a powerful reversal of roles she, the "Visiting Black Poet," now imagines her white audience as a threat in order to show them the perverse power of the white colonial gaze. Jordan (1995) even refers to her audience in the same language as white colonizers once referred to their colonial subjects: "natives ... aborigines ... *bitch*" (pg. 171). In Jordan's subversion of *Heart of Darkness*, white supremacy, represented by the overwhelming, white Minnesota snow, is the thing to be deconstructed, pacified, and ultimately destroyed.

The sarcastic question Jordan ends this paragraph with ("Oh, what should I do?") is echoed at the end of her essay ("What should I do?") with a double meaning and a reverberating answer. Of course, the first meaning of her question is rhetorical because the answer lies in recognizing what has already been done: the raping, pillaging and murdering of colonized peoples. The second meaning puts her in a position of power as the audience is captive to her keen imagination and observation through a "Third World" lens. I can picture some of the white people in the audience squirming in their seats, yet unable to look away, as she outlines the various ways that white folks avoid facing the truth of their collective history. Her question does not allow them to ignore or forget the crimes against humanity perpetrated by white colonial power, and it demands a fully human response. She invites them to join her in a "radical plan" to value the humanity in all "Third World" peoples, to love them instead of subjugating them to more violence and erasure of their cultures, to stop running away from their complicity by stepping into the shoes of a "Visiting Black Poet" for one evening (Jordan, 1995, p. 176–177).

If I had read June Jordan's speech in my high school English class, I would have garnered a greater respect for Dr. R and his curriculum. I might have even taken more ownership of my learning and acquired the language to critique *Heart of Darkness*. Instead, I continued through high school rarely questioning the validity, bias or credibility of the texts my teachers assigned me to read. I also took for granted my own bias and perspective as a reader.

But all of that changed when I took my first course on literary criticism in my sophomore year of college. Reading Jacques Derrida's theories about deconstruction expanded my definition of "text" and opened up a whole new way for me to use and analyze language in literature. Edward Said's theories about postcolonialism gave me a language to fight racism rooted in colonialism that I experienced as an Asian American. The following quote by bell hooks (1994) encompassed yet another reason why critical literary theory changed my life:

> I came to theory because I was hurting—the pain within me was so intense that I could not go on living. I came to theory desperate, wanting to comprehend—to grasp what was happening around and within me. Most importantly, I wanted to make the hurt go away. I saw in theory then a location for healing [p. 59].

In my junior year of college, I experienced a traumatic event that caused me to question my self worth. Theorists like bell hooks and Toni Morrison made me realize that I did not have to be defined by my trauma; I am so much more than the world will ever know, and therein lies my power. I suddenly understood that if my identity was fluid, then I could shape who I wanted to be, rejecting what others thought of me. I could be free from the hurtful stereotypes that had haunted me throughout grade school.

In my twelve years of attending a predominantly white, suburban public school system in the Northeast, I had always felt like an outsider because I was a bilingual, biracial, Asian American immigrant. I was born in Taiwan, attended preschool in Nepal, and arrived in the U.S. just in time for kindergarten, where my teachers told my mother she should only speak English to me so that I would not fall behind. While some may say these teachers had good intentions, I believe holding onto my Chinese language was about so much more than just "falling behind"; the Chinese language was my connection to my culture and my ability to communicate with family in Taiwan. Thus, early on, I experienced how language could be used to both facilitate access to power and take power away.

The racism, however, did not end in preschool. I was bullied in elementary school for eating "weird food" at lunch, for wearing clothes some classmates would describe as "fresh off the boat" and for having a Chinese name which almost no one could pronounce. I even had a math teacher in middle school who refused to help me with a math problem because he said, "Asians are supposed to be good at math," which ironically was my worst subject. In high school, I started to wonder why I did not see Asian Americans represented in my history textbooks or in any curriculum.

Someone who knew me in high school might say that I fit the "model minority" stereotype because I looked and sounded like a quiet, polite, friendly Asian American girl, who got good grades, wanted to please everyone, and said "sorry" a lot. It was not until recently that I learned that the type of behaviors I was exhibiting had a name: fawning. Most people have heard of the "fight, flight or freeze" responses to trauma, but not this fourth one, which can often be a result of complex and sustained trauma (V, J., 2021, p. 1). I did not realize until joining an online Asian American affinity group during the pandemic that "fawning" could also be a response to experiencing systemic racism. In this group, we theorized that Asian Americans in particular are susceptible to "fawning" as a response to trauma because of how Asians have been racialized to be silent and submissive in this country (Dhingra, 2021). Fawning, I finally understood, was my way of surviving the people who had threatened my mental, emotional and physical well being.

Throughout my schooling, I rarely questioned the racist message that the Asian part of my identity was inferior to white, Western culture. Thus, using critical theories to understand the world and my experiences as a "perpetual foreigner" was both liberating and healing because it helped me see that the "model minority" myth was not only a harmful fiction used to silence Asian Americans, but also a dangerous tool used to further anti–Blackness (Chow, 2017, p. 2).

Because critical literary theory helped me understand why I should matter to myself and the world, I wanted to give that powerful feeling to my students, too. With this in mind, I began to revamp my former school's 12th grade Humanities curriculum in my third year of teaching by including literary criticism. My main goals for including literary criticism, or what I called "Literary Lenses" in my curriculum, were to give students a language of resistance and to make them aware of the biases and theories that each author and reader brings to a text. On the first day of learning about literary criticism, many of my students were surprised to learn that the standardized tests they had been taking required them to read and analyze a text by using a "Formalist" lens. In addition to Formalism, I introduced my students to Queer Theory, Critical Feminist Theory, Critical Race Theory, Postcolonial Theory, Marxist Theory, and Psychoanalytic Theory. To help students understand how to apply different literary theories in their own writing, I compared it to putting on a new pair of sunglasses each time they switched "lenses." I then had students practice using these "literary lenses" in small groups by analyzing trailers of different Disney movies, such as *Aladdin* and *Pocahontas*. Also, on an anchor chart, I posted three essential questions students could ask themselves if they got stuck on how to use these lenses: *What stories are left unsaid? Whose voices get represented and/ or left out? How does this piece of work challenge or reinforce stereotypes?*

My next step in teaching literary criticism was getting students to apply these "lenses" to a work of literature. So, I asked students to choose one of the literary theories to use when writing a literary analysis paper about Chinua Achebe's novel *Things Fall Apart*. Before students wrote their paper, we looked at models of literary analysis essays written by college students. I intentionally showed my students examples of college students' essays to make the point that they can achieve that same level of rigor and sophistication in their own writing. Given that many of my students are the first in their families to pursue a college education, it is essential that they experience college-level work before entering college. Furthermore, Gholdy Muhammad (2020) argues that teachers should both learn and teach critical theory because:

> Criticality calls for teachers and students to understand the ideologies and perspectives of marginalized communities (especially Black populations all over the world) and their ways of knowing and experiencing the world.... Criticality is feeling for those who are not treated in humane ways regardless of what the law, policy and norms dictate [p. 120].

When I teach critical literary theory, I am quite explicit with my students that many scholars use these theories to fight oppression in its different forms. It is my hope that students are able to transfer this "criticality" when reading *any* text so that they do not leave high school as I did, unaware of how to think critically about what I was reading and writing. Instead, they will leave high school with a toolkit of "lenses" they can use to analyze and critique any text.

The following excerpt is from one of my former students, a Haitian American girl, who exemplifies multiple layers of "criticality" in her essay where she uses a feminist lens to analyze and critique *Things Fall Apart*:

Uchendu tells his family that women are important because they are the out-let in which a child can unload their emotions unto. The words "sorrow," "bit-terness," and "refuge" connote to the idea that a woman's place in this life is to nurture those weakened by misfortune. A woman can go beyond this connec-tion, whereas a man cannot. As a result, women are seen as more important figures simply because their connection to their children provides an insight into themselves as well as the people they supply emotional comfort for.

Earlier in her essay, this student also discussed the role of toxic mascu-linity in shaping the main male characters, such as Okonkwo and his son Nwoye. Not only was her essay a powerful piece of literary criticism, but it also indirectly related to her life because, as a Black girl who was raised by a single mother, she knew from firsthand experience that women in her life were the main source of strength and emotional comfort. Women had always played a sacred role for her, so by analyzing the importance of women in this novel about African culture, she was also affirming her own existence and importance in the world.

Freedom to Question and Make Mistakes

One of the most important lessons I have learned from my students is the power of admitting that I do not know something and the beauty that comes with making mistakes. In this section, I describe two strate-gies I have used to teach the value of asking questions and making mis-takes. The first one I learned from taking a workshop led by Dan Rothstein and Luz Santana, co-founders of the Right Question Institute, and it is called the Question Formulation Technique. The second strategy is called asset-based feedback, which I learned about from reading Zaretta Ham-mond's book *Culturally Responsive Teaching and the Brain*.

It was my seventh year of teaching, and my 12th grade Humanities class was in the midst of learning about the history and culture of Afghan-istan in preparation for reading the novel *The Kite Runner* by Khaled Hosseini. A bright and loquacious Dominican boy raised his hand and asked me why the U.S.-supported elections in Afghanistan did not solve much of the ethnic conflict between Hazaras and Pashtuns (two ethnic groups mentioned frequently in the novel). What a complex question that demanded a thoughtful answer, but I had none prepared, so as I panicked to think of something smart to say, I just made up an answer that sounded good. After class, I berated myself by asking, *What was it that got in the way of me being honest with my students about not knowing something?* I have had more awkward moments than I care to remember where I could have just said, "I'm not sure, let me get back to you tomorrow," or "Let's research this together" instead of trying to pretend I knew the answer. Over the years, I have blamed my "teacher ego" or the fact that my own teachers in high school rarely admitted to not knowing something. Either way, it was a problem because, how could I expect my students to feel comfortable being curious, taking risks and admitting when they did not know something if I did not model that for them?

One way I have tried to combat this fear of not knowing in myself and in my classroom is by using a strategy from the Right Question Institute called the Question Formulation Technique (QFT). This strategy, when used consistently and over time, honors not knowing and puts the person and/or people asking the questions in a position of power, in a position to manipulate language to get to the answer they are looking for, in a collaborative way. The first time I teach the QFT, I always begin by asking my students to list all of the different reasons they might need to ask a question in life. I record their responses on the board. I then pause for effect and survey the results once our list is done and say, "Given how important the skill of asking questions is in life, how many of you have explicitly been taught or asked to practice this skill?"

One student says, "Never."

"Yeah, our teachers mostly ask the questions and we answer them," another student chimes in.

I then pull up a graph with data by the Right Question Institute that shows the steep decline in students asking questions between kindergarten and 12th grade. I ask for possible reasons why, and inevitably one student will say they are afraid to look stupid or not know something in front of their peers. I admit, "Me too." This fear does not disappear in adulthood; in fact, it often gets worse to the point that people will make up a story instead of the truth if they do not know something. Before students experience the QFT for the first time, I take them through this process of unearthing the fear of not knowing, which sets them up to be more open to asking questions later.

The first step in doing the QFT is that students start off by asking as many questions as they can in small groups about a teacher-created "Question Focus," which could be a short quote, image, graph, diagram, etc. (basically anything but a question). Right before they do this step, the teacher presents four basic rules to follow while asking questions:

1. Ask as many questions as you can.
2. Do not stop to answer or discuss the questions.
3. Write down every question EXACTLY as it is stated.
4. Change any statements into questions. (Rothstein & Santana 2017)

These rules encourage students to focus on generating questions (a type of divergent and creative thinking). Then, once students have generated as many questions as they can, they begin refining and narrowing down their focus to figure out what the most relevant questions are. To do this, they must first label each question as closed-ended or open-ended (see Appendix A for definitions) and change one question from closed to open and one from open to closed by rephrasing it. In this way, students are becoming more aware of how to manipulate a question to fit a particular purpose. Furthermore, this practice of labeling questions as open-ended and close-ended levels the Bloom's Taxonomy hierarchy that privileges "higher order questions" over "lower order questions." It makes students realize that *all* questions, whether simple or complex, are important depending on what function they serve. An example I often give after students experience the QFT for the first time is: a journalist may decide to speed up or slow down an interview by asking close-ended or open-ended questions, so all questions can serve a purpose, and therefore should be valued.

Lastly, as a group, students select their three most important and relevant questions based on criteria from the teacher or student-generated criteria (a type of convergent, evaluative thinking). For example, I might ask students to pick which questions they want to discuss in a Socratic Seminar or which questions would make good "essential questions" for a unit. By giving students a specific purpose for selecting questions, I am reinforcing the idea that different types of questions are needed for different purposes. Essentially, the QFT teaches students there is no such thing as a "bad" question because it all depends on what information you are trying to find. The implications of using the QFT regularly are that if students have more practice with the skill of asking questions, they will be more prepared to use questions to advocate for themselves and others in the future.

The collaborative aspects of the QFT are tied to culturally responsive teaching methods, such as using pedagogy that honors collectivist cultures. In her research on Black literary societies of the 19th century, Gholdy Muhammad (2020) points out that, "these societies were highly collaborative and prompted social responsibility to share knowledge gained from acts of literacy rather than keep education to one's self" (p. 26). In her book *Culturally Responsive Teaching and the Brain*, author Zaretta Hammond (2015) defines culturally responsive teaching as "The process of using familiar cultural information and processes to scaffold learning. Emphasizes communal orientation. Focused on relationships, cognitive scaffolding, and critical social awareness" (p. 156). Thus, both Hammond and Muhammad emphasize that culturally responsive learning environments are designed to be collaborative and focused on relationships and valuing one's ability to contribute to the learning of others. Similarly, I have seen students write in their post–QFT reflections that they were inspired to ask more questions by listening to their group members' questions. For example, the following is a sampling of my students' responses in 2016 to the reflection question "What did the QFT make you learn about the process of asking questions?":

- Doing the QFT today made me realize that at first questions may be simple but then each question after gets better and better
- It literally makes me think more about the meaning of what's going to happen in this unit
- I learned to ask different types of questions
- It makes me think and expand my ideas
- Open questions allow for more opinions
- Questions can get very deep with a change in one word
- It takes a lot more effort than just thinking straight off hand. You need to work with others in order to make more complex questions.
- How people can get inspired off each others' questions
- Understanding the text and uncovering some of the hidden facts in between the words
- You think about different perspectives when asking questions
- Some questions are more important than others. Some questions have more to tell than others.

In this group of student responses, two students cited the importance of working as a group to ask questions: One student said, "You need to work with others in order to make more complex questions" and another said, "How people can get inspired off each others' questions." In my classroom, the QFT functions as what Hammond (2015) would call a cognitive routine: "The ultimate goal of culturally responsive instruction is to help students build inside their heads a 'cognitive power plant' that allows them to do more complex and challenging work by building on their cultural ways of learning through the explicit focus on *cognitive routines*" (p. 131). The QFT is not only a successful strategy for building up students' cognitive abilities, but also for improving students' question-asking skills because it allows students to do divergent, convergent and metacognitive thinking (Rothstein and Santana, 2011, p. 11).

In addition to asking questions, feedback is such a critical part of learning, yet it can often feel like the most time consuming and frustrating part of teaching; however, in a recent webinar, Hammond (2020) suggested an approach for how to give and use feedback as a tool for improving learning outcomes, especially for students who she identifies as dependent learners. Hammond argued that teachers should get students to see their own errors as useful data instead of something to hide or be ashamed of. She gave an example of a teacher who posted responses to "The Power of Not Yet," where students and teachers wrote down skills they are working toward mastering, such as cooking, skateboarding and writing a research paper (Hammond, 2020). In much the same way that the QFT reframes "not knowing" and asking questions as purposeful, Hammond's theory reframes mistakes as useful and something to learn from.

Another benefit of Hammond's approach to giving feedback is that it asks teachers to focus on students' strengths while also suggesting specific areas a student can improve upon, which can motivate students to respond to feedback meaningfully: "the teacher has to convey faith in the potential of the student while being honest with the student about the gap between his current performance and the standard he is trying to reach" (Hammond, 2015, p. 104). Although in her book Hammond often focuses on what asset-based feedback looks like on an individual level, last year I attempted to apply that same approach on a class-wide level. For example, each time I graded a set of essays, I recorded patterns of strengths and weaknesses and then shared these observations with the class on the day I passed back their graded work. This process of sharing feedback allowed me to highlight my observations in a non-judgmental way and suggest specific actions students could do to improve their writing. When I pass back their essays, I emphasize that how students respond to my feedback and revise their work is where the most learning happens. I also ask for volunteers to publicly share what types of errors they make and what they learned from them. Lastly, I share errors in my own writing to model risk taking and framing mistakes in a positive way.

Freedom from White Supremacy Culture

In the book *Heteropatriarchy and the Three Pillars of White Supremacy: Rethinking Women of Color Organizing* Andrea Smith (2016) describes a framework called "Three pillars of White Supremacy" for people of color to organize politically and avoid the pitfalls of "oppression olympics" (p. 66). In describing this framework, Smith asserts that there is not only one type of racism and white supremacy; rather, there are three interconnected "pillars" that constitute these systems of oppression. The first pillar of this framework is Slavery/Capitalism, which is the idea that exploiting and treating Black people as property, whether through slavery, sharecropping or prison, is inherently part of a capitalist system. Another pernicious part of the false racial hierarchy created by Slavery/Capitalism is the idea that if "you are not Black, you have the opportunity to escape the commodification of capitalism ... [which] helps people who are not Black to accept their lot in life, because they can feel that at least they are not at the very bottom of the racial hierarchy—at least they are not property" (Smith, 2016, p. 67). As someone who identifies as Asian American, this first pillar helps me understand why Asians have historically been used to further capitalist practices of filling a need for cheap labor, while also being used to drive a wedge between Asians and other racial groups in order to promote anti–Blackness.

The second pillar is called Genocide/Colonialism, which is the myth that indigenous people must be going extinct in order to justify colonizers taking over their lands. This second pillar operates differently than the first pillar. For example:

> African Americans have been traditionally valued for their labor, hence it is in the interest of the dominant society to have as many people marked "Black," as possible, thereby maintaining a cheap labor pool; by contrast, American Indians have been valued for the land base they occupy, so it is in the interest of dominant society to have as few people marked "Indian" as possible, facilitating access to Native lands [Smith, 2016, p. 71].

Though they are related systems of oppression, it is important to understand the distinctions between Slavery/Capitalism and Genocide/Colonialism because racism towards Black people may look and sound different than racism toward American Indians due to their different positions in this historical and political hierarchy.

The third and final pillar that Smith (2016) explains is called "Orientalism/War," which is the idea that civilizations and people from the "Orient" or Asia are not only inferior to Western cultures and civilizations, but also a threat. "Consequently, orientalism serves as the anchor for war, because it allows the United States to justify being in a constant state of war to protect itself from its enemies" (Smith, 2016, p. 68). This third pillar has helped me understand where Islamophobia and the "perpetual foreigner" stereotype that I have experienced comes from. Furthermore, the first and second pillars have helped me see how I, too, have been complicit in a white supremacist system. For example, I thought I was being antiracist by including a racially diverse group of authors in my Humanities curriculum. While representation is important, that alone "does not address the nuanced structure of white supremacy, such as through these distinct logics of slavery, genocide, and Orientalism" (Smith, 2016, p. 70); however, representation paired with "criticality" can be a powerful tool for teachers and students to work together to challenge these systems of oppression.

Furthermore, teachers must reflect on and examine their own practices and beliefs in order to dismantle the hierarchy of power dynamics set up in their classrooms so that they are not continuing to replicate the societal hierarchy of white supremacy and heteropatriarchy. Thus, as part of the process of dismantling the hierarchy of power set up in my own classroom (which privileges the teacher above the student), I had to reflect on my own school experience to examine and unlearn the toxic, racist, sexist, transphobic and homophobic, classist and ableist practices and beliefs I had absorbed along my educational path. I also had to assume that these systems of power and oppression potentially existed in my classroom, which meant that I needed to identify how they are playing out in my teaching practices and in my school.

At the end of last school year, my administrators offered me the opportunity to do just that by attending an online antiracist workshop led by speaker and activist J.T. During the workshop, teachers were introduced to the characteristics of White Supremacy Culture (WSC), as defined in an article by Kenneth Jones and Tema Okun (2001):

> Below is a list of characteristics of white supremacy culture which show up in our organizations…. The characteristics listed below are damaging because they are used as norms and standards without being pro-actively named or chosen by the group. They are damaging because they promote white supremacy thinking. They are damaging to both people of color and to white people. Organizations that are people of color-led or a majority people of color can also demonstrate many damaging characteristics of white supremacy culture. Perfectionism…. Sense of Urgency…. Defensiveness…. Quality over Quantity…. Worship of the Written Word…. Only One Right Way…. Paternalism…. Either/Or Thinking…. Power Hoarding…. Fear of Open Conflict…. Individualism…. Progress is Bigger, More…. Objectivity…. Right to Comfort [p. 1–8].

After reading the entire article, teachers in the workshop were then asked to identify which of these characteristics played a role in their lives and in their work. What was so powerful about this article is that it gave me a language to name many of the systemic problems that I had encountered in my previous educational experiences, both as a teacher and as a student. I was shocked to realize that I could identify most, if not all, of these characteristics in my current and former school. Ironically, my school, which is a diverse, urban public school, prides itself in being quite progressive. For example, my current school is undergoing a transformation in its philosophy around grading practices by moving from a traditional grading system, where assignments are given points or letter grades, to a project-based and competency based assessment system, where students are given multiple opportunities to demonstrate mastery of certain skills or "outcomes." Yet, our data continues to show that a disproportionately higher percentage of students failing their classes are Black boys, and this points to the fact that inequitable systems are still in place. I wondered, *How had I overlooked these aspects of our school culture? Why had I not associated these things with White Supremacy Culture before?* By the end of the workshop, I came to the conclusion that my answer to these questions was the same reason I had not been able to identify those characteristics when I myself was a student: because they were "normal" and standard practices that most people accepted.

Each WSC characteristic was paired with "antidotes" about how to challenge or address that characteristic, so J.T. asked how we would apply these antidotes to make our places of work more antiracist. We were then asked to write down and reflect on these characteristics in an online workbook. I wrote down that the area I felt I most needed to work on was: "Perfectionism … mistakes are seen as personal, i.e., they reflect badly on the person making them as opposed to being seen for what they are—mistakes" (Jones and Okun, 2001, p. 1). I had often been too hard on myself for making mistakes as a teacher, which was not a healthy mindset to model for students. Some of the "antidotes" to "Perfectionism" are: "develop a learning organization, where it is expected that everyone will make mistakes and those mistakes offer opportunities for learning; create an environment where people can recognize that mistakes sometimes lead to positive results" (Jones and Okun, 2001, p. 1). Hence, I needed to unlearn perfectionism by modeling for students that my errors gave me valuable information about what I could do better next time, which is also a practice that Hammond (2015) affirms.

The Toxicity of Character Education

During my self reflection in this workshop, I also realized that I had been guilty of promoting another type of White Supremacy Culture not named in J.T.'s workshop: Character education. In Bettina Love's book *We Want to Do More Than Survive*, character education refers to the type of education reform that focuses on improving the "character" of black and brown children through measuring qualities like grit and zest. For example, an organization called KIPP thinks students should graduate high school with a GPA and a CPA (Character Point Average). But, as Love points out, by KIPP's CPA standards, Donald Trump would be given an A+ for having passion, grit and zest. The character of dark kids is not the problem, she points out. What is problematic is the fact that they are being measured against inherently racist white standards of success and behavior (Love, 2019, p. 69–77).

In my 6th year of teaching, I had learned about a form of character education from a white female teacher. It was the spring of 2013 and this teacher, who I will refer to as Ms. Ryan, excitedly burst into my classroom after school one day to tell me about a TED talk she had just listened to about "Grit" by Angela Duckworth. She talked about it like Ms. Duckworth had just figured out the silver bullet to urban education. Her excitement was contagious, so I agreed to have my students read and discuss an article about grit as part of a college essay unit in the fall.

After reading the grit article in class, my mostly black and brown students were not nearly as impressed by the article as Ms. Ryan and I were. I expected them to be inspired and uplifted, but instead one student asked, "How is this going to help us write the essay?" Understandably, they were more concerned with figuring out how to write an essay that would get them into college than this article. At the time, I was puzzled by why they did not get as excited about "grit" as I was, but looking back through the lens of Love's critique of character education, I now see how foolish I was. My assumption that they needed "grit" to succeed was not only foolish, but racist and deficit-based. What my students really needed was the wealth, resources and opportunities afforded to white suburban and private school kids who were competing for the same spots in college. Most of my students had experienced levels of trauma and stress that your average adult would not be able to handle without having a mental breakdown. Many were helping their families stay financially afloat, often one or two steps away from homelessness. A few were actually homeless and still managed to come to school almost every single day. If that is not grit, I do not know what is.

"Character education" that measures the potential of black and brown kids is essentially a distraction from the real issue of systemic racism underlying many of our education policies. Love argues compellingly that the potential of black and brown kids must be protected, not measured. Love (2019) says we should focus on civics education, which she defines as:

> the practice of abolitionist teaching rooted in the internal desire we all have for freedom, joy, restorative justice (restoring humanity, not just rules), and to matter to ourselves, our community, our family, and our country with the profound understanding that we must "demand the impossible" by refusing injustice and the disposability of dark children [p. 7].

Love brings in the work of Civil Rights activist Ella Baker as an example of what is possible with civic education that can lead to civic action and change. Students need to know how our systems work before they can change them. The hidden message behind character education is: conform, not change. Love's response to this is very clear: we must focus on *changing*, not conforming to, a system that does not value black and brown children.

I distinctly remember one student in my sixth year of teaching, Anthony, whose spirit would have been killed by any sort of "character education." I uplift Anthony's story because to me he represents what so many of my students of color go through in schools—a process of forced assimilation to heteronormative White Supremacy Culture. Ultimately, his story is neither a tragedy nor a success; it is simply a reality and a possibility that our students of color face on a daily basis.

Anthony made quite an impression on his first day in my class. It was the beginning of November, and he had just moved from a city down South to the Northeast with his aunt. My administrators said he had an IEP from his previous school, but no one could seem to access his records. So, I knew very little about Anthony when he arrived at my school with his boisterous laugh, a striking 6'4" figure and a Ru Paul fashion sense. He wore a black, glittery, cropped T-shirt, which skimmed right above his belly button, ripped jeans, a rainbow belt and Doc Martens. I did not know much, but one thing was clear: he was a queer, black boy in a new school. I sensed the other kids might give him trouble, so I went out of my way to welcome him.

"I love your shoes, Anthony!" I exclaimed.

Without skipping a beat, he smiled broadly and said, "Thanks Miss, your outfit is on point, too!" I went back to teaching, but Anthony had other plans. He stood up, wandered around the room, looking at posters, chatting randomly with other students, and finally ending up at my desk. He opened up the top drawer and asked, "Miss, you got any gum?" My jaw dropped before I could respond. No one opened my drawer without asking for permission. It did not even need to be stated, every student just knew. But, of course, this was Anthony's first day in class, so as calmly as I could muster I said, "I'm sorry, I don't have any gum, but could I show you something?"

I led him to the Do Now bin and explained, "The Do Now is like a get-the-day-started activity. I keep it by the door, so that you can easily grab a worksheet as you walk to your seat when you enter my class. Sound good?"

He nodded, but instead of heading towards his seat with the Do Now, he left it on a random desk and said, "I'm going to the bathroom now."

Before I could stop him, he was out of the room. I wondered, with exasperation, what I was going to do with this new student.

One day in March, Anthony really messed up my day. I was short on sleep from grading papers the night before, and I knew I was going to be observed that day, so I strongly hinted to the class that they should be on their best behavior. I began the lesson by explaining the Do Now. I looked over to see what Anthony was doing, and he was drawing something inappropriate on his paper. Luckily, I was able to remove that paper and give him a new one before my administrator walked in with a clipboard in hand. I shot Anthony a *"not today"* look before continuing my lesson. He seemed not to notice and continued with his own agenda that day. During the group work phase of the lesson, Anthony started an argument with Angel from across the room. I looked over at my administrator scribbling notes down, and I was mortified and shouted, "Anthony, meet me outside of the classroom now!" I told him how disappointed I was in his behavior and sent him back inside. Anthony put his head down for the rest of class.

When class was over, I tapped him on the shoulder to see if he was awake. He looked up and I noticed tears in his eyes. I was shocked. Anthony always had a big grin on his face, even when he was being reprimanded.

"Miss, my cousin in Baltimore was shot and killed last night. I just wanted you to know that."

"Oh my God. Anthony, I am so sorry. I shouldn't have yelled at you today. I can't even imagine what you are going through right now." Now it all made sense to me why Anthony had been acting out earlier. He was not trying to ruin my day, but rather to cry out for help in the only way he knew how.

Looking back on this lesson, I realize that my behavior during class was wrong. Though I did not realize it at the time, I was exhibiting the WSC of "Defensiveness" when I yelled at Anthony. One aspect of "Defensiveness" is defined by Jones and Okun (2001) as: "because of either/or thinking ... criticism of those with power is viewed as threatening and inappropriate (or rude)" (p. 2). I had interpreted Anthony's arguing with another student and not doing the Do Now as defiance and disrespect. On top of that, I felt the pressure to conform to my administrator's definition of "good" classroom management when I was being observed, so I took out that pressure on Anthony by yelling at him; however, the story does not end there because I was later able to display one of the "antidotes" to Defensiveness, which Jones and Okun (2001) describe as: "understand[ing] the link between defensiveness and fear (of losing power, losing face, losing comfort, losing privilege)" (p. 2).

Anthony mentioned to me the next day that I was the only teacher he had told about the death of his cousin. From that day on, we had an unspeakable bond. He would often eat lunch in my room or just stop by during my free period to tell me a funny story. At the end of the school year, I wrote him a letter saying how much I had grown to love him as a student and how much he had taught me about how to be a better teacher. After reading the letter, he gave me a big hug and thanked me. Then, he said something unexpected. "You know, Miss, even when you were mad at me, I knew you cared about me."

"You did? How?"

"Because you would always apologize afterward, and you never held any grudges."

Now I understood why I was the only teacher Anthony had told about the death of his cousin. In his other classes, he was labeled as the "trouble maker" or a "freak" because of how he dressed in ways that did not fit neatly into binary gender norms. But in my class, Anthony had a fresh start, no matter what happened the day before, and he always forgave me if I was impatient with him. He also taught me to forgive myself for days when I did not handle a situation well, which allowed me to save face and learn from my mistakes. In essence, we gave each other the gift of redemption that only comes from a relationship built on mutual love and respect. Hammond (2015) compares an ideal teacher-student relationship to an alliance, where "in the alliance, the student commits to being an active participant in the process and taking ownership of his own learning as he works toward his learning goals" (p. 95). By creating this partnership, the teacher builds trust with the student, which then leads to more of a commitment by the student to persevering through the times when learning gets tough.

Using Writing to Move Beyond the Education Survival Complex

One of the ways that I have attempted to combat racist practices and White Supremacy Culture at my former school is to use teacher writing groups to fight against what Love (2019) calls the "educational survival complex [which] has become so rationalized and normalized that we are forced to believe, against our common sense, that … there is nothing that can be done about school shootings … that the only way to measure a child's knowledge is through prepackaged high-stakes state tests" (p. 101). As it turns out, I did not win my battles against the "education survival complex," but I did win the war collectively.

It was September of 2017, my first year in the role of Humanities co-department head. I wanted to make a good impression on my Black female principal, whom I greatly respected, but my jaw almost dropped to the floor when I heard her start our first department meeting by pushing the benefits of yet another standardized test that the district wanted to pile on our already full plates. This did not seem like her typical approach to school leadership, so I was willing to give it a shot and try to "sell" the idea to the other teachers in my Humanities department. My co-department head Yvonne and I strategized beforehand and decided we would go through the motions of explaining what everyone needed to do to implement the test, but when it came time to actually using the data from the test, we would let teachers decide what would be the best course of action.

October and the first cycle of testing came and passed. The district condescendingly sent a central office representative into one of our department meetings to make sure we knew how to analyze the data. As Yvonne and I had predicted, the test results did not tell us anything we did not already know about our students and their supposedly "mediocre" skills. In fact, the tests highlighted what was "wrong" with our students, rather than all of the brilliance we knew they possessed. Plus, the texts chosen by the test-makers were esoteric, devoid of context, and not relevant to our students' lives. Basically, we felt that the testing cycle and data analysis were a waste of time, but we could not tell our principal that because we knew she was pressured by the superintendent to implement these tests. So, Yvonne and I strategized again, and privately polled the teachers in our department to see what they would like to do during our meeting time.

Yvonne and I offered teachers in our department several options, and the one that got the most votes was to spend our time reading and writing together to solidify our community of teacher-learners. This was especially important to us given the impending merging of our school with another school that we shared a building with, and we knew this potentially foreshadowed a closing of our school the year after that (turns out we were right). Yvonne and I formed writer response groups with the goal of building community and solidarity amongst educators, instead of discussing test data. In these response groups, we used a writing and feedback protocol (Appendix B) which I had learned from taking a summer institute with the Boston Writing Project in 2008. I still remember one teacher named Rochelle's journal entry that moved me deeply. She wrote that as a black woman experiencing racism all of her life, it made her feel numb to see violence toward people of color, such as videos of police brutality on social media, so feeling any emotion at all was like an act of rebellion for her.

Yvonne shared next. She tearfully read aloud a poem she wrote about explaining to her teenage son why she was against the metal detectors in our school and at the same time would take a bullet for her students if there were ever a school shooter in the building. She read this the week after we had an active shooter drill, so the event was fresh in everyone's mind. After she read this poem, we reflected on how some of our students froze and sat numbly, like Rochelle, during the drill, while others buried their faces in their shaking hands, trying to still the rising panic. This drill especially triggered painful and traumatic memories for those who had lost loved ones to gun violence. Yet, our administrators gave no training on how to support students emotionally during the "lock-down." By the time we finished processing what happened during this drill, we were all left wondering, *Why did we not discuss how to handle this protocol as a school?* We brought this concern to our principal at our next staff meeting, but very little was done about it. Though we could not get rid of the district-mandated test or the active shooter drill, Yvonne and I fought against the "educational survival complex" (Love, 2019, p. 101) by creating a space for teachers to be seen, heard, and healed.

Our writer response groups showed us the power of collective, rather than individualistic, action. Similarly, in his essay "Freedom Schooling: Reconceptualizing Asian American Studies for Our Communities," Glenn Omatsu (2003) argues, "that changing society also meant transforming oneself—i.e., accepting the ideological challenge to remold one's own values and worldview. This remolding, activists emphasized, could not happen individually but only by participating with others in movements to serve the community" (p. 14). The radical act of writing together and sharing our writing, allowed us to "remold" ourselves into a stronger collective group and think critically about how to respond to oppressive systems. What are the possibilities when teachers are given a sacred space to do that kind of collective writing, sharing, and response? When teachers are given this space to think, write, and validate each other, a critical freedom can grow and flourish.

If Bettina Love's book *We Want to Do More Than Survive* had been published back when I first started that writer response group for teachers, I undoubtedly would have shared her writing with the group. I am truly inspired and energized by Bettina Love's (2019) concept of "Freedom dreaming," as I embark on my fourteenth year of teaching this fall: "Freedom dreaming gives teachers a collective space to methodically tear down the educational survival complex and collectively rebuild a school system that truly loves all children and sees schools as children's homeplaces" (p. 102). The double pandemics of Covid-19 and racism have spurred me to write more poetry as a form of resistance. Poetry has become my way of "Freedom dreaming." One of the pieces I wrote after attending J.T.'s antiracist workshop is a poem is about my path to overcoming internalized racism:

The "Bad" Asian

In elementary school
I asked for a break from math homework
And my mother said,
"No, your cousins in Taiwan
Are already doing calculus."

In middle school
I asked for help with a math problem
And my white algebra teacher
Said with a sly smile,
"Aren't Asians supposed to be good at math?"

In college
I spelled the word "juice" wrong once
And a white professor
Asked me with a grin,
"Is that how Asians spell it?"

When I became a teacher
I once said to a Vietnamese American boy
Who preferred the hallways
to my classroom,
"You're a bad Asian like me."

What I should have said was:
Our token will never fit
Into the jukebox of whiteness.
We may be minorities
But we're no models.

When Yuri shook hands with Malcolm
She opened the door
To liberate other "bad" Asians
To be *badass* and get into
Good trouble.

The first three stanzas of my poem capture the origins of my internalized racism, while the fourth captures my transference of racism toward other Asian Americans. Finally, the last two stanzas are about how I have used history and criticality as empowerment to resist the Asian stereotypes that I had internalized.

Experiencing the antiracist workshop forced me to confront not only my internalized racism, but also an uncomfortable question that had been bothering me for awhile: why did I grow up assuming that "liberal" was synonymous with "antiracist"? After having several honest conversations about racism with my extended family members about this, the hard truth finally dawned on me: I simply did not want to believe that my own "liberal" family could be racist. I was in denial. When I asked my friends about their families, I realized I was not alone in my denial. I am still working to find ideas that challenge my biases. For example, Amy Cooper was apparently a "liberal," but that did not stop her from using white privilege to threaten a black man in a public space; "the conversation about white liberal racism is long overdue" (Burton, 2020). This past summer I was working to challenge my biases and assumptions by reading books by Black scholars, such as Ibram Kendi, Mikki Kendall, Gholdy Muhammad, Bettina Love and June Jordan. Each of these authors has given me an intersectional way to look at how racism coupled with sexism and capitalism (just to name a few -isms) have created invisible "toxins" that we are all breathing in, making it difficult to be truly free. Yet, there is hope in this story. I see the writings of these Black authors and theorists as "antidotes" to those toxins. As bell hooks (1994) once said, the academy is not paradise. But learning is a place where paradise can be created. The classroom, with all its limitations, remains a location of possibility. In that field of possibility we have the opportunity to labor for freedom, to demand of ourselves and our comrades, an openness of mind and heart that allows us to face reality even as we collectively imagine ways to move beyond boundaries, to transgress. This is education as the practice of freedom [p. 207].

Like hooks, I too want to "move beyond boundaries" and reimagine myself and my classroom as a place of possibilities, curiosity, love, hope, joy and freedom. This work of liberation cannot simply be performative; it is a life-long endeavor.

Pedagogical Resource A: The Question Formulation Technique (QFT)[1]

1. THE QUESTION FOCUS: (insert below)
    RULES FOR BRAINSTORMING & PRODUCING QUESTIONS:

    - Ask as many questions as you can.
    - Do not stop to answer or discuss the questions.
    - Write down every question EXACTLY as it is stated.
    - Change any statements into questions.

Choose a scribe and type the questions you and your group think of here:

2. IMPROVE YOUR QUESTIONS:

    - Classify each question as Closed-ended (C) or Open-ended (O):
    - Closed-ended questions: Can be answered with "yes" or "no" or with one word.
    - Open-ended questions: Require an explanation and *cannot* be answered with "yes" or "no" or with one word.
    - Change two questions by rewording them (add them to your list of questions above):
    - Change one question from *closed* to *open*
    - Change one question from *open* to *closed*

3. PRIORITIZE THE QUESTIONS:
    - Choose 3 questions you and your group believe to be the most important and write them here (you will be sharing these questions with the whole group):

4. REFLECT (as a group)

What did you learn today? What is the importance of learning to ask your own questions?

Pedagogical Resource B: Writer Response Group Guidelines

Reading

Each group member should have a copy of your writing. Read your paper aloud to the group; then keep silent till someone responds. Resist the impulse to defend, apologize, explain, clarify, or amplify immediately after reading. However, once the first group member has responded, the writer should become part of the dialogue about the paper, and may even wish to direct comment to certain areas or questions.

Usually there is silence immediately after the reader finishes. Sometimes it's long, sometimes it's short. This is normal. Group members need time to look back over the paper, make notes, put their thoughts in order, or find the right words to begin talking about the paper.

Responding

1. Responders should begin by commenting on what they feel was the strongest or most positive aspect of the paper. BE POSITIVE AND SPECIFIC. This may include comments on particularly striking or effective words, images, constructions, etc., or on larger aspects such as organization, tone, humor. Pick an aspect of the part that was effective for you as a listener/reader and describe its effect. What did you hear and see in the paper, how did it make you feel?

2. After the group has commented on the most positive aspect of the part, responders should move to the second step which is to point out/ask about any part, word or assumption that they found confusing for any reason. Is there something the writer assumed you knew that you didn't know? Are there spots which are awkward, repetitious, out of place, unclear?

3. Next the group should move to giving the writer suggestions on where the piece might go next, possibly around questions such as the following: Is it in nearly final form? Should it be continued? If so, what would you like to hear more about? Are there really two or three subjects vying for attention, and should the piece be split into two or three separate pieces? What direction should rewriting take? How should the writer go about expanding this piece of writing? How does

the writer feel about the piece? Is there some specific part of the writing that the writer would like feedback on or some specific question?

4. Finally, the group members should point out any grammatical, usage, or spelling corrections that need to be made. THIS STEP SHOULD ALWAYS BE DONE LAST. The writer may also want to ask the group for help in some specific area of grammar or usage that proved difficult in the paper.

(NOTE: Each group should have a timekeeper so that an approximately equal amount of time is spent on critiquing each paper.)

NOTE

1. Source: The Right Question Institute (RQI). The Question Formulation Technique (QFT) was created by RQI. Visit rightquestion.org for more information and free resources.

REFERENCES

Burton, N. (2020, May 27). It looks like Amy Cooper, the white woman in the viral Central Park video, is a liberal. That's important. *The Independent*. https://www.independent.co.uk/voices/amy-cooper-central-park-racist-dog-walker-trump-a9533581.html.

Chow, K. (2017, April 19). *"Model Minority" Myth again used as a racial wedge between Asians And Blacks*. NPR. https://www.npr.org/sections/codeswitch/2017/04/19/524571669/model-minority-myth-again-used-as-a-racial-wedge-between-asians-and-blacks.

Conrad, J. (2020). *Heart of darkness by Joseph Conrad*. Independently published.

Dhingra, P. (2021, March 19). *Racism is behind anti–Asian American violence, even when it's not a hate crime*. The Conversation. https://theconversation.com/racism-is-behind-anti-asian-american-violence-even-when-its-not-a-hate-crime-157487?utm_source=linkedin&utm_medium=bylinelinkedinbutton&fbclid=IwAR0uRkG3BDuvZTVHKawp8ILfc9QiEaurM1KUuIqkW8i2pRRPUX5NT2aEflg.

Hammond, Z.L. (2015). *Culturally responsive teaching and the brain: Promoting authentic engagement and rigor among culturally and linguistically diverse students* (1st ed.). Corwin.

Hammond, Z.L. (2020, August 5). *The 4 steps to creating intellectually-safe classrooms anywhere* [Slides]. Webinar. https://vimeo.com/445101556/55b2f69683.

Hong, C.P. (2021). *Minor feelings: An Asian American reckoning* (Reprint ed.). Random House.

hooks, b. (1994). *Teaching to transgress: Education as the practice of freedom (Harvest in translation)*. Routledge.

hooks, b. (2018). *All about love: New visions (765th ed.)*. William Morrow Paperbacks.

Jones, K., and Okun, T. (2001). *White supremacy culture: Characteristics*. Showing Up for Racial Justice—SURJ. https://www.showingupforracialjustice.org/white-supremacy-culture-characteristics.html.

Jordan, J. (1995). *Civil wars* (Reprint ed.). Touchstone.

Kendi, I.X. (2019). *How to be an antiracist* (First Edition). One World.

Love, B. (2019). *We want to do more than survive: Abolitionist teaching and the pursuit of educational freedom* (Illustrated ed.). Beacon Press.

Morris, M., Conteh, M., & Harris-Perry, M. (2018). *Pushout: The criminalization of Black girls in schools* (First Trade Paper ed.). The New Press.

Muhammad, G. (2020). *Cultivating genius: An equity framework for culturally and histori-cally responsive literacy.* Scholastic Teaching Resources (Teaching Strategies).

Omatsu, G.K. (2003). Freedom schooling: Reconceptualizing Asian American stud-ies for our communities. *Amerasia Journal, 29*(2), 9–34. https://doi.org/10.17953/amer.29.2.b67p8561140171x3.

Pulido, L. (2006). *Black, Brown, Yellow, and left: Radical activism in Los Angeles (Volume 19) (American Crossroads)* (First ed.). University of California Press.

Rothstein, D., Santana, L., & Puriefoy, W.D. (2011). *Make just one change: Teach students to ask their own questions.* Harvard Education Press.

Smith, A. (2016, July 7). *Heteropatriarchy and the three pillars of white supremacy: Rethink-ing women of color organizing.* Taylor & Francis. https://www.taylorfrancis.com/chapters/mono/10.4324/9781315680675-46/andrea-smith-heteropatriarchy-three-pillars-white-supremacy-rethinking-women-color-organizing-carole-mccann-seung--kyung-kim.

V, J. (2021, April 19). *Fawning: The fourth trauma response we don't talk about.* The Mighty. https://themighty.com/2020/01/fight-flight-freeze-fawn-trauma-responses/?utm_source=yahoo&utm_medium=referral&utm_campaign=in-text-link.

Waxman, O.B. (2021, March 30). A "History of Exclusion, of Erasure, of Invisibility." Why the Asian-American story is missing from many U.S. classrooms. *Time.* https://time.com/5949028/asian-american-history-schools/.

Pedagogical Practices to Thwart Voicelessness Among America's Silenced Students

PATRICE W. GLENN JONES
and KEVIN A. ROLLE

The message of voicelessness sounded loudly during the 2020 social justice protests that ensued after the murders of George Floyd, Breonna Taylor, Ahmaud Arbrey, and others. These murders, like so many others, and the lack of accountability that followed many of these incidents, highlighted the social inequity that exists between White Americans and citizens of color, particularly Black Americans. Though not new in association with the experiences of Black Americans in the United States, for many Black American youths, the sense of powerlessness and the marginalization of Black perspective has become an issue worth fighting for. In many ways, the 2020 protests and accompanying messages are reminiscent of those that took place in the 1950s and 60s. Among Black American youth, who have conveyed frustration and demanded change, being silenced is no longer acceptable. In a video featured on the BlackLivesMatter website, the video's narrator indicated that the 2020 movement was "a watershed moment that brought the world to its knees." The narrator went on to say, "we fall to our knees and we can't breathe, but we rise up using our voices and creativity."

As Black Americans, the present authors have faced social inequity and felt voiceless. For both of us, a message of voicelessness, be it for our own protection or as a reflection of racially fracture society or in response to racial discord, started young. For one us of, as a Black boy raised in the 1960s, racial inequity and the consciousness of being Black, male, and of significant stature, were protected by directives to maintain a low profile and speak only when spoken to. When addressed by a White person, the expectation was to (a) maintain humility and (b) behave as to not draw attention to yourself.

For the other author, racism became an evident quality of life at age six. It is still difficult and still evokes emotion to recall an incident when a little White girl pointed, laughed, and spewed racial slurs. The girl was cruel in her words and behavior. Instead of correcting her daughter's rudeness, the mother said, "She doesn't matter; she is just a nigger."

The goal of many anti-voiceless campaigns, as well as social justice efforts, is the antitheist of that mother's message—Black Americans, as do all Americans, matter. Their perceptions matter. Their experiences matter, and the disparity they face also matters.

The literal meaning of voicelessness is a lack of voice, but the figurative meaning goes back to the sense of powerlessness and marginalization of perspective. For Black American youth, who have been silenced by communal, social, and judicial structures, voicelessness begins early, as does the apparent perpetuation of racist ideals, as represented by the mother's response to her daughter. While communal and familial groups aim to provide fortification, the disparity among social and judicial groups regularly evolve from racism.

For that matter, literal voicelessness is behavioral. As elementary children, students are regularly expected to remain quiet. Effective classroom management is commonly characterized by quiet student groups. Furthermore, students' ideas about teaching, their own learning, and social issues are rarely solicited. Students are minimally asked, "What do you think?" Such limitations serve as catalysts for perpetual voicelessness.

Ultimately, educators play a pivotal role in how all students perceive their sense of power and perspectives. One goal of education is to encourage knowledge production and to create independent learners who can think critically, solve problems, and contribute to a global society through innovation. How can students accomplish any of the aforesaid if they are not given the permission, power, and provision to do so?

Seminal silencing research reveals that more than any other student group, Black youths are America's silenced students (Fine, 1987; McLaughlin & Tierney, 1993). As a supplement to previous research (viz., Jones, 2020), this research amplifies the theme of voicelessness among Black American students and provides teachers and educational leaders with practical pedagogical strategies and approaches to give voice to Black American students. Nevertheless, Black American college students' perspectives on these strategies and approaches are captured through qualitative means.

Voicelessness

Voicelessness is both a concept from critical psychology and a statement of condition. Ultimately, having a voice is a positive social condition. Thus, the lack thereof is widely perceived as negative.

Permission

In addition to its role in psychology and society, voicelessness is manifested as a theme through rhetorical studies among women and Black American literature. For both women and Black Americans, the significance of voicelessness is related to their respectively subsidiary positions in U.S. society, which has historically recognized White American men as holding a dominant role. Thus, voicelessness represents a deficient in one's ability to be considered, heard, or recognized when communicating personal concerns, perspectives, or ideas. It lends itself to authority. When a person has a voice, he or she is sharing in the authority that is largely given to White American men. The women's suffrage movement, for example, was a demand for permission to take part in something White men had always possessed the right to do—vote. Black Americans first sought the "permission" to be seen as human beings and subsequent "requests" have evolved to what is now an urgent demand to be heard. The word "permission" may promote uncomfortable feels, but the truth is in the U.S., White men have always possessed most of the power and all others have sought to share in it.

Power

While the definitions of voicelessness converge between the literal and figurative, ultimately, the meaning is associated with powerlessness and the mitigation or marginalization of perspective. Bolker (1979) offered an early definition as:

> The inability to write or speak our central concerns. Or to write but as a disembodied persona who bears no relation to our inherent voices. We say only what we think we're expected to say and end up telling lies or half-truths. Voicelessness is also feeling powerless to speak and sensing that there is no one out there who speaks for us [p. 908].

Prior to the 2020 protests, Jones (2020) explored Black American high school and college students' perceptions of prosocial behavior (i.e., activism and organizing) and identified four themes and related ideas. Voicelessness was one of the most powerful themes identified.

The participants in Jones' study communicated a sense of voicelessness, which included frustration from lack of control, powerlessness, and invisibility as a condition of being a Black American youth. One participant indicated, "Hey, nobody listens to what I have to say. I'm young and Black, so nobody listens except when I get very loud" (Jones, 2020, p. 7). Another participant indicated, "...But they [teachers] don't get it, and they don't even want to hear what we have to say. They just want to keep us under control" (p. 7).

Provision

Reactions during the height of the 2020 protests ranged from peaceful assemblies to unlawful looting. For some, the riotous actions were an opportunity to victimize, but for many others, the actions of riot were authentic responses to voicelessness. Martin Luther King, Jr., said,

> But it is not enough for me to stand before you tonight and condemn riots. It would be morally irresponsible for me to do that without, at the same time, condemning the contingent, intolerable conditions that exist in our society. These conditions are the things that cause individuals to feel that they have no other alternative than to engage in violent rebellions to get attention. And I must say tonight that a riot is the language of the unheard. And what is it America has failed to hear? It has failed to hear that the plight of the negro poor has worsened over the last twelve or fifteen years. It has failed to hear that the promises of freedom and justice have not been met. And it has failed to hear that large segments of White society are more concerned about tranquility and status quo than about justice and humanity [King, 1968].

This portion of King's speech, "the Other America" given March 14, 1968, feels, for some, just as relevant today.

Reciprocal to having a voice is being heard. The implication is that those who have permission and power to communicate their perspectives and experiences are also heard. However, being voiceless means that your social and psychological needs are not met. Therefore, being voiceless can lead to rebellion. For those not faced with voicelessness, any measure of rebellion is deemed unacceptable because, by in large, far too many cannot see the injustice and the inhumanity because they are not targets of it. Thus, a voiceless person is a person who lacks provision.

Purpose

This study aims to identify strategies to promote voice-encouraging behaviors among Black American students. The strategies identified serve to counteract or prevent voicelessness. While the strategies emphasize Black American students, we contend that these strategies would benefit any students.

Method

To identify voice-encouraging pedagogical strategies, we conducted a systemic review of literature. We identified instructional strategies that encourage voice promotion among Black American students. These pedagogical strategies were then shared with twenty-three (23) Black American college and university students. Three focus groups were held via an online video communication platform. All focus groups were held in September of 2020. Three themes were identified from the data analysis.

Pedagogical Strategies to Activate Student Voice

We posit that promoting voice among Black American students begins with a self-examination of personal perception. As educators, we are responsible for how we perceive our students and the level of expectation we place on them. Far too many educators take a deficit perspective toward Black and poor students.

Eradicate the Cultural Deficit Perceptive

Even those with good intentions can view all Black American students as a homogenous group. Even the classification "Black" is a misleading label that suggests congruence in experiences. Black students represent various ethnicities, have diverse backgrounds, practice numerous cultures, and have ranges of experiences and exposures. This misalignment of Black students results from stereotypes and conjecture and can cause teachers and educators to lower their expectations of Black American students.

Cultural deficit perspective derives from racism (Valencia, 2012), and it is a view that causes a person to hold low expectations of a student merely because of his or her cultural background (Silverman, 2011). Thus, a teacher who examines a group based on individual perception of what does not exist (i.e., deficiency) as oppose to what does exist (i.e., asset) and even what can be (i.e., potential) formulates an inherent disparity. That disparity is not authentic; it is a psychological construct that begins in the mind of the teacher or educator.

The bigger issue is that teachers, like other individuals, behave based on the perspective they hold. A teacher who has low expectations of his students will not bother to facilitate learning in a way that promotes creativity, critical thinking, innovation, or knowledge production because he does not think this student group will "get it."

As teachers, we—the present authors—shared the behavior of demanding greatness from our students. Whether as an English teacher of middle school students from an urban inner city or as a college-level professor, the expectation was that our students were capable, strong, and needed only the right catalyst to amplify their own strengths. Neither of us lowered our expectations nor did we allow our students' personal circumstances to shape that expectation. In many ways, because our students were among those others would view through a cultural deficit perspective, we had higher hopes for and stronger expectations of them. Our perspectives were asset based. To foster voice among Black students, it is imperative that we employ an asset framework by eradicating our deficit perceptions of who they are, what they are not capable of, and the stereotypes that foster our biases (Toldson & Johns, 2016).

Students have mixed degrees of potential. In addition, rates of development, as well as the age of readiness (Biemiller, 1974), vary from one learner to the next. Thus, it is grossly arrogant for any teacher to assume he or she knows what another person can do, become, or accomplish. Who are we to assume that what we see in an individual is all there is? We cannot. Therefore, educators must always see students as works in progress whose potential is unfinished. If we fail to begin to adopt an asset perspective, we will fail our students and, in various ways. We will fail them beyond just the promotion of power and perspective.

Demonstrate Care

The saying, "children won't care about what you know until they know that you care" is an important factor of any student-teacher relationship. Teachers must demonstrate they that care. Beyond caring about a child, in general, teachers must also convey that they care about students' feelings, ideas, thoughts, and perspective. To demonstrate concern for students' individuality is a catalyst that causes students to feel comfortable to share their ideas and perspectives. According to Delpit (2012), care, along with high expectations and strong demands, foster acceptance of concern and encourages students to do well.

For Black American students culturally relevant critical care, which intersects critical race theory and African American caring pedagogy, recognizes students' backgrounds and the impact on a universal level.

Culturally relevant critical care affirms individual humanity through collaboration, reciprocal trust, and care among community members. According to Watson, Sealey-Ruiz, and Jackson (2016), culturally relevant critical care promotes personal freedom and fosters student voice.

Explicitly Teach About Perspective

In many classrooms and among many student groups, there exists the misconception that every scenario, problem, or question has one correct and many incorrect answers. The notion of perspective is grossly ignored in elementary and secondary schools. The meaning of the term perspective, as well as the associated term "point of view," can vary based on the field or its use. For the purpose of this study, the term perspective refers to an individual's personal reactions to, thoughts about, feelings toward, or position on a topic or subject.

Perspective is often shaped by experience. Thus, with consideration of experiences in number, it is easy for an adult to assume that his or her perspective has stronger implications or value than an elementary-aged student. It is likely that the adult has had more years of experience. However, regarding perspective and the significance of individual power and voice, quantity of years does not dictate worth. For example, a fourth grader who has lost his mother and father to violence could offer an adult who has never faced such a profound and gripping perspective on death. Maybe that young child would have witnessed ordeals that the adult could not even conceive. Thus, an elementary-aged students' perspective, and by default, his or her experiences are just as personally and, in some case more socially, salient as those of the adult.

As educators, we must realize that teaching a subject involves teaching a whole child who has been influenced by communal beliefs and practices, as well as personal attitudes, experiences, and his or her own personality. To ignore those experiences, attitudes, and such is to reduce a child to our own preconceived ideology that is probably based in stereotype. Thus, we must teach children that perspectives vary, and we must embrace individuality.

In addition to teaching about perspective, we must also embrace perspective as a factor of knowledge production. For example, helping a child formulate an effective essay means nurturing his or her ability to think critically and communicate clearly. Perspective certainly factors into these behaviors. Therefore, teachers must foster an environment that encourages students to develop and communicate their own perspectives. Likewise, students must be encouraged to use their individual perspective to help them make greater meaning of global issues.

Perspective Taking. A tangent skill to honing individual perspective is the ability to empathize with another person's perspective. Regarded as an important social skill, perspective taking involves "...overcom[ing] your own egocentric perspective, 'put[ting] yourself in another person's shoes,' and try[ing] to perceive a situation from another person's point of view" (Eyal, Steffel, & Epley, 2018, p. 547). Previous research has examined the impact of power on perspective taking, and while converging outcomes result, the common finding is that perspective taking is an important practice that has a relationship to power (Anderson & Berdahl, 2002; Blader & Chen, 2012; Blader, Shirako, & Chen, 2016). Thus, to foster power and voice among students, it is critical that educators explicitly teach students about perspective and examine subjects and situations from various perspectives, include those of the students represented in the group.

In addition to taking the perspective of their students, teachers and educators must also promote perspective taking among students. This can be assumed through role playing and many other strategies to help students examine situations from other students' or groups' perspectives. The benefit of perspective taking is empathy (Herrera, Bailenson, Weisz, Ogle, & Zaki, 2018; Miklikowska, 2018; van Loon, Baileson, Zaki, Bostick, & Willer, 2018). Encouraging empathy for others has the potential to strengthen social relationships and foster a more equitable system.

Foster a Questioning Community

Questioning, as an instructional strategy, is about general investigation. A school of questioning research examines the efficacy of the strategy as a technique used by teachers. Therefore, asking questions is something teachers are expected to do. Hannel and Hannel (2005) asserted that teachers who ask questions promote critical thinking. Hannel and Hannel further developed methods of teacher-generated questioning strategies to promote student engagement. The use of questioning in reading is common (viz., Anisah, Fitriati, & Rukmini, 2019; Bataineh & Al-Shbatat, 2019; Marzona & Astria, 2019), but it is also perceived as an effective strategy to teach other subjects (viz., Dahal, Luitel, & Pant, 2019; Suprapto, 2019) or in not traditional modalities (viz., Hu, Chiu, & Chiou, 2019). Caram and Davis (2005) agree that the effective use of teacher-initiated questioning has the potential to engage students and improve learning, as well as performance.

Questioning is a strategy that should be promoted as a student-led activity. We both remember being told, "there is no stupid question." However, we could also recall teachers taking offense to our questions and promoting feelings that discouraged us from asking further questions.

Far too often, teachers position themselves as sages on stages and keepers of knowledge. This perception and behavior places students in roles as knowledge consumers, as opposed to knowledge producers.

To the contrary, teachers must embrace questioning as a student-led strategy that helps students (a) make personal meaning of content, (b) explore content from varied perceptions, (c) build upon existing knowledge, (d) reflect upon their own thinking, and (e) innovate. Therefore, teachers cannot react negatively when students pose questions that the teachers, themselves, don't fully understand, questions the teacher doesn't like, or to which the teacher doesn't know the answers. The reality is that not all teachers are sensitive to the cognitive development process or remove their egos from instruction. Teachers must begin to view students, no matter how young or how different from themselves, as partners in the cognitive processes of knowledge development. Teachers cannot view student-initiated questioning as a threat.

Even more, teachers must encourage questioning. Like the present authors, some students avoid asking questions because of their teachers' or their peers' responses. Even more, when students do ask questions, teachers must abruptly stop negative responses from other students. Questioning has to be normalized, and if a problem with questioning is unacceptable, it should be with the students who do not ask questions, not with those who do ask them.

Erect a "Ladder" of Democratic Participation

Children's ladder of participation and democratic classroom are two concepts that have been included in the discourse about student engagement in the U.S. and internationally. Rarely, however, have the two concepts been discussed in tandem. The combination presented herein aims to help educators empower students and promote their voices by viewing students, no matter their ages, as valuable citizens who can contribute in a democratic participatory manner.

Children's Ladder of Participation. The children's ladder of participation model was first published in 1980 and derived from Arnstein's like model for adults (viz., Arnstein, 1969). Children's ladder of participation gained further attention as a power distributing method to involve children in everyday participatory activities in the 1990s when the model was featured in a UNICEF publication (Hart, 1992). Hart developed the model to help adults arrange settings for interaction and everyday conversation between children and adults. Burr (2003) asserted that through everyday conversations, power relations manifest. According to Hart (2008), the ladder is metaphorical and "...is primarily about the degree to which adults and institutions afford or enable children to participate" (p. 23), which in turn provides students with a degree of power. The ladder features eight levels of participation: (1) manipulation, (2) decoration, (3) tokenism, (4) assigned but informed, (5) consulted and informed, (6) adult-initiated shared decisions with children, (7) child-initiated and directed, and (8) child-initiated shared decisions with adults. Hart (2008) argues that:

> The highest possible degree of citizenship (i.e., level 8 child-initiated, shared decisions with adults) … is when we, children or adults, not only feel that we can initiate some change ourselves but when we also recognize that it is *sometimes* appropriate to also invite others to join us because of their own rights and because it affects them too, as fellow-citizens [p. 24].

Democratic Classroom. Research on democratic classrooms includes foci on citizenship (viz., Beista, 2011; Geboers, Geiljsel, Admiraal, & ten Dam, 2013; Westheimer & Kane, 2004), students' involvement in decision making (viz., Harell, 2020), how teachers resolve conflicts (viz., Harell, 2020), equity (viz., Bickmore, 2014; Parker, 2010; Schniedewind & Davidson, 2006), and classroom discussion and everyday conversations (viz., King, 2009). Many models of democratic educational practice have been offered, and most acknowledge Dewey's *Democracy and Education* as seminal scholarship. Democratic education addresses the global society and the politics of the people (Hess, 2009) while emphasizing justice and equality to close the gap between ideals and practice (Banks & Nguyen, 2008). Morrison (2008) defined democratic education as a "freedom-based education," and in the same way that political democracy is based on individual freedoms, the foundation of educational democracy is student freedoms.

Thus, a democratic classroom is one that operates through distributed power, where teachers and students actively participate in the management of the environment, decision making, the curriculum, knowledge production, and conversation. A democratic classroom allows students to participate in what and even how they learn. While students cannot change course objectives and standards, they can contribute to how and through what methods the course content can be taught and the mastery demonstrated.

When combined with the highest degree of participation from the children's ladder of participation, practices dominant in a democratic classroom help to create a foundation for student voice. The shared power, ability to initiate change, reciprocal consideration, and distribution of decision-making help to formulate a learning environment that communicates a student's value.

In such a setting, the teacher would begin the year by engaging students in a meaningful discussion about democracy and participation. At this point, the ladder of democratic participation is a conceptualization of levels of participation that emphasize decision making, discussion, and empowerment (see Figure 1). The fundamental elements of such a classroom would (a) include an asset-based culture, (b) promote constructive response and have no tolerance for negative reactions or bullying, and (c) embrace individuality. Stages in the ladder are ascending.

Figure 1: "Ladder" of Democratic Participation

				Respect others' decisions even in disagreement; Value each other's ideas and perspectives; Willingly share power
			Openly question content and perspectives but demonstrate empathy	Individuality is encouraged through choice
Participant Behaviors		Share responsibility in class management, curriculum choices, and knowledge production	Are encouraged to asked questions and engage in active listening	Are empowered through shared responsibility
	Are taught to reflect upon their learning	Are taught about varied perspectives and experiences	Feel safe to share their ideas	**Individuality embraced**
Are regularly asked their opinions	Are taught the importance of questioning	Learn about democratic behaviors and shared accountability	**Asset-based culture**	**Promote constructive responses, no tolerance for negative reactions or bullying**

Facilitate Creative Problem Solving Through Project-Based Learning

Twenty-first century employers seek employees who can solve problems and devise creative solutions. Likewise, college and university professors regularly identify the lack of problem solving and creativity skills as deficits among many undergraduate students. Ultimately, solutions to life's problems are copious, and the potential solutions come from a place of creativity, experience, and individuality. As educators work to prepare students for post-secondary study and employment in an increasingly globalized society, the need for problem solving skills, as well as project-based decision making, will likely increase.

Problem solving involves isolating solutions to a problem. Greenstein (2012) identified a five-stage process for problem solving: (a) understand the problem, (b) identify all possibilities for solution, (c) design a plan to solve the problem, (d) execute that plan, and (e) evaluate the outcome. Early instruction that promotes creative problem solving helps prepare students for global competition and success (National Education Association, 2012).

Kubaitko and Vaulova (2011) identified a positive relationship between project-based learning and problem solving. Project-based learning is a term that refers to a broad array of instructional and learning methods that foster student understanding through their active involvement in meaningful projects. These projects are often based in real world problems and reflect social need. Project-based learning promotes personal perspective and self-reflection. According to Kizkapan and Bektas (2017), project-based learning also (a) promotes collaboration, (b) encourages students to ask questions, (c) fosters discussion of ideas, (d) supports student observations, and (e) actively involves students in decision making processes.

Black College Students' Views

This portion of the study sought to examine Black American college and university students' perceptions of the six strategies identified to foster voice among Black American students. Following qualitative methods, purposive, directed sampling was used among twenty-three (23) participants, which included 12 women and 11 men. All participants met specific criteria: (a) self-identify as Black American, (b) at least 18 years old, (c) college or university enrollment, and (d) self-expressed view that Black American students are voiceless. Table 1 shows participant characteristics.

Table 1: Participant Characteristics

Participant	Gender	Age
Andrea	Woman	21
Brandon	Man	19
Chantel	Woman	19
Debra	Woman	20
Everette	Man	19
Fran	Woman	18
Glenn	Man	22
Hampton	Man	19
Iana	Woman	18
Jayden	Man	20
Kimberly	Woman	19
Landon	Man	19
Monica	Woman	20
Nia	Woman	20
Opal	Woman	19
Paul	Man	19
Quincy	Man	23
Rose	Woman	18
Sam	Man	19
Tami	Woman	20
Usher	Man	19
Valerie	Woman	18
William	Man	23

Some participants (i.e., eight of them) were involved in previous research (viz., Jones, 2020). Jones (2020) identified four themes related to Black student activism: (a) voicelessness, (b) awareness of inequity, undirected desire to participate in social activism, and (d) a focus on group participation and collectivism. Thus, participants in the present study confirmed their ideas about voicelessness among Black American students. Using the snowball effect, other like-minded participants were identified. One pre-screening question was asked to determine participant suitability: How do you view Black American perspective and what are your ideas about voicelessness?

Focus groups were the chosen method of data collection to encourage participant interaction and to uncover a wider range of ideas and reactions. Three focus groups were held with three different groups of participants in September 2020. The lengths of the focus groups were 68, 73, and 92 minutes. Table 2 shows the demographics of the focus groups.

Table 2: Focus Group Demographics

Group	Participants	Gender Make Up	Length
1	8	5 Women / 3 Men	73 minutes
2	7	4 Women / 3 Men	68 minutes
3	8	3 Women / 5 Men	92 minutes

The three focus groups took place virtually using a web-based information communication platform (ICP). Participants' ICP video was enabled at first, and after initial identity authentication and introductions, participants had the choice to dis-enable their videos. Participants were presented with the purpose, a brief discussion about voicelessness, and a table of the six strategies (i.e., [a] eradicate cultural deficit perspective, [b] demonstrate care, [c] explicitly teach about perspective, [d] erect a ladder of democratic participation, [e] foster a questioning community, and [f] facilitate creative problem solving through project-based learning), along with brief explanations. The focus groups were facilitated by one researcher and an assistant. The researcher fostered a relaxed environment, guided the discussion, and managed the relationships among the participants. The assistant documented the discussion and participants' nonverbal responses.

Although a focus group question protocol was developed, questions also developed from participant responses. To engage participant discussion, the researcher followed the process for each of the six proposed strategies:

1. The strategy was named and explained. All jargon-specific terms, like "cultural deficit perspective" and "project-based learning," were defined.
2. Examples of the strategies were shared.
3. Tables and figures were shared when appropriate (i.e., the ladder of democratic participation).
4. Participants were allowed to ask questions.

The discussion was focused on the strategies, and participants were encouraged to share their reactions and thoughts about the strategies. With participants' permission, the sessions were audio recorded. Recordings were transcribed. The audio transcripts were analyzed by the same researcher and assistant.

Geboers, E., Geijsel, F., Admiraal, W., & ten Dam, G. (2013). Review of the effects of citizenship education. *Educational Research Review, 9,* 158–173. Doi: http://www.sciencedirect.com/science/article/pii/S1747938X12000176.

Greenstein, L. (2012). Assessing 21st country skill: A guide to evaluating mastery and authentic learning. Corwin.

Hannel, G.I., & Hannel, L. (2005). *Highly effective questioning,* 4th ed. Hannel Educational Consulting.

Harell, K.F. (2020). The value of conflict and disagreement in democratic teacher education. *Democracy and Education, 28*(1), 3.

Hart, R. (1992). *Children's participation: From tokenism to citizenship.* UNICEF Innocenti Essays, 4. International Child Development Centre of UNICEF.

Hart, R.A. (2008). Stepping back from "The Ladder": Reflections on a model of participatory work with children. In A. Reid et al. (eds). *Participation and learning* (pp.19–31). Springer. http://kinderrechtenonderzoek.nl/wp-content/uploads/2015/11/Hart-stepping-back-from-the-ladder.pdf.

Herrera, F., Bailenson, J., Weisz, E., Ogle, E., & Zaki, J. (2018). Building long-term empathy: A large-scale comparison of traditional and virtual reality perspective-taking. *PloS one, 13*(10), e0204494.

Hess, D.E. (2009). *Controversy in the classroom: The democratic power of distribution.* Routledge.

Hu, H.W., Chiu, C.H., & Chiou, G.F. (2019). Effects of question stem on pupils' online questioning, science learning, and critical thinking. *The Journal of Educational Research, 112*(4), 564–573.

Jones, P.W.G. (2020). *Activism deferred among Black American students.* Samuel Dewitt Proctor Institute for Leadership, Equity, and Justice. Rutgers Graduate School of Education. https://proctor.gse.rutgers.edu/sites/default/files/Activism%20Deferred%20Among%20Black%20American%20Students.pdf.

King, J.T. (2009). Teaching and learning about controversial issues: Lessons from Northern Ireland. *Theory & Research in Social Education, 37*(2), 215–246. Doi: http://www.tandfonline.com/doi/abs/10.1080/00933104.2009.10473395.

King, M.L. (1968). *The other America.* Grosse Pointe Historical Society. https://www.gphistorical.org/mlk/mlkspeech/.

Kizkapan, O., & Bektas, O. (2017). The effect of project based learning on seventh grade students' academic achievement. *International Journal of Instruction, 10*(1), 37–54.

Marzona, Y., & Astria, W.J. (2019). The effect of questioning strategy and students' motivation toward reading comprehension of narrative text at the eleventh grade social science of SMA Negeri 1 Talamau Pasaman Barat. *Jurnal Ilmiah Pendidikan Scholastic, 3*(2), 32–39.

McLaughlin, D., & Tierney, W.G. (1993). *Naming silenced lives: Personal narratives and processes of educational change.* Routledge.

Miklikowska, M. (2018). Empathy trumps prejudice: The longitudinal relation between empathy and anti-immigrant attitudes in adolescence. *Developmental Psychology, 54*(4), 703.

Morrison, K.A. (2008). Democratic classrooms: Promises and challenges of student voice and choice, Part One. *Educational Horizons, 87*(1), 50–60. https://files.eric.ed.gov/fulltext/EJ815371.pdf.

National Education Association. (2012). Preparing 21st century student for a global society: An education guide to the "Four c's." National Education Association.

Parker, W.C. (2010). Listening to strangers: Classroom discussion in democratic education. *Teachers College Record, 112*(11), 2815–2832.

Schniedewind, N., & Davidson, E. (2006). *Open minds to equality: A sourcebook of learning activities to affirm diversity and promote equity.* Rethinking Schools.

Silverman S.K. (2011). Cultural deficit perspective. In: Goldstein S., Naglieri J.A. (eds) *Encyclopedia of child behavior and development.* Springer. https://doi.org/10.1007/978-0-387-79061-9_750.

Suprapto, N. (2019). Development and validation of students' perception on learning by questioning scale in physics. *International Journal of Instruction, 12*(2), 243–258.

Toldson, I.A., & Johns, D.J. (2016). Erasing deficits. *Teachers College Record, 118*(6), 1–7.

Valencia, R.R. (Ed.). (2012). *The evolution of deficit thinking: Educational thought and practice*. Routledge.

van Loon, A., Bailenson, J., Zaki, J., Bostick, J., & Willer, R. (2018). Virtual reality perspective-taking increases cognitive empathy for specific others. *PloS one, 13*(8), e0202442.

Watson, W., Sealey-Ruiz, Y., & Jackson, I. (2016). Daring to care: The role of culturally relevant care in mentoring Black and Latino male high school students. *Race Ethnicity and Education, 19*(5), 980–1002. Doi: 10.1080/13613324.2014.911169

Weis, L. (1993). *Beyond silenced voices: Class, race, and gender in United States schools.* SUNY Press.

Westheimer, J., & Kahne, J. (2004). What kind of citizen? The politics of education. *The American Educational Research Journal, 41*(2), 1–30. Doi: http://aer.sagepub.com/content/41/2/237.

Post-Pandemic Solidarity Through Social Justice Pedagogy in America and Beyond

An AsianCrit Autoethnographic Account of Race, Justice, and Education

Aaron Teo

An Autoethnographic Account: Part One

It was an average year thus far. Having miraculously completed my teaching qualification (reasonably unscathed) at the end of last year, here I was three months into my very first *real* teaching job. I was one of a fortunate few, not just because I had secured a teaching position *before* graduating, but also because the position was at an up-and-coming government school just half an hour north of Metropolitan Brisbane. However, as my more experienced colleagues constantly lamented, a large proportion of the students at this school *seemed* to hold education in low regard—certainly in *lower* regard than the students I had encountered on practicum, at least up to this point of my teaching career. Of course, this meant that there was *much* more behaviour management than I was used to, but at least nothing severe had happened ... yet. Behaviour management aside, it had been a steep learning curve as a beginning teacher, made even steeper by the fact that despite being trained in (and incredibly passionate about) Business, Legal Studies and Special Needs, I was thrust into a Mathematics teaching position. I had learned by this point that being "Asian" conferred some sort of unspoken stereotypical mathematical aptitude, you see. Nevertheless, if necessary—the important thing was that I had a job and besides, by this point in the year, I was starting to feel like, for the most part, I had begun to find my feet, both within the school

131

and in the subject area. Perhaps this was an arrangement I *could* be content with?

However, serendipitously or otherwise, my contrived contentment as a pseudo-Mathematics teacher was disrupted in the humdrum of the fourth week of term two by an urgent meeting with the deputy principal, who informed me that, as a result of ongoing health issues with the current Business teacher, I would no longer be teaching Mathematics. Instead, effective the following day, I would be taking on the incumbent teacher's timetable, composed entirely of Business classes from grades nine to 12—indeed, it looked like my average year *would* be getting a lot better.

* * *

As I fling the classroom door open in a hurry, I am cognizant of the adrenaline and nervous anticipation coursing through my body—a cocktail of an earnest desire to make a good first impression in a subject I actually enjoy teaching, and the nervousness that inevitably emerges every time I am about to meet one of my classes for the very first time. I feel the perspiration on my back and the clamminess in my palms and remind myself to take a deep breath. After all, my maiden lesson with the grade 11 Business students just before this had gone relatively smoothly—how bad could the next 70 minutes with the grade nines be?

With two minutes to spare, I connect my laptop to the projector, display the seating plan and write my salutation up in capitals on the whiteboard, leaving myself just enough seconds to take another deep breath and look like I have everything under control.

My nervousness begins to subside as I step through the routine of letting all 28 students into the classroom, ushering them to their allocated seats and outlining my expectations for the year. Most of the class appears to be paying attention, and for those looking slightly distracted, a small dose of non-verbal physical proximity brings them back on track—so far, so good.

I press on with the lesson, but feel my mind returning to high alert as I notice a few more students disengaging. I double down on my movement around the classroom, alternating between physical proximity, visual cues, removal of distractions and subtle one on-one verbal redirection. Before I know it, 20 minutes passed, and we are on to our first activity—a group discussion brainstorming and ranking entrepreneurial characteristics.

I provide activity instructions and behavioral expectations and split the 28 students into groups of four based primarily on seating location. I start the ten-minute countdown timer, simultaneously spurring the groups into action while raising the sound level in the classroom exponentially. As I float around, I notice from the corner of my eye that Joe's back is intentionally turned to the rest of his group, preventing him from engaging in the discussion. I make my way over to the group and attempt to redirect him.

"Everything good over here, guys? Joe, what are we supposed to be doing?" Joe shrugs his shoulders without making eye contact with me.

"Well, I can see your back is turned. You do know this is a group discussion, yeah?"

"Yeah, but I don't want to work with them—they were rude to me!"

Momentarily taken aback by Joe's accusation and bent on resolving the issue speedily so that I could return to monitoring the class, I ignored Joe's snickering groupmate and reacted on my first instinct.

"Well, mate, the three of them look like they're working pretty well together and you're the one who's got your back turned to them, so I think it might be *you* who's being rude here. I need you to physically swivel around so you can actually get the work done with your group."

"URGH! This isn't fair! Why won't you believe THEY were rude to me?? Is it because I'm Black?!"

Joe's last question cuts straight through the classroom commotion—in an instant, I notice that following a few outbursts of laughter, everyone has ceased work and all eyes are on me. I notice, from a quick scan of the classroom, that Joe *is* the only dark-skinned (visibly Aboriginal) student in the classroom. I feel my cheeks flush and the adrenaline come rushing back as I stand there for what seems like an eternity. My head doesn't seem forthcoming with a reply, so I fall back on my first instinct yet again.

"Err, I don't know what *that* has to do with anything at all, Joe. I gave everyone clear instructions and you weren't following them—simple as that. Please work productively with your group. Same for the rest of you—everyone ought to be contributing."

My response seems sufficient enough to placate the class and everyone returns to work. Joe scoffs at me and begrudgingly turns around to face his group. I breathe a sigh of relief and give myself an imaginary pat on the back—after all, I'd made the best of a bad situation, hadn't I?

An Autoethnographic Account: Part Two

It was later in that first year of teaching on a day after an emphatic All Blacks victory over the Wallabies. As a devout All Blacks fan, I *knew* the only sensible thing to do after such a fortuitous outcome between two of Rugby Union's longest-standing rivals was to make sure that *everyone* knew who had won the night before. And so, I donned my All Blacks supporter's jersey, a pair of jeans and sneakers and made my way to school. As

I waltzed through the school grounds, I winked at the few knowing smiles, and smiled cheekily at the rest who feigned disgust at my choice of outfit.

Just as I am about to reach the staffroom, I am stopped in my tracks by Reagan, a White male student from one of my classes.

"Sweet kit, sir! You must have caught the game last night?"

"Thanks, Reagan—yeah, of course! Wouldn't miss it for the world."

"Oh, okay, right. Cool.... But umm, don't you support Japan though?"

I nearly reel back as I process the racist undertones of Reagan's essentializing comment. When my head finally catches up, I manage to muster a question in retort. "Well, I'm not Japanese, and I've never said *who* I support, so what makes you say that?"

"Err, because they're the best Asian team around, and *you're* Asian, so..."

"So? So, what, Reagan? What does *that* have to do with anything?"

"Umm.... Like, umm.... Err.... I actually have to get to class now—I might see you later, sir."

Reagan slinks away in record time before I have the opportunity to address his comment any further.

I storm into the staffroom and collapse into my roller chair, livid from being on the receiving end of yet another microaggression—for a fleeting moment, I regret my choice to become a teacher and curse the fact that there was no way to avoid interacting with students like Reagan.

A Reflexive Re-turn: Part One

As I think back on these two incidents—from a time when my understanding of racism was highly simplistic and limited to individual acts of prejudice, without consideration for the larger structures and systems shaped by the ideology of White European supremacy and colonialism (Taylor, Gillborn & Ladson-Billings, 2009)—I realize my response to Joe was, in fact, *far* from best. As it turns out, I found out later that Joe was reacting to a microaggression.

Indeed, my initial "unwillingness to approach teaching from a standpoint that includes awareness of race ... [was] rooted in the fear that [my] classroom ... [would be] uncontrollable" (hooks, 1994, p. 39). As a result, my subconsciously Whitewashed expectations of group work were "based on certain normative definitions of what knowledge is valuable, what is good pedagogy and how ... students are best assessed" (Rizvi, 1990, p. 172).

Alas, as an unwitting cog in the White supremacist machine, I had centered my own discursively constructed understandings, disregarded Joe's voice and acted "unconsciously in complicity with a culture of domination" (hooks, 1994, p. 173), ultimately failing to realize the "eminently political" (Giroux, 2010, p. 336) nature of education and neglecting what should have been a commitment to transformative politics and practice (hooks, 1994).

Should I have known any better? Definitely. *Would* I have known any better if the same thing had not happened to me and entreated me to "come to theory" (hooks, 1994)? Definitely not. Consequently, with the hope that you, the reader, will not have to repeat my mistakes, this essay aims to explore a different, more critical way of doing things—a critical, more socially just type of pedagogy a way forward. However, before I move into this, I touch briefly on the underpinning methodological and theoretical influences.

An Autoethnographic Assemblage: Methodology and Theory

This essay uses autoethnography, a type of post structural methodology that *combines* research, writing and story and *connects* personal lives to culture, society and politics (Ellis, 2004). Put differently, autoethnography advocates for the validity of individual experiences as a sociological starting point on the basis that attempting to distinguish each person from their social milieu is a chimera (Wall, 2008). In particular, autoethnography features individual experiences as "concrete action, emotion, embodiment, self consciousness, and introspection portrayed in dialogue, scenes, characterization, and plot" (Ellis, 2004, p. xix) to ensure the accessibility to, participation in, and empathy of, a range of traditional and non-traditional audiences (Ellis, Adams & Bochner, 2011). Consequently, I use the conventions of literary writing (Ellis, 2004) to allow a "back-and-forth movement between experiencing and examining … and observing and revealing" (Ellis, 2007, p. 14) in conjunction with sprinklings of conventional academic writing as a way of carrying out and presenting research (Vasconcelos, 2011) that foregrounds and empowers personal knowledge while resisting dominant discourses (Ellis, 2004). As hooks (1994) reminds us, the shift away from relying solely on conventional academic formats are "political decisions motivated by the desire to be inclusive, to reach as many readers as possible in as many different locations" (p. 71).

This political decision to engage in transformative practice (hooks, 1994) is enhanced by the use of critical autoethnography in particular, which connects individual lived experiences with intersections of oppression such as race, sexuality, gender, and language to the larger realm of society and education (Marx, Pennington & Chang, 2017). Specifically, critical autoethnography *validates* personal encounters with discrimination and exclusion in order to *critique* racism, sexism and colonialism as forms of clandestine domination (Boylorn & Orbe, 2014), while simultaneously engaging with politics at all levels (Allen-Collinson, 2013) both within and outside the classroom. Indeed, because critical autoethnography can "democratize the representational sphere of culture by locating the particular experiences of individuals in tension with dominant expressions of discursive power" (Neumann, 1996, p. 159), I am, as a high school teacher, able to use critical autoethnography to "enmesh the personal within the political and the political within the personal in ways that can, do and must matter" (Holman Jones, 2005, p. 774).

The personal-political impetus for transformation is also consistent with Asian critical race theory (AsianCrit) (Iftikar & Museus, 2018), which is one of the theoretical lenses through which my story is framed. Similar to its critical race theory counterpart, AsianCrit is concerned with intersectionality, social justice praxis and the use of (counter)stories as a vehicle for societal transformation (Museus & Iftikar, 2013). Specifically, counter stories (or counter narratives) conceptualize personal narrative as a valid form of evidence (Kraehe, 2015), and aim to convey the unique yet delegitimized voices, experiences and knowledge systems of people of color in order to confront the purported objectivity of dominant discourses like Meritocracy and Whiteness (Chang, 2013). Such discourses, championed by "master narratives" (Solórzano & Yosso, 2002), are a disguise for the perpetuation of the dominant groups' interests (Gillborn, 2015), which reaffirm the status quo and espouse the deficit discourse that racial minorities (whether Indigenous Australian like Joe or "Asian" like me) are different and biologically, culturally or intellectually inferior to Whites (Tate, 1997). From an AsianCrit perspective in particular, this deficit discourse is based around "an intense opposition to an internal minority on the grounds of its foreign connections" (Chang, 1993, p. 1253). The deficit discourse thus essentializes diverse individuals from the Asian diaspora with manifold ethnic, class, and migration experiences into a single "cultural" entity based on stereotypes of yellow perils to be feared or overachieving model minorities to be disdained (Yu, 2006). Counter-storytelling thus question these implicit presuppositions upholding the asymmetrical power relations inherent in society (Cho, 2017) to resist what Solórzano and Yosso (2002) refer to as the persistent rhetoric of (biological, cultural and intellectual) deficit inherent in master narratives.

The other theoretical lens and final piece of the personal-political puzzle is Critical / Social Justice Pedagogies (SJP). As Ayers, Quinn and Stovall (2009) point out, SJP as classroom practice is kind, hopeful, justice-oriented and academically engaging; it is grounded in the lives of students while remaining critically reflexive in its approach to itself and the world. Under SJP, teachers are responsible for "equip[ping]students with knowledge, behaviour and skills needed to transform society into a place where social justice can exist" (Ayers et al., 2009, p. 590). Simultaneously, as a framework, the enactment of SJP provides the means for examining schools from a sociocultural perspective (Breunig, 2011), making it apropos for the next installment of my (counter)story.

And so, in pressing ahead with critical autoethnography framed by AsianCrit and SJP, I engage on a personal-political-pedagogical level in what Holman Jones (2005) refers to as "a radical democratic politics committed to creating space for dialogue and debate that instigates and shapes social change" (p. 763).

A Reflexive Re-turn: Part Two

Having explicated the methodological and theoretical foundations of this essay, I provide a brief note on my positionality before I press on with my story. I am a middle-class, heterosexual, able-bodied male—the firstborn grandchild of both my maternal and paternal extended families. Before migrating to Australia for higher education, I attended two of Singapore's most elite private schools, all while receiving significant social, emotional and economic support from friends and family. Consequently, I did reasonably well at school and was never deprived of opportunity—indeed, prior to migrating, my skin color never conferred any sort of disadvantage.

I am fully aware that these privileges have limited my experiences and so, do not profess to represent the experiences of the Asian diaspora; I also do not attempt to speak for all migrants or people of color. Instead, this essay functions as a platform for personal stories and reflections that may contribute to a more nuanced understanding of race and racism in the context of Australian and American high school education.

An Autoethnographic Account: Part Three

"All right, for the last part of class today, let's move on to something else. With our exam coming up in the next fortnight, I just want to be *really* sure that we're all on the same page when it comes to the cognitions that you'll be assessed on in this subject. We've spent a fair bit of time previously talking about what we need to do for Comprehending as well as Analyzing, so I'm hoping to talk a bit more about Evaluating in this lesson. I've looked over some of the Evaluate responses that we submitted for homework from the previous fortnight, and I personally reckon there's definitely still some room for improvement—what do we think? How are you all feeling about this last cognition?"

Anne volunteers that while it may not represent the views of everyone, she would certainly appreciate the practice. I scan the room and notice a unanimous nodding of heads. "Okay, thanks for clarifying that. Right, well, if that's the case, what is the synonym that *should* come to mind when we see the word 'evaluate'?"

A number of hands in my grade 11 Legal Studies class shoot straight up. "Lachlan, tell us!"

"Judgment, sir—when we evaluate, we need to make a judgment about something."

"Spot on—thank you, Lachlan. Specifically, we need to determine the merit of a particular situation, policy or piece of legislation, after which we need to discuss alternatives to reach a recommendation. Are we all comfortable with this process so far?" The wave of nodding heads across the classroom tells me that they are. "Right, well, who can tell me what we base our judgments on or against?"

No luck with the hands this time, so I default to the old teaching trick of counting to ten (full) seconds in my head while gliding around the classroom—perhaps the introverts needed time to formulate their thoughts.

The ten seconds elapsed, and no one seemed any closer to offering a response—it was time to follow-up.

"Jimmy, what do you think? Do we just make arbitrary decisions, or do we use something as a benchmark?"

Jimmy ponders for a split second, and in the following split second, I see the light bulb light up at the back of his eyes.

"Ohhh, criteria! We evaluate against criteria!"

"Well done, Jimmy! Yes, when we evaluate, we need to do so against criteria. Now, some of your homework responses started addressing that. I think some of you talked about how fair or just something was—that's a good starting point. For the exam, and the rest of this course really, I'm going to give you an acrostic to help you remember what types of criteria we can evaluate against. You ready?"

The ayes have it.

"Okay, I hope we like our fruit, because the acrostic is PEARS, which stands for Protection of individual rights, Enforceability, Accessibility, Resource efficiency and Society's needs. Did we all catch that? So basically, when we make a judgment about something, we need to refer to at least one—ideally two—of these criteria."

Once everyone has finished jotting down the information, I continue.

"All right, looks like we're good with this in principle. Let's have a go at some practice. I'd like you to spend three minutes discussing with your elbow partner how well you think the Queensland criminal justice system works. Because you're *evaluating* it, I want you to ensure you use at least one of the PEARS criteria when you make your decision. If you have no questions, your three minutes starts … now."

I start the timer on my watch and the class immediately flies into discussion.

"30 seconds to go!"

"10 seconds…"

"and 5, 4, 3, 2, 1…. Time's up! Please wrap up and face me when you're ready!" "So, what did we come up with…? Yes, Jimmy?"

"So, sir, Sam and I used the S in the PEARS acrostic, and we said that the criminal justice system works because it meets society's needs in the sense that it protects society from criminals. I mean, since criminals have done bad things, they deserve to be locked up, and from what we know, everyone who is meant to be locked up is locked up, so that keeps society safe, which is why we feel it meets society's needs."

"Okay, let's try to dissect that further. Jimmy and Sam, when you say everyone who is meant to be locked up, you're referring to…?"

"Oh, murderers, thieves, domestic abusers, Aboriginals…. That sort of thing." My eye twitches and my heart races when I hear Jimmy's last qualifier. Having since learned my lesson about grounding White supremacist perspectives that glossed over issues of race, I was impelled to deal with the racialized situation differently *this* time—I instinctively knew I had to do something more. At that moment, my head takes a while to catch up with my heart as I organize my thoughts in deciding how to address the comment.

"Okay, let's hold that thought for a second. First of all, we *do* know that Nikki and Sam here have Aboriginal lineage, yes? Let's think for a moment what implications that assumption might have on them. Secondly, who here has been following what's been happening with the Black Lives Matter protests both here and in America?" With the exception of a few nods, most of the class shake their heads.

"Okay. This will be a good learning opportunity for everyone then, I reckon. Now I could go on for days about this topic, but I don't think it would be fair for me to do so without letting Nikki and Sam speak first, but only if they are comfortable with doing so…. As a minority myself, I'm aware that we need to foreground non–White voices, but not at the expense of the potential trauma and Racial Battle Fatigue (Pizarro & Kohli, 2020) that can accompany always having to be the one to speak."

Nikki tells me that because she's not particularly in touch with her Indigenous heritage, all she knows is that it has something to do either with police brutality or incarceration. Sam, however, is nodding his head vigorously, so I encourage him to share.

"I haven't read *that* much, and it hasn't directly affected me *or* my immediate family—I mean we've heard *of* distant relatives being involved and so on—but from what I understand, it's because of the ongoing unfair treatment that Black Americans regularly face. I think what sparked it all was the death of George Floyd, which was caused by police brutality, and that really upset people. Whereas here it has more to do with unfair treatment in the form of disproportionate imprisonment rates of Aboriginal people."

"Absolutely, Sam—some would argue that police brutality on Indigenous Australians is a problem too. So why the large scale protests?"

Sam gathers his thoughts and explains that the unfair treatment in both scenarios have been more than just isolated incidents.

"Exactly, this is something that has been going on for *ages*. And I might open this up to everyone else—why do we think that it's targeted mainly at Black Americans or Indigenous Australians?"

10, 9, 8, 7, 6, 5, 4 ... James pipes up.

"Well, sir, probably because they're discriminated against because of their skin color?"

"Everyone's on fire today—I'm really loving the contributions! Yes, there's a terrible history of racial discrimination against Black Americans and Indigenous Australians, and for Indigenous Australians in particular, this sadly continues in the form of Indigeneity being a significant predictor of imprisonment (Snowball & Weatherburn, 2007) because of the very harmful assumption that Black people will tend to commit more crimes, and more of the sorts of crimes that result in them being caught up in the criminal justice system (Jeffries & Bond, 2012)—quite similar to what Jimmy asserted earlier actually. Within the system, there's also police neglect while in custody (Klippmark & Crawley, 2018) and outside of it, more systemic issues like disadvantage, social exclusion, lack of access to housing and healthcare that lead to a cycle of recidivism (Macdonald, Scholes & Powell, 2016). So yes, these forms of institutional and structural racisms (Klippmark & Crawley, 2018) in both the U.S. and Australia have created a real urgency for people to speak up against injustice in the form of protests." I pause to catch my breath and let the words sink in. A brief moment passes before Sam ventures a response.

"Hmm.... Okay, that makes a lot more sense now. I'm not outraged per se—not at this moment at least—but it's certainly annoying thinking about it. I'd definitely say that something *needs* to be done. At this stage, I'm not quite sure about joining in with a mass group of people with all that's been going on with Covid, but yeah, I think we *should* all think about some way we can raise awareness about it, even if it's as small as talking about it within our own friendship groups or something along those lines—I'm glad we managed to talk about it today."

Sam was right—I was glad about it too. Yes, we had deviated from the original activity around Evaluating, but I cannot help but smile to myself as I noticed the rest of the class nodding their heads while they digested the conversation. Just as I'm about to launch into a spiel about how Covid-19 has made societal inequities even more apparent and how an activist stance to issues of racial inequities is key, I am abruptly interrupted by the end-of-lesson bell.

* * *

As I disconnect my laptop from the projector and clean the whiteboard, I reflect on what had just happened; I breathe a deep sigh of relief at how the discussion had played out. Could I have predicted the outcome? Probably not. Could the outcome have been different? Could the outcome have been worse? Probably. Even so, I knew by this point that SJP was "pedagogical risk-taking" (Breunig, 2016, p. 5) and cognizant that possible failure, student disinterest or self-embarrassment was much better than engaging in an "act of complicity" (hooks, 1994, p. 66) by remaining silent, or worse still, devaluing the already-silenced voices in the room like I had with Joe. I smile to myself again as I realize that I had, in my own way, become part of a "project and provocation that challenges students to critically engage with the world so they can act on it" (Giroux, 2010, p. 336). Even more excitingly, there had been a shift in emphasis to my students, allowing them to relate their own experiences to what was being taught and in so doing, "making visible the relationships among knowledge, authority and power" (Giroux, 2010, p. 336).

A Reflexive Re-turn: Part Three

Invariably, questions of domination, power and privilege continue to accompany me on my journey as an "Asian" migrant teacher in Australia. As a minority, I am, like Indigenous Australians and Black Americans, subsumed into the politics of discrimination, marginalization and exclusion by the White (Australian) majority (Rizvi, 1990). Simultaneously, while it is beyond the scope of this essay, I remain aware that "racism against Aboriginals and Asians … represents distinctive modalities of racism with their own history and structures of meaning [stemming from] quite distinct patterns of historical development" (Rizvi, 1990, p .174). Consequently, as a migrant settler who refuses to perpetuate settler colonial logics (Klippmark & Crawley, 2018), I continue on this personal and professional journey with theory as my guide, knowing full well that it is both the content of curriculum *and* methods of pedagogy that teach politically transformative lessons

(Breunig, 2016). As hooks (1994) reminds me, theory around AsianCrit and SJP *must* work hand in hand with my praxis as a teacher, for failing to let one inform the other "den[ies] the power of liberatory education for critical consciousness, thereby perpetuating conditions that reinforce our collective exploitation and repression" (hooks, 1994, p. 69).

Indeed, this personal is political is pedagogical AsianCrit counter story *about* SJP has been an effort to acknowledge "power, history, memory ... as the issues central to transnational democratic struggles" (Alexander & Mohanty, 1997, p. xix) and a way of writing in intra-national and international solidarity "to build those coalitions, affiliations and social movements capable of ... promoting substantive social change" (Giroux, 2010, p. 339).

At the same time, I *shall* not make any claims that what has been explored here serves as the *only* way forward. On one hand, this essay hopes to counter the dearth of research that explores classroom teachers' critically conscious practice (McDonough, 2009), but on the other, very much remains part of an ongoing "process of multiple avenues of insightful moments" (Sleeter, Torres & Laughlin, 2004, p. 83). In other words, this essay's overarching goal was not to offer "class plans for duplication, but [to illustrate a] path to praxis" (Hinchey, 2008, p. 20). Indeed, engaging with SJP means that we need to remain vigilant against establishing a set of recipes for praxis (Keesing-Styles, 2003) or expecting a uniformity in practice (Tilley & Taylor, 2013), particularly because insisting on a blueprint undermines the premise that SJP acknowledges that each classroom is different and that strategies must be changed and reconceptualized for each new teaching experience (hooks, 1994). Where I *will* make a claim though, is that because "schools and classrooms, as microcosms of society and as primary sites of knowledge construction and production, are key determinants of how we think, feel and talk about race and racism" (Rudnick, 2019, p. 217), I *can*, *will* and *shall* press forward with a continued commitment to a transformative politics and practice (hooks, 1994) through SJP.

REFERENCES

Ayers, W., Quinn, T.M., & Stovall, D. (2009). *Handbook of social justice in education.* Routledge.

Boylorn, R.M. & Orbe, M.P. (2014). *Critical autoethnography: Intersecting cultural identities in everyday life.* Left Coast Press.

Breunig, M. (2011). Problematizing critical pedagogy. *International Journal of Critical Pedagogy, 3*(3), 2–23.

Breunig, M. (2016). Critical and social justice pedagogies in practice. In Breunig, M. & Peters, M.A. (Eds.), *Encyclopaedia of educational philosophy and theory.* Springer.

Chang, B. (2013). Voice of the voiceless? Multiethnic student voices in critical approaches to race, pedagogy, literacy and agency. *Linguistics and Education, 24*(3), 348–360. doi:10.1016/j.linged.2013.03.005.

Chang, R.S. (1993). Toward an Asian American legal scholarship: Critical race theory, post structuralism, and narrative space. *California Law Review, 81*(5), 1241–1323.

Cho, H. (2017). Racism and linguicism: Engaging language minority pre-service teachers in counter-storytelling. *Race Ethnicity and Education, 20*(5), 666–680. doi:10.1080/1361 3324.2016.1150827.

Ellis, C. (2004). *The ethnographic I: A methodological novel about autoethnography*: AltaMira Press.

Ellis, C. (2007). Telling secrets, revealing lives: Relational ethics in research with intimate others. *Qualitative Inquiry, 13*(1), 3–29. https://doi.org/10.1177/1077800406294947.

Ellis, C., Adams, T.E., & Bochner, A.P. (2011). Autoethnography: An overview. *Historical Social Research / Historische Sozialforschung, 36*(4), 273–290.

Ford, L. (2010). *Settler sovereignty: Jurisdiction and indigenous people in America and Australia, 1788–1836.* Harvard University Press.

Gillborn, D. (2015). Intersectionality, critical race theory, and the primacy of racism: Race, class, gender, and disability in education. *Qualitative Inquiry, 21*(3), 277–287. doi:10.1177/1077800414557827.

Giroux, H.A. (2010). Paulo Freire and the crisis of the political. *Power and Education, 2*(3), 335–340. https://doi.org/10.2304/power.2010.2.3.335.

Holman-Jones, S. (2005). Auto ethnography: Making the personal political. In Denzin, N.K. & Lincoln, Y.S. (Eds.), *Handbook of Qualitative Research* (pp.763–791). Sage.

hooks, b. (1994). Teaching to transgress: Education as the practice of freedom. Routledge.

Iftikar, J.S., & Museus, S.D. (2018). On the utility of Asian critical (AsianCrit) theory in the field of education. *International Journal of Qualitative Studies in Education, 31*(10), 935–949. https://doi.org/10.1080/09518398.2018.1522008.

Jeffries, S., & Bond, C.E.W. (2012). The impact of indigenous status on adult sentencing: A review of the statistical research literature from the United States, Canada, and Australia. *Journal of Ethnicity in Criminal Justice, 10*(3), 223–243. https://doi.org/10.1080/1537 7938.2012.700830.

Keesing-Styles, L. (2003). The relationship between critical pedagogy and assessment in teacher education. *Radical Pedagogy 5*(1), 1–19.

Klippmark, P., & Crawley, K. (2018). Justice for Ms Dhu. *Social & Legal Studies, 27*(6), 695–715. https://doi.org/10.1177/0964663917734415.

Kraehe, A.M. (2015). Sounds of silence: Race and emergent counter-narratives of art teacher identity. *Studies in Art Education, 56*(3), 199–213. doi:10.1080/00393541.2015.11 518963.

Macdonald, J., Scholes, T., & Powell, K. (2016). Listening to Australian indigenous men: Stories of incarceration and hope. *Primary Health Care Research & Development, 17*(6), 568–577. https://doi.org/10.1017/S1463423616000256.

Marx, S., Pennington, J.L., & Chang, H. (2017). Critical autoethnography in pursuit of educational equity: Introduction to the IJME special issue. *International Journal of Multicultural Education, 19*(1), 1–6. https://doi.org/10.18251/ijme.v19i1.1393.

McDonough, K. (2009). Pathways to critical consciousness: A first year teacher's engagement with issues of race and equity. *Journal of Teacher Education, 60*(5), 528–537.

Museus, S.D., & Ifitikar, J.S. (2013). Asian critical theory (AsianCrit). In M.Y.G. Danico, J.G. (Ed.), *Asian American Society.* Sage.

Neumann, M. (1996). Collecting ourselves at the end of the century. In Ellis, C. & Bochner, A.P. (Eds.), *Composing ethnography: Alternative forms of qualitative writing* (pp.172–197). Altamira.

Pizarro, M., & Kohli, R. (2020). "I stopped sleeping": Teachers of color and the impact of racial battle fatigue. *Urban Education, 55*(7), 967–991. https://doi.org/10.1177/0042085918805788.

Rizvi, F. (1990). Understanding and confronting racism in schools. *Unicorn, 16*(3), 169–176.

Rudnick, D.L. (2019). Walking on eggshells: Colorblind ideology and race talk in teacher education. *Multicultural Education Review: Policy Influences and Practical Contributions of Multicultural Education in Diverse Contexts, 11*(3), 216–233. https://doi.org/10.10 80/2005615X.2019.1644043.

Sleeter, C., Torres, M.N., & Laughlin, P. (2004). Scaffolding conscientization through inquiry in teacher education. *Teacher Education Quarterly, 31*(1), 81–96.

Snowball, L., & Weatherburn, D. (2007). Does racial bias in sentencing contribute to indigenous overrepresentation in prison? *Australian & New Zealand Journal of Criminology, 40*(3), 272–290. https://doi.org/10.1375/acri.40.3.272.

Solórzano, D., & Yosso, T. (2002). Critical race methodology: Counter-storytelling as an analytical framework for education research. *Qualitative Inquiry, 6*(1), 23–44.

Tate, W.F. (1997). Critical race theory and education: History, theory, and implications. *Review of Research in Education, 22*, 195–247.

Taylor, E., Gillborn, D., & Ladson-Billings, G. (2009). *Foundations of critical race theory in education*: Routledge.

Vasconcelos, E. (2011). "I can see you": An autoethnography of my teacher-student self. *The Qualitative Report, 16*(2), 415–440.

Wall, S. (2008). Easier said than done: Writing an autoethnography. *International Journal of Qualitative Methods, 7*(1), 38–53. doi:10.1177/160940690800700103.

Yu, T. (2006). Challenging the politics of the "model minority" stereotype: A case for educational equality. *Equity & Excellence in Education, 39*(4), 325–333. https://doi.org/10.1080/10665680600932333.

Under-Resourced, Underfunded, and Covid

What a Pandemic Can Teach Schools Seeking Racial Equity

N.J. Akbar, Jennifer L. Martin,
Christie Magoulias, *and* Dayle Rebelsky

> Racial equity is about applying justice and a
> little bit of common sense to a system that's been
> out of balance. When a system is out of balance, people
> of color feel the impacts most acutely, but, to be clear,
> an imbalanced system makes all of us pay.
> —Glenn Harris, President, Race Forward
> and Publisher, Colorlines

Introduction

Horace Mann argued that education is society's great equalizer. The push for equality in education has led to multiple yet unsuccessful reform movements. These movements were promulgated on Mann's 1848 premise, yet school funding inequities remain. There are many funding issues that serve as mechanisms for creating inequitable schools across the country. Districts and schools already confronted with funding challenges found themselves on the brink of funding peril with the unforeseen necessities related to Covid-19. The global pandemic fundamentally altered the way schools operate.

In mid–March 2020, the lives of all Americans dramatically changed for the foreseeable future. School buildings were forced to close as Covid-19 swept this country. Administrators, teachers, and parents were given no time for preparation. Schools were forced to change their historical delivery method of teaching and learning with the transition to remote learning, while some families faced limited broadband access, food and housing insecurity, and massive unemployment. The pandemic intensified already disparate conditions facing students and families, which propelled these conditions to the forefront for many school board members and district staff. Districts were now no longer able to disregard disparities such as lack of broadband access, food insecurities, etc., which were previously ignored because it did not hinder the school delivery model.

Some districts throughout the U.S. were prepared to move to the challenge of full remote learning as they had already invested in technology for all students. However, as Black and Brown students are more relegated to underfunded schools and districts, they bore the brunt of additional issues of inequities brought on by the pandemic. Many underfunded urban and under-resourced rural districts scrambled to find quick solutions to fill digital gaps. Along with the pandemic and the social inequities that were heightened by the crisis, the country also experienced major protests calling for racial justice—inspired by several incidents of police brutality, typified by the murder of George Floyd. Surrounding this event, the pandemic political rhetoric was laden with racial animus, particularly targeting Chinese, Asian, and individuals perceived to be Chinese. In 2020, Americans experienced uncertainty, fear, and anxiety as word of the pandemic spread and lockdowns began to occur. These feelings were inflamed by frustration and outrage at the persistent acts of state sanctioned violence in the murdering of Black citizens and subsequent attacks on the Black Lives Matter movement.

As school districts considered the complexities brought about by the pandemic as well as the nation-wide calls for racial justice, leaders were positioned to make sustainable change for long-term racial equity. This was the time and opportunity for district leaders to be innovative and transformative in making decisions regarding our educational systems. This essay will discuss funding inequities spotlighted by the Covid-19 pandemic intersecting with the pressing need and fight for racial justice in our schools and communities. It will showcase these two distinct crises separately; however, we argue that both deserve to be considered as they intersect in ways that exacerbate systemic inequities to further marginalize the same people and communities.

Background

Racial equity in under-resourced and underfunded schools has always been a pressing issue (Kozol, 2012; Milner, 2018; Noguera, 2001;

Ngounou & Gutierrez, 2017). Scholars have long since identified the achievement gap, now more commonly known as the opportunity gap (Carter & Welner, 2013), as a deficit that exists between Black and Latinx children when compared to their white peers (Ladson-Billings, 2006; Yosso, 2005). These gaps, however, have historically not been attributed to the inequities that exist within the underserved, under-resourced, and under-funded school districts. The prevailing ideology still positions the problem belonging to the students themselves as opposed to the systems that created the inequities among U.S. racial lines.

Along with this deficit framing of students and families, it is necessary to acknowledge and address the challenges that school districts face, namely inequities in funding. Challenges include access to broadband, technology availability, and food insecurity. Additionally, access to early childhood education, which is a critical component for closing opportunity gaps, is less readily available for families and young children in underfunded school districts. In many districts, early childhood funding is solely dependent upon grant dollars and ancillary money after compulsory needs are met by districts. As Covid-19 has overwhelmed districts, underfunded schools face fewer possibilities for offering extended early childhood education opportunities for the students who most need it. Ostrander (2015) argues that funding inequities and over-reliance on federal funding and local property tax with little accountability has a disparate impact on urban school districts.

Boston and Warren (2017) noted that racial identity and belonging is critical to student achievement. Schools that do a better job of cultivating the cultures of the students they serve promote stronger student-teacher relationships and increase the achievement of Black students who often feel disconnected from the school. A greater focus on racial equity would include the integration of culturally relevant pedagogy. Policy would support these practices if racial equity were considered a priority. When considering the fact that many schools have turned to remote learning as the primary mode of teaching students during Covid, culturally relevant pedagogy is even more important because of the physical distance that this type of learning places between the students and the school.

Ngounou and Gutierrez (2017) discuss the need for district leaders to take action toward institutional change promoting racial equity. Racial equity necessitates moving beyond the uncomfortable conversations around race, and involves the daily decisions made within the district. Noguera (2001) highlights the fact that politics complicates the issue of addressing race in education. Political fears can impede districts from attempts at racial equity thus widening opportunity gaps. School leaders must be courageous by directly challenging the political forces which detract from achieving racial equity goals.

A major component of racial equity is the disproportionate disciplining of Black and Brown students. Alexander (2010) evidences how differential discipline leads to the school to prison pipeline which has exacerbated the mass incarceration of People of Color, specifically Men of Color. Johnson, Jabbari, Williams and Marcucci (2019) indicate that there is a need to balance safety in schools with responsive discipline to achieve racial equity, concluding that restorative justice positions districts to better achieve racial equity goals.

In sum, racial equity policies are more necessary than ever in response to the Covid-19 pandemic in order to not worsen the inequities that already exist. Funding inequities and the overreliance on property taxes may present future challenges as they relate to students being further disadvantaged because of the lack of early childhood education in already underfunded areas. School leaders must focus on moving beyond simply providing lip service to inequities based on race, and move toward true racial understanding and healing by committing to action to dismantle institutional and systemic inequities. Additionally, district leaders should be aware of the political forces that pose conflicts for acting in the best interests of racial equity within underfunded school districts. This includes moving beyond the interest convergence principle. Interest convergence involves societal changes occurring historically only because said policies and practices benefited white citizens (Bell, 1980; Zion & Blanchett, 2011).

Comparable Glances: A Snapshot of Two Districts

The global pandemic that is Covid-19 forced all school districts to transform their learning models virtually overnight. There have been many responses to the pandemic, based upon existing resources and those that were added out of necessity. Below is a brief snapshot of two districts. The first is a midsize urban school district with 21,000 students located in a Midwestern state. The second is a small middle class rural-suburban district with 2,100 students in a different Midwestern state.

Ohio School District (Urban)

In mid–March, the state where this district is located ordered all schools closed because of the Coronavirus as a precautionary measure to reduce the spread. The overall purpose was to prevent hospitals from being overloaded with sick patients, and to protect the people of the state. Citizens were placed on stay at home orders besides essential travel (e.g., work, doctor visits, grocery store trips, etc.). This school district closed its doors for in-person learning, and within three days was offering remote learning. A few years earlier, the district began investing in tablets for each of its students to supplement their in-class learning. These tablets were used for different applications (i.e., Google Classroom and iReady) to teach students various lessons with technology. The students were already in the habit of using many of the platforms, and most parents were already familiar with the technology being used at home.

Despite all this, there were many equity issues highlighted in this district because of the pandemic. Broadband access was no longer a luxury, but a necessity to perform daily academic tasks. Additionally, there were many households that lacked quality access to high-speed broadband services. Before the pandemic, some students used their cellular devices to do their homework, either using its internet connection or using it as a hotspot. The pandemic demonstrated that this model was not sustainable when students were required to utilize their tablet devices, and connect to the internet as a means for attending class. Therefore, the district purchased mobile hotspots and delivered them to students who lacked adequate broadband access. The district also paid the monthly usage charges. This solution filled the gap temporarily, but it was not sustainable; technology access is an ongoing challenge that the community must soon address in a systemic manner.

Lastly, the public schools have become increasingly recognized as essential resources for the community. During the school year and the summer of the pandemic, this school district provided meals at most of its school buildings to ensure that students had the nutrition they needed. After the pandemic began, community members lauded the district's meal program, which provided more than 100,000 meals in the first month following Covid-19 school closures. Remote learning services, hotspots/internet access, and accessibility to meals are three essential components provided by schools in this district. Districts made the necessary expenditures due to the essential needs of the community as uncertainty of federal support loomed. Later, Covid Relief and Elementary and Secondary Schools Emergency Relief (ESSER) funds covered the cost for the increased expenses caused by the pandemic as allowable by the federal stimulus packages passed by Congress.

There were a host of other issues that the district needed to solve to support students and their families, such as monitoring attendance because of compulsory education laws. This district employed "connectors" who visited homes and contacted families in non-traditional ways to ensure that students and families were ready to engage in the online classroom. This resource was invaluable for the district and is one that will continue to support students and families with the resources that they need inside and outside of the school building.

Illinois School District (Rural-Suburban)

After the governor closed schools state-wide on March 13, 2020, state school boards and superintendents navigated new territory with requisite remote learning through the end of the 2019–2020 academic year with little to no preparation time for teachers and staff. Evidence Based Funding (EBF) is an Illinois initiative begun in 2017 to provide more equity in funding between all districts. The higher a district's funding adequacy, the lower the EBF it would receive, and vice versa. After decades of equity funding studies, two years of EBF payments, and a pandemic threatening long-term shutdowns, would districts continue to operate as silos or would this be the defining pivot toward unity and equity for school districts in this diverse state? Operating in a new and foreign landscape, requiring maneuvering of finances, districts piloted new models of teaching. As the school year moved into summer 2020, Illinois announced that Evidence Based Funding, the new and much needed school funding reform, was stalled and no new EBF dollars would be distributed to any districts across the state. In Illinois, despite the removal of the funding meant to provide more equity across districts, all school district administrative teams acquired additional devices, increased access points to the internet, scheduled food delivery, and provided teachers a crash course in remote instruction.

In a middle class, mostly white, rural-suburban Illinois district of 2,100 students, the funding adequacy measurement is 71 percent and $8,500 district spending per student. During the summer of 2020, the school board and superintendent tackled the strict guidance and regulations from the Illinois governor and the Illinois Department of Public Health with a decision to begin the 2020–2021 academic year with remote-only instruction. Despite pressure from neighboring districts attempting a hybrid or minimally changed weekly schedule, the district leadership cited the recommendations of regional health professionals to remain remote. Despite the remote only decision, the school board promised the community to provide more than the darkened, empty school buildings that were the symbol of the previous spring.

All district stakeholders (students, families, and staff) were surveyed multiple times for feedback with high response rates each time. A robust remote learning plan was written, and investments were made for teachers and students to improve educational access and learning outcomes. The district invested in Canvas as a learning management system for use in first through twelfth grades. Chromebooks, which were already owned and used by fourth through twelfth grades, were purchased and distributed to first–third graders as well. Teachers were provided forty-four hours of professional development geared toward teaching remotely with fidelity and efficacy. The investment in teacher training equated to 50 percent of each teacher's three-year professional development requirement. The entire school district began the year with students in synchronous class meetings and asynchronous learning planned into each day. As the district moved through the first quarter, metrics and data were reassessed as state guidelines and state allowances shifted slightly. The district began serving six days of lunches to all children under the age of eighteen who arrived at lunch pickup times. The district also progressed in October to a hybrid learning model with two days of full attendance for 50 percent of the students twice each week.

Comparable Inequities

As we consider these two district snapshots, there were several noticeable differences. These differences can be categorized as parent engagement, food insecurity, and broadband access. In the more affluent district, parental voice was not only more present but also more authoritative. Parents in the urban district became more engaged in sharing their perspective but not in an authoritative way. Secondly, food insecurity was a major issue for families in the urban district; the district was charged with providing food for students during the initial quarantine and throughout the summer. Both public school districts fed any student eighteen years old and younger who arrived during the meal distribution times regardless of enrollment. The urban district supplied upward of 14,000 meals per day, while the rural-suburban district provided approximately 2,000, which further financially constrained the urban district. Furthermore, the urban district experienced greater participation in their meal program from the abundance of residents attending charter schools. The students receiving the meals in the urban districts were largely supporting basic needs, whereas the rural-suburban district had fewer students using the food distribution for necessity while many used it for convenience.

Lastly, broadband access was another area where families from both districts experienced disparities. In the U.S., personal broadband access has historically been viewed as a luxury. However, the Covid-19 pandemic and the shift to remote learning has demonstrated that our society has moved personal broadband access from a want to a need to fully function in our society. Some students and families have insufficient internet access solely on their cellular device, which does not provide them with adequate service to engage in everyday life, particularly during the global pandemic.

To conclude, the pandemic exacerbated inequities for an already underfunded urban district to provide the basic needs necessary for students to successfully participate in remote learning. The rising costs associated with providing meals and broadband access ballooned, particularly in the urban district amid pandemic provisions. As districts are continuing to adjust, we predict these inequities will widen.

Education in the Time of Covid-19

Superintendent Responses to the Pandemic

During the pandemic, district superintendents were tasked with synthesizing a variety of federal, state, and local guidelines in order to create new pandemic policy guidance for their districts. For many superintendents, this was an onerous task completed independently. County and state guidelines were required, yet support to implement mitigations was not provided to districts. Pressure from parents, school boards, teacher and staff unions, combined with health, athletic, and state education agencies, created an unprecedented quandary for superintendents. Interpretation for guidelines varied such that some public school districts began the 2020–2021 academic year fully remote, some in a hybrid format, and some with in-person attendance.

Baker Tilly, an advisory, tax, and assurance firm, conducted a survey of 78 superintendents in Minnesota to get an understanding of the effectiveness, changes, and challenges that have resulted from the Covid-19 pandemic. Superintendents could answer questions with follow-up comments. The survey asked superintendents about their management and movement to remote learning during the pandemic after states forced school closures (Lifto, 2020). Those who were highly or moderately prepared had high expectations, firm deadlines, common learning management systems, and emergency operations plans to help guide and propel their responses. Comparatively, those who were minimally or not at all prepared lacked technology and training, possessed no online or remote learning programs prior to Covid-19, and experienced technology inequities (e.g., not possessing a 1:1 policy, or one device per student).

The transition to remote learning was not difficult for districts that were already comfortable with technology, had students and faculty who were already using tech tools, and were able to provide support to those who were not. Whereas districts that had difficulty with the transition had large numbers of students without internet access, low communications with struggling or busy parents, and issues creating robust remote learning experiences comparable to what they did in the in-person classroom (Lifto, 2020). Overall, Lifto (2020) found that the biggest challenges reported by participants were teacher training and technical infrastructure (29 percent). This puts the digital divide between districts into perspective: some districts are working on catching up to those who already had access and infrastructure to support remote teaching and learning prior to the pandemic.

Gustavo Balderas, 2020 National Superintendent, and Eugene SD 4J Superintendent in Oregon, was interviewed about his experiences with leading during Covid-19 as well as on education in general. In response to how his district dealt with the global pandemic, Balderas indicated:

> It's really all revolved around teams and structure and getting people trained on that pretty quickly. We're also focused on helping people understand their jobs and responsibilities during this time and making sure people are responsible for their areas. We're also thinking a lot about how we communicate. It's always communication that seems to be the issue. Right now, that's compounded by the tension people are having because this is fast-moving and evolving [as cited in Pitts, 2020, para. 4].

Balderas, when asked if the pandemic is making educators change their thinking, said, "Absolutely. I was telling my team that there's a real opportunity to look at systems that we don't have that probably should've always in place" (para. 7). Balderas had already been focused on equity within his district. His thoughts on equity challenge the current way many think about the issue:

> I think equity is about intentionality. Equity means intentionality around access and opportunity. I also talk a lot about having a global perspective. I don't believe that the most affluent should have the most influence. How do we make sure that we're doing what's right for all kids? [as cited in Pitts, 2020, para. 20]

Pitts (2020) asked Balderas what teachers and administrators can do to increase equity. Balderas indicated that teachers and administrators need to examine data and information, ensure the correct systems for data are in place, and use data to make the most informed decisions. In terms of data collection, he believes it will be difficult to collect over the next few months but will work to continue assessments to make sure students' needs are being met.

Parental and Teacher Concerns

As a member of the Covid at-risk group and suffering from the loss of two family members, Gladys Marquez, a public school teacher in Chicago, changed from optimism to fear for her, her children, and her students returning to school in the fall of 2020. She did not believe that putting the health of both faculty and students at risk was the best option at that time. With an increase in younger adults and children contracting the virus, she believed it to be premature and unsafe to resume school as "normal" (Cullotta & Sherry, 2020). The position of the Chicago Teachers Union as the 2020–2021 school year approached, was that schools would not be able to open safely; this conflicted with district plans to move to a blended format, requiring both in-person class and virtual learning. Parents and teachers in the Chicago area shared the concerns of the union. Teachers whose students come from lower socioeconomic and historically marginalized racial groups felt that the virus spike would severely impact their children, especially in households with members who had a preexisting condition or elderly relatives who are at a greater risk of contracting the virus (Cullotta & Sherry, 2020).

For working class families, the pandemic created a frustrating situation. Ruzanna Yesayan, a parent of four-year-old twins, expressed her thoughts on the school reopening plan for the New York City schools, which required students to attend in-person class twice a week and virtually the rest of the week. According to Yesayan, "The school reopening plan proposed by the mayor and the Education Department is a disaster for working families. Parents will be forced to provide alternative child-care arrangements on the days when the children are not in school" (as cited in Leonhardt, 2020, para. 2). Families like Yesayan's, who do not have close family nearby or cannot afford childcare, are in a dangerous predicament. Yesayan feels conflicted with the need for schools to reopen in order for her and her husband to work to support their family, but also does not feel it is the right time for schools to open indicating, "I don't understand how is it even worth it to put children in school for two days a week? Why would I compromise my family's safety at all? It doesn't make sense" (Leonhardt, 2020, para. 4).

In response to the increasing uncertainty of the safety of sending children back to school, parents began to examine other alternatives for their children's education. Parents reached out to Pete Baroody, who leads summer camps in North Virginia, about creating groups, or learning pods, that are held within homes. Baroody allowed parents to put groups together, giving them control over the space being used. Herdawit Balcha, who heads Bright Mind Preschool, opened a new location and instead of holding the pod within a home, she signed a lease on a space where children can be dropped off. Both have worked to limit the pods to less than six students per instructor and eliminate any contact between pods, thus reducing the risk of spreading the virus (LeBlanc & Wolf, 2020).

Baroody and Balcha were interviewed about different aspects of learning pods. In terms of new services that will be offered, Balcha responded:

> Most of our parents were utilizing our service for the summer. But now they are going to need us for the fall, too. So, for the elementary kids, we have expanded and created a learning pod and hired an elementary teacher. So that way, they don't lose another school year, so they can help them facilitate that virtual learning [as cited in LeBlanc & Wolf, 2020, para. 15].

Baroody, when asked what a pod facilitator would do, responded, "It's hard to understand because there's so many different needs out there. We have a whole menu of items that we can provide." He added, "It is not just the one size fits all for anybody because the comfort level, because of the needs of the kids, because of the financial needs and that sort of thing is like, okay, we're trying to adapt to all these different things" (as cited in LeBlanc & Wolf, 2020, para. 24).

Although learning pods are one solution to the impact of Covid-19, they are not a viable financial option for low income families. Families who have been working on organizing these pods can pay for teachers, tutors, and facilitators who can work on creating structure for their children, in small groups, for the day. Some nonprofits have stepped in to help support low income families with similar services (Childress, 2020). This also raises the question of what school districts are doing to help their low-income families. Some districts, such as Zeta Charter Schools, located in New York, and Durham Public Schools in North Carolina, have created teacher or tutor facilitated pods with a tiered pricing structure to make this option available for lower income families. However, parents are beginning to question why they must pay for these services when their districts are already being supported by their tax dollars (Childress, 2020). The learning pods should be accessible to everyone, especially disadvantaged students. If not, it is likely that the pods will create greater disparities than were previously present within the traditional in-person public school system (Fox, 2020).

The Pandemic's Impact on Education

The pandemic led many districts into a spiral of deep questioning and examination of their capabilities of fully transitioning to remote learning practically overnight. Some districts who made the early investments into one-to-one technology for students arguably had a much easier time adjusting to this new reality. Other districts, especially those with limited resources, may have experienced more challenges making the transition. Regardless of the transition time, the pandemic launched a period of innovation such as learning pods, hybrid learning models, and many others.

Paul Reville, former secretary of education in Massachusetts had great insight into issues that the pandemic brought to the forefront for schools. Because mass closures on this scale in the U.S. have never occurred, school districts entered uncharted territory (Mineo, 2020). Reville believes the lesson to be learned for all school districts is the necessity of a back-up system. However, he believes not only are districts going to need to create a backup, but also design new systems that close gaps in student learning as well as opportunity gaps. Marginalized students are more affected, inside and outside of the classroom. Many of these students do not have access or exposure to similar opportunities as their affluent peers; such exposure is required to achieve academic parity based upon biased learning assessments (Carter & Welner, 2013). Reville sees this as an opportunity to change the status quo, rather than repair the existing one, and to fix a system that attempts to hold to a "one size fits all" mentality, which ultimately hurts students, particularly Black, Brown, and low-income students. This may begin to shift now that parents are noticing inequities on a larger scale with Covid closures and shifts to remote learning (Mineo, 2020).

Racism in the Time of Covid

Racial Impact

Although racial disparities have existed for decades within U.S. schools, economic opportunities, and healthcare systems, Covid-19 shines a spotlight upon them. With many Black and Brown families living in multi-generational households, an added danger is created for older family members if their children or grandchildren have in-person school attendance requirements. This is compounded by inequities their families may already face within the healthcare system. Overall, 30 percent of all K–12 students are disadvantaged in remote learning with either inadequate access to devices or internet connections (Fox, 2020).

As the education system adapts and changes in the wake of Covid-19, the inequalities faced by students from marginalized populations are not likely to change without an intentional plan to pursue racial justice. There are many newsworthy stories demonstrating racism being enacted on Black and Brown children within U.S. schools. For example, a six-year-old Black girl was arrested on school grounds for a temper tantrum, and placed in handcuffs (Seale, 2020). Although many were outraged by this incident, it is a pattern of the treatment of Black girls in schools (Morris, 2016). Black girls make up only 16 percent of the student population, yet are 42 percent of the recipients of corporal punishment, 45 percent with one or more suspension, and more than one-third are arrested on school grounds (Seale, 2020). School personnel and policy makers must create a new "normal" where racial justice is one of the main foci, in addition to race-based academic gaps.

School personnel and policy makers need to change the school system from within by actively searching for areas where explicit bias exists and implementing implicit bias and diversity training requirements for all levels of staff (Seale, 2020). This may involve disciplining and removing staff who engage in racism, microaggressions, and other biased actions. There have been several reports this year where teachers and staff were terminated for racist social media posts. In sum, societal views toward Black and Brown students affect them more than just academically; anyone advocating to close opportunity gaps in schools must turn toward racial justice.

The racial reckoning of 2020 demanded a national call to action around acknowledging the existence of the legalized mistreatment of Black people. This clarion call demands that the country see the humanity of Black people. Furthermore, it is a petition to the consciousness and soul of this country to coalesce around a standard value that Black people do not deserve the presumption of guilt, criminality, and ultimately sentencing to death due to the hue of their skin. Policy makers must acknowledge that the problem exists, and actively work to address these concerns as foundational to this advocacy.

Another aspect of the impact of Covid-19 also involves racial bias and racist sentiments being leveled against persons of Asian descent. The discrimination toward Asians and Pacific Islanders after the outbreak of Covid-19 had not only a societal impact, but also an impact on student academics. Angie Hong, an Asian American mother, asked her son if other students at school had made any comments toward him about Covid-19. "Yeah," he said. "They yelled across the room, 'You're Chinese, you have coronavirus!'" (Hong, 2020). This is not an isolated incident perpetrated toward Asian American students across the nation. If the students speak up, they are told by their peers to lighten up, or are left to defend themselves if their teachers do nothing (Hong, 2020). In addition to addressing this racism with her son, Hong confronted the principal. Armed with a slideshow presenting facts versus myths about Covid-19, Hong expressed to the principal that she was not only advocating for her son, but also for any child who may experience racial harassment. Hong states (2020) she felt ridiculous explaining this, but she felt she needed to address it directly since overt racism leveled toward Asian Americans seems to not have clicked for many, "Asians/Asian Americans residing in the U.S. who have not traveled to China (recently or *ever*) are no more at risk than non–Asians/Asian Americans to contract the Coronavirus" (Hong, 2020, para. 8).

Hate crimes spiked amid the Covid-19 outbreak, with regional news-casts reporting the occurrences. One case occurred at a Sam's Club in Texas, where the perpetrator stabbed a two and a six-year-old because he thought the family was spreading the disease because of their race. Another case occurred when teens attacked a 51-year-old woman, bombarding her with anti–Asian statements and accusations that she started the virus (Liu, 2020). The importance of explaining the truth about the virus to children and adults is important, including the choice of words used to describe the virus. There is no need to include China or Chinese in the description and, if necessary, define that the virus started in a geographical region, and not by the people who descend from there. Parents and educators need to let their children know that if they see their peers being bullied to inform a teacher and to show their Asian peers compassion, respect, and acceptance. Children also need to be taught that memes and jokes pertaining to the virus are unacceptable, and how they may be stereotyping Asians by using these mediums (Liu, 2020; National Association of School Psychologists, 2020).

George Floyd and School Learning

In addition to facing the virus and all of its many implications, the uprisings of the summer of 2020 certainly impacted students of all ages, and found its way into schools. The death of George Floyd sparked outrage across the nation that led to uprisings across the globe. It remains unclear how schools will respond to the murder of George Floyd, and other incidents of state sanctioned violence—but to ignore them does not do justice to anyone—particularly those students who experience personal race related trauma. Mikkel Storaasli, superintendent of Grayslake High School District 127, posted a brief statement on the impact of Floyd's death, "Our students are naturally trying to process their feelings and determine the best way to express their sadness and anger. As a human being, so am I. But today we stand with our black students and their families, and families grieving everywhere" (Storaasli, 2020, para. 2). Storaasli has since furthered the conversation about race and is working directly with promoting and teaching antiracism through training and professional development.

One key feature that the district has updated, using Sims Bishop's concept of windows and mirrors, is to provide materials that allow students to understand and build empathy through learning the lived experience of others, "windows," and to see material that represents people like themselves, "mirrors." However, Storaasli has also called attention to the immediate impact of Floyd's death on his students, who are experiencing confusion, anger, and sadness. The students are encouraged to contact their school counselors, deans, social workers, administrators, teachers, or trusted adults to help them process their thoughts and emotions (Storaasli, 2020).

Some school districts across the nation, including in Minneapolis, Denver, and Portland, began to receive anonymous calls to eliminate their districts' contracts with the police. Derrianna Ford, a 16-year-old is one of many teens protesting police presence in schools. The school resource officers (SRO) present at her school, she said, do not make her feel safe and that money could be better spent. Her school currently employs three SROs, has one counselor, and no full-time nurse. "Even if you hurt yourself, they're calling the SRO," Ford said. "The first thing you should call is a nurse—but our nurses are only here Tuesday. If you're not hurt on Tuesday, it's your loss" (as cited in Balingit, Strauss, & Bellware, 2020, para. 6). Ford is not the only person to think money could be better spent. The American Civil Liberties Union found that across the United States, more than a million students attend a school who have a police officer, but no counselor or social worker; twenty-two million students attend schools that do not have funding for counselors or social workers, but do for police officers. A city council member in D.C. desires to work toward funding mental health professionals, rather than spending more on police. Some districts are concerned about feeding into the school-to-prison pipeline, and creating an unsafe atmosphere for their students (Balingit, et al., 2020).

Two St. Louis County school districts responded to a social media post by two white male students from their districts. One of the students knelt on the other student's neck, mimicking the murder of George Floyd, and included the hashtag #GeorgeFloydChallenge on their post. NAACP president John Bowman called on the districts to make a firm and quick response, and also for parents to take action. "There's no excuse for being insensitive and inhumane toward other people," Bowman said. "We have to show empathy toward other people who have losses. It's just a basic skill of being a human being." He added, "This is going to be a period where we're going to have to deal with being a little uncomfortable because in my community people have been uncomfortable for a long time" (Banker, 2020, para. 10).

Jason Lukehart, a fourth-grade teacher in Oak Park, Illinois, held a special Zoom meeting for his students to talk about the issue of racism. With a majority of his students joining the meeting, Lukehart said he wanted his students to know they could share their thoughts and feelings. "We've talked about the concept of white privilege and I was able to go back to some of those discussions," Lukehart said. "I want my white students to have the right perspective on this stuff in an age-appropriate way. For my black students, I hope they feel like I care about them" (para. 4). For many, school is a place where students can wrestle with difficult concepts with the presence of a teacher or counselor. However, with Covid-19's impact, these conversations are difficult to hold, especially if students turn off their microphones or cameras, which makes participation and feedback difficult for teachers (Mahoney, 2020; Richards, 2020).

One major obstacle, outside of the virtual learning impact, is that discussing the topics of race and racism, especially against Black Americans, is difficult and uncomfortable for many teachers. This may be because many of the teachers who would lead these discussions, approximately 80 percent, are white (Bureau of Labor Statistics, 2019). Studies have shown that compared to People of Color, whites are less likely to habitually talk about race, which creates a major hurdle to overcome in terms of discussing this issue (Milner, 2018). However, studies also reveal that children who talk about race with their families not only are able to navigate racial situations better, but also have an easier time speaking up for themselves and have better performances on conflict resolution and anger management tests (Richards, 2020).

Jesse Hagopian, a Black teacher at Garfield High School in Seattle, like most educators, has struggled to teach his students in a virtual format. Kamenetz (2020) interviewed Hagopian about why it is important and what it means to teach for Black lives. When asked to give advice to parents, Hagopian states, "They should take this opportunity to have these hard conversations with their kids about what's happening in our world today" (para. 6). In terms of what is missing from the curriculum in schools most, Hagopian responded, "Too often black people are reduced to slavery, and the only way that kids learn about black history is learning about enslavement. And, you know, we wanted to say, actually there is this incredible legacy of struggle and contributions to our country that are far bigger than our oppression" (para. 15). He added that, in a mixed-race setting, some of the most powerful moments occur when some of his white students have breakthroughs and come out with a better understanding of themselves and their Black peers, allowing them to become and commit to being allies with their Black peers. According to the Black Lives Matter at School movement, there are four needs required for antiracist school reform: "Counselors, not cops," ending "zero-tolerance" policies, mandating Black history and ethnic studies, and the hiring of more Black teachers (Kamenetz, 2020, para. 21, 27). In order to address the needs of previously underserved and racially diverse student populations, school boards must advocate for curricular and policy changes with these four needs in mind. School boards should make budgetary decisions with these needs in mind so that additional counselors can be hired to support student needs. Schools boards should also seek to fund equity audits and curriculum reviews in order to facilitate more culturally relevant and responsive curricula, which includes Black history and ethnic studies throughout K–12 systems. Finally, school systems must actively work to recruit and retain Teachers and Staff of Color.

Racial Inequities: An Overview

The standards or "accountability" movement in the U.S., often associated with the No Child Left Behind Act (2001), led to a narrowing of the curriculum in general. For example, in some elementary schools, subjects such as science and social studies, those that are not assessed on standardized measures, are no longer taught—especially in those schools servicing Black and Brown students. This short-term solution leads to major issues. In an effort to hold schools "accountable," students are being harmed; students are less knowledgeable about their government and their world, which may potentially lead to the deterioration of democracy (Pinar, 2012). To compound this fact, the inclusion of the cultures of Black and Brown students is critical.

Such curricular revision involves a necessary revolt against teaching children using one-size-fits-all curricula, pre-packaged curricula, and drill-and-kill mandates with the sole purpose of increasing scores on standardized tests. Teachers must, especially now, band together to insist upon the value of their own knowledge to create curricula, in conjunction with their students, for the purpose of empowerment and freedom. We must revolt against systems designed only to preserve the status quo.

During the global pandemic of 2020, the classroom pushed into the world. The great majority of these uprisings in the spring and summer of 2020 were peaceful—with the goal of collective action for long overdue racial justice. In the U.S., state sanctioned violence against Black and Brown bodies for the first time in recent memory was publicly acknowledged; previously, these stories were used by the majority to deceive and deform the racial inequities that remain a stark reality in the U.S. This long overdue change is happening *because* of the public and political protests of untold numbers of people in the U.S. and across the world—standing in solidarity and in outrage about the death of George Floyd, and the deaths of untold People of Color by police. We have also been witnessing many white youths using their privilege to protect Black and Brown bodies from the shields and batons of police. Some educators have been worried about the impact of Covid-19 on education. We submit that the summer of activism (2020) has done more to educate our young people than what they have missed in the months of remote learning.

Funding for Equity
and School Boards for Equity

Current state based educational funding models are largely driven by property taxes and thus disadvantage students who live in high poverty areas. However, the equity we need must be more complex and inclusive (Aleman, 2007; Morgan & Amerikaner, 2018). Racial equity and racial consciousness should be a primary factor for analyzing and developing policy (Aleman, 2007).

The impact of mandatory school closures, and the remote learning that followed, may include a rollback of the more equitable funding model finally enacted in Illinois in 2017 (Evidence Based Funding, or EBF). The future of EBF in Illinois is currently in question. The tragic irony of this is that the most vulnerable students and neediest districts are susceptible to falling even further behind with fewer resources after years of being underfunded. The pandemic has and will increase the disparity between the top funded and lowest funded school districts in the state.

School boards are the governing bodies for districts focusing on setting vision and policy. It is incumbent upon boards to take the lead on the equity issue by setting it as a priority within the vision of the district, adopting policies which ensure greater credence and instructing district leaders to fully vet their recommendations through equity lenses prior to submitting them for approval. This process will also require districts to engage in equity audits. The lead author of this essay discusses the importance of equity audits further in another essay within this series.

When districts are considering equity, all decisions should be examined through critical race lenses. Darden and Cavendish (2012) argue that school boards are responsible for inequities within districts through their non-monetary resource allocations in favor of more affluent schools. There is little accountability placed on school boards or board leaders when decisions are made on spending, facilities, and other matters that may appear on the surface as immaterial to equity. All business before the board directly affects the students within the district. Because of this, said decisions can also have a disparate impact on racial and other educational inequities.

Board level decisions and inequities have been evidenced across the country more prominently because of their responses to the Covid-19 pandemic. It caused districts to re-evaluate their policies and practices to attend to the unique and varying needs of the students that they serve. Families were introduced to issues and inequities resulting from those decisions more often in many cases than they were previously. Many boards moved their meetings to virtual platforms, which allowed for greater levels of public participation. This increased level of participation also meant more issues were presented that likely always existed, but were not seen as critical to address as they did within a remote learning environment. Other challenges have presented themselves with districts choosing to return to in-person learning in the Fall of 2020. At this time, it is hard to determine whether these decisions will lead to more disparate outcomes for Students of Color. Ultimately, this has showcased the need for strong board leadership on the monitoring of issues of equity in all decision making.

Reimagining Schools

Recommendations for Justice from Antiracist Pedagogues

Paulo Freire reminds us that "…education is a political act" (Freire, 1998, p. 63). Educator choices within the classroom determine our position: does our pedagogy perpetuate the status quo, e.g., tracking students into categories that are always already predetermined for success or failure? Or, are we truly educating for the practice of freedom? If we choose the latter, we should let the students lead, which is exactly what happened in our streets during the uprisings of 2020.

It is critical that we take the lessons from the uprisings of the summer of 2020 and bring them into the classroom. This applies to both the higher education classroom and the K–12 classroom. Beautiful, brave, and creative actions, art, satire, and acts of resistance were collectively created in the summer of 2020 in support of Black Lives Matter and in response to the murder of George Floyd. People can change the world, and the world is changing swiftly. In just two weeks, collective protests across the U.S. leveraged charges being brought against violent, corrupt, and murderous police officers, and the banning of chokeholds in MN; changes were made to funding/militarization of police budgets in some cities, and symbols of the confederacy were brought down in many areas within the south and abroad (e.g., the statue of Robert E. Lee in Richmond, Virginia, and the statue of Edward Colston in Bristol, UK). There are other injustices that remain blatant and unsettled, such as not charging the officers responsible for the murder of Breonna Taylor. At the time of this writing, one police officer was charged for firing bullets into a different residential dwelling, and not into the body of a Black woman. In effect, a police officer was charged for damaging property, but not for killing a Black woman while she slept. We must consider how this tragedy impacts our students, particularly our Students of Color.

As teacher educators, do we think about the material conditions of our students? Do we think about the systems that perpetuate poverty, racism, and disenfranchisement? Do we engage in these epistemological discussions in our teacher education programs? We are beginning to study Trauma Informed Care and Social Emotional Learning in the United States, but these are relatively new lines of inquiry. Teacher education programs are slow to critically question systems, as most teacher candidates have been successful within said systems and come from white and middle-class homes. Now is the time to question all of the systems.

Despite the increasing diversity of our K–12 student population, the vast majority of the K–12 teaching force remains white; according to the Bureau of Labor Statistics (2019), there are currently 9,313,000 teachers, 81.5 percent of whom are white. Hegemonic teacher training programs, or programs that do not provide antiracist instruction to pre-service teachers, is another system that must be eradicated. We must, as educators, continue to critically reflect on our material conditions, and our own cultural contexts—and insist that our teacher education students do the same—engaging in a dialectic between theory and practice. Without critical conversations about racism and how to be antiracist in our classrooms, our democracy lives in untruths.

We have witnessed, across the world, young people organizing outside of the classroom in political protests to change the world. Where did they learn this? Did they learn this from us, or did they learn this despite us? Can we learn from these youth organizers and bring this knowledge to our classrooms? Matias' work (2016) demonstrates how white teacher candidates cloak their racism in "emotional diminutives." According to Matias and Zembylas (2014), "...the politics of disgust maintains whiteness in ways that are often taken for granted as natural and innate" (p. 329). Moreover, the authors further argue that notions of "caring" and "empathy" are empty and inauthentic because they "fail to be accompanied by action" (p. 321), e.g., through antiracist work, moving beyond colorblindness, electing to engage in professional development or readings on cultural responsiveness. Because of all of this lack of awareness, training, and overall caring for Students of Color, schools remain sites of "hegemonic social control" (Matias & Zembylas, 2014, p. 322). Matias (2016) argues that racialized disgust is also about maintaining a sense of superiority over racialized Others. We have, in the summer of 2020, witnessed this cultural conflict on the street. At this crucial time in our world, we look to reimagining and re-inventing our existence: toward acceptance, toward inclusion, toward peace. We are inspired by the global support for Black Lives Matter and against state sanctioned violence.

As Kohl (1994) describes, the phenomenon of "not-learning" occurs when students, consciously or not, resist learning from a teacher who they perceive as not respecting their identity, their language, their culture, their gender, their sexuality, their race, etc. According to Kohl, "Not-learning tends to take place when someone must deal with unavoidable challenges to her or his personal and family loyalties, integrity, and identity. In such situations there are forced choices and no apparent middle ground. To agree to learn from a stranger who does not respect your integrity causes a major loss of self" (Kohl, 1994, p. 6). Thus, authentic and caring relationships are necessary in developing educational experiences that move beyond perpetuating the status quo and maintaining oppression.

In fact, a recent study by Goff, Jackson, Di Leone, Culotta, and DiTomasso (2014) examined why Black minors are 18 times more likely to be charged and sentenced as adults than their white counterparts; one of the reasons for this differential result lies in the dehumanization of Black and Brown children in general. Such dehumanization is based in part on white perceptions of Black and Brown children as being older (thus more culpable) than they actually are and being deemed less worthy of the "privilege of innocence" which results in "violent inequalities" (p. 14).

Students of Color may be exhibiting acts of fugitivity, as described by Patel (2019), in response to schooling that does not reflect, support, or embrace them, and, effectively, dehumanizes, demonizes, and diminishes them. Hegemonic characterizations of disengagement, disrespect, discipline, and truancy may be perceived as delinquency and highly problematic. However, it may be an attempt to save the self that the school neither values nor respects. In other words, fugitivity represents a flight toward freedom and a desire to maintain humanity.

We must reframe fugitivity, and work to create equitable schools for all our students.

If we have learned nothing from the dual public health crises that reached the schoolhouse steps, we should have learned that there is a need to directly address inequities. There are social inequities, which impact learning and the maintenance of equitable schools and there are systemic racial inequities embedded in every facet of the country. All of these inequities cannot be solved by the schools; however, equitable schools cannot be formed without the acknowledgment that institutional racism has influenced the education of all of a school district's students equitably.

Students of this generation have embarked upon a more activist culture than in the more recent past. The students will demand the innovation of education either due to the intersections spotlighted by the pandemic and racial equity outcry, or educational leaders can willingly transition to a culture of racial equity innovation. The goal is to forge an educational system where each student's academic achievement is on par with their peers in other racial groups. This can only happen through racial equity educational practices, which accept the lessons of 2020 as opposed to insistence on a radical return to pre-pandemic schools.

One of those lessons requires states and school districts to specifically attend to the funding inequities that exist between districts with larger proportions of marginalized communities. Districts can craft their own funding equity formula for the funds that they do receive which accounts for racial inequities and other social inequities that were exacerbated by the pandemic to begin the journey. The choice is yours. What will you choose?

REFERENCES

Alemán E., Jr. (2007). Situating Texas school finance policy in a CRT framework: How "substantially equal" yields racial inequity. *Educational Administration Quarterly*, 43(5), 525–558.

Alexander, M. (2010). *The new Jim Crow: Mass incarceration in the age of colorblindness.* The New Press.

Balingit, M., Strauss, V., & Bellware, K. (2020). Fueled by protests, school districts across the country cut ties with police. *The Washington Post.* https://www.washingtonpost.com/education/2020/06/12/schools-police-george-floyd-protests/.

Banker, A. (2020). *St. Louis County school districts investigating photo of students mocking George Floyd's death.* FOX 2. https://fox2now.com/news/st-louis-county-school-districts-investigating-photo-of-students-mocking-george-floyds-death/.

Boston, C., & Warren, S.R. (2017). The effects of belonging and racial identity on urban African American high school students' achievement. *Journal of Urban Learning, Teaching, and Research, 13*, 26–33.

Carter, P.L., & Welner, K.G. (Eds.). (2013). *Closing the opportunity gap: What America must do to give every child an even change.* Oxford University Press.

Childress, S. (2020). Gallup: Parents give schools low marks on reopening plans. What happens next? *Forbes.* https://www.forbes.com/sites/staceychildress/2020/08/16/parents-give-schools-low-marks-on-reopening-plans-what-happens-next/?sh=4ef78b4b4874.

Cullotta, K.A., & Sherry, S. (2020, July 17). As schools weigh whether to reopen in the fall, anxiety is high among Illinois parents and teachers: "This is not the time to be getting students back together." *Chicago Tribune.* from: https://www.chicagotribune.com/coronavirus/ct-coronavirus-illinois-back-to-school-anxiety-20200717-g7o6duxj5rf2xes3i7vui3ddvi-story.html.

Darden, E., & Cavendish, E. (2012). Achieving resource equity within a single school district: Erasing the opportunity gap by examining school board decisions. *Education and Urban Society, 44*(1), 61–82.

DiAngelo, R.J. (2018). *White fragility: Why it's so hard to talk to white people about racism.* Beacon Press.

Eberhardt, J.L. (2019). *Biased: Uncovering the hidden prejudice that shapes what we see, think, and do.* Viking Press.

Fox, M. (2020). *Coronavirus has upended school plans. It will also worsen racial and economic inequalities, experts warn.* CNBC. https://www.cnbc.com/2020/08/12/impact-of-covid-19-on-schools-will-worsen-racial-inequity-experts-say.html.

Freire, P. (1998). *Teachers as cultural workers: Letter to those who dare teach* (D. Macedo, D. Koike & A. Oliveira, Trans.). Westview Press.

Goff, P.A., Jackson, M.C., Di Leone, B.A., L., Culotta, C.M., & DiTomasso, N.A. (2014). The essence of innocence: Consequences of dehumanizing Black children. *Journal of Personality and Social Psychology, 106*(4), 526–545.

Hong, A. (2020). *Amid the coronavirus outbreak, Asian-American students like my son face racist taunting. Let's change that.* Chalkbeat. https://www.chalkbeat. org/2020/3/12/21178748/amid-the-coronavirus-outbreak-asian-american-students-like-my-son-face-racist-taunting-let-s-change.

Johnson O. Jr., Jabbari, J., Williams, M., & Marcucci, O. (2019). Disparate impacts: Balancing the need for safe schools with racial equity in discipline. *Policy Insights from the Behavioral and Brain Sciences, 6*(2), 162–169.

Kamenetz, A. (2020). Q&A: *How to talk to kids about Black lives and police violence.* NPR. Retrieved from: https://www.npr.org/2020/06/04/868600478/q-a-how-to-talk-to-kids-about-george-floyd.

Kendi, I.X. (2019). *How to be an antiracist* (1st ed). One World.

Kohl, H. (1994). *"I won't learn from you" and other thoughts on creative maladjustment.* The New Press.

Kozol, J. (2012). *Savage inequalities: Children in America's schools.* Broadway Books.

Ladson-Billings, G. (2006). From the achievement gap to the education debt: Understanding achievement in U.S. schools. *Educational researcher, 35*(7), 3–12.

LeBlanc, P., & Wolf, Z.B. (2020). *Analysis: There's still no plan for schools, so parents are making up their own.* CNN. https://www.cnn.com/2020/09/03/politics/what-matters-september-2/index.html.

Leonhardt, M. (2020). *"I am definitely panicking": Parents say school reopening plans leave them without any good options.* CNBC. https://www.cnbc.com/2020/07/16/parents-say-school-reopening-plans-leave-them-without-any-good-options.html.

Lifto, D.E. (2020). *Leadership matters: Superintendents' response to COVID-19.* Baker Tilly |Advisory, Tax and Assurance—Baker Tilly. https://www.bakertilly.com/insights/leadership-matters-lessons-learned-in-the-trenches.

Liu, E. (2020). *COVID-19 has inflamed racism against Asian-Americans. Here's how to fight back.* CNN. https://www.cnn.com/2020/04/10/opinions/how-to-fight-bias-against-asian-americans-covid-19-liu/index.html.

Love, B. (2019). *We want to do more than survive: Abolitionist teaching and the pursuit of educational freedom.* Beacon Press.

Mahoney, B. (2020). *School response to George Floyd killing/Remote learning participation rates.* Arlington Community Media, Inc. https://acmi.tv/videos/school-response-to-george-floyd-killing-remote-learning-participation-rates/.

Matias, C. (2016). *Feeling white: Whiteness, emotionality, and education.* Sense Publishers.

Matias, C.E., & Zembylas, M. (2014). "When saying you care is not really caring": Emotions of disgust, whiteness ideology, and teacher education. *Critical Studies in Education, 55*(3), 319–337.

Milner, H.R. (2018). Relationship-centered teaching: Addressing racial tensions in the classroom. *Kappa Delta Pi Record, 54*(2), 60–66.

Mineo, L. (2020). *The pandemic's impact on education.* Harvard Gazette. https://news.harvard.edu/gazette/story/2020/04/the-pandemics-impact-on-education/.

Morgan, I., & Amerikaner, A. (2018). *Funding gaps 2018: An analysis of school funding equity across the U.S. and within each state.* Education Trust. https://edtrust.org/resource/funding-gaps-2018/.

Morris, M.W. (2016). *Pushout: The criminalization of Black girls in schools.* The New Press.

Muhammad, G. (2019). *Cultivating genius: An equity framework for culturally and historically responsive literacy.* Scholastic.

National Association of School Psychologists. (2020). *Countering COVID-19 (Coronavirus) stigma and racism: Tips for parents and caregivers.* National Association of School Psychologists (NASP). https://www.nasponline.org/resources-and-publications/resources-and-podcasts/school-climate-safety-and-crisis/health-crisis-resources/countering-covid-19-(coronavirus)-stigma-and-racism-tips-for-parents-and-caregivers.

Ngounou, G., & Gutierrez, N. (2017). Learning to lead for racial equity. *Phi Delta Kappan, 99*(3), 37–41.

Noguera, P. (2001). Racial politics and the elusive quest for excellence and equity in education. *Education and urban society, 34*(1), 18–41.

Ostrander, R. (2015). School funding: Inequality in district funding and the disparate impact on urban and migrant school children. *BYU Educ. & LJ*, 271.

Patel, L. (2019). Fugitive practices: Learning in a settler colony. *Educational Studies, 55*(3), 253–261.

Pinar, W.F. (2012). *What is curriculum theory?* (2nd ed.). Routledge.

Pitts, C. (2020). How a superintendent of the year is responding to COVID-19 and looking to the future. *Teach. Learn. Grow.* https://www.nwea.org/blog/2020/superintendent-of-the-year-is-responding-to-covid-19-looking-to-future/.

Richards, E. (2020). Kids need to talk about George Floyd, protests and racism. With coronavirus school closures, it's hard to do. *USA Today.* https://www.usatoday.com/story/news/education/2020/06/04/george-floyd-protests-kids-coronavirus-school-closures/3128780001/.

Seale, C. (2020). Education after COVID-19 cannot be reimagined without a racial justice plan. *Forbes.* https://www.forbes.com/sites/colinseale/2020/05/27/education-after-covid-19-cannot-be-reimagined-without-a-racial-justice-plan/?sh=60085d6845ee.

Storaasli, M. (2020). *D127 statement on racial equity & George Floyd protests.* Grayslake Community High School District 127. https://www.d127.org/north/blog/162 2079/d127-statement-on-racial-equity-and-george-floyd-protests.

Strauss, V. (2020). An old story made new again: Why students of color are primed to be left behind in the coronavirus crisis. *The Washington Post.* https://www.washingtonpost.com/education/2020/04/24/an-old-story-made-new-again-why-students-color-are-primed-be-left-behind-covid-19-crisis/.

Yosso, T. (2005). Whose culture has capital? A critical race theory discussion of community cultural wealth. *Race ethnicity and education, 8*(1), 69–91.

Zion, S.D. & Blanchett, W. (2011). (Re)conceptualizing inclusion: Can critical race theory and interest convergence be utilized to achieve inclusion and equity for African American students? *Teachers College Record, 113*(10), 2186–2205.

Isolation, Incarceration, and Institutions

Exploring Abolitionist Policies for Post-Pandemic Education

Ebony L. Perro *and* Ted Nelson

In a cacophony of crises, educational institutions rushed to remote learning to protect the lives of students, staff, and faculty from Covid-19. As classrooms closed and Zoom rooms opened, many teachers and administrators replicated structurally violent practices. Online learning became the subject of online scrutiny, mainly as people used online platforms to express their frustrations about the shift in learning environments. Even in "unprecedented times" underscored by violence and divisive politics, school officials expected students to perform academically. With months of isolation and shelter-in-place phases waxing and waning, new waves of protest pedagogy, "pedagogy *about* protest, *through* protest and *in* protest" (Cussans, 2011, p. 1), emerged on social media, in the streets, and at schools. Protest pedagogy in schools typically focused more on information and less on demands and actions. As many people desired a return to pre-pandemic normalcy, activists and agitators—galvanized by the murders of Ahmaud Arbery, Breonna Taylor, Tony McDade, and George Floyd—protested a normal underscored by racism. Despite the pandemic requiring social distancing and solidarity to "flatten the curve," police brutality and vigilante violence defined 2020. The violence gone viral presented a sample of the dynamics informing Black life in the United States. In addition to this violence, epistemic and institutional violence against Black students made headlines, illuminating ways the school-to-prison pipeline surfaced in virtual learning. The nation's struggle to contain a virus and eradicate viral injustices called attention to historical and institutional narratives that plague Black students and inform their treatment in educational spaces. The reproduction of structural violence in online settings incited activism that rewrote narratives of children impacted by isolation and carceral states. The intersecting violence of the pandemic advanced conversations surrounding the abolition of the prison system and parallel disciplinary practices permeating primary and secondary education.

This essay explores viral stories that illuminate the continued criminalization of Black children in educational spaces. We highlight the Black Lives Matter Movement and adjacent resistance work's influences on academic discourse and reform demands to articulate challenges to the criminalization of Black youth through hashtag activism and collective work. Civil unrest (a driver of movements) and restlessness (driven by isolation and quarantine) encouraged shifts in praxis and amplified the need for trauma-informed, healing-centered policies. As communities move toward liberatory consciousness, they push to revise narratives surrounding Black children. We assert that the amplification of Black student voices and stories is critical to the abolitionist work needed for students to thrive. Changing the narratives can aid in restructuring and reimagining the many systems creating barriers to Black students' success. Love and Jiggetts (2019) note that liberatory consciousness relies on four features: awareness, analysis, action, and accountability/allyship (p. xiii). Through the essay, we reflect on these features and their manifestations through digital counterpublics. We explore alternatives to policing and surveilling Black students to envision post-pandemic education in K–12 schools. We look to our experiences with/in education to discuss the present and future of discipline in public schools and its relationship to present movements and policies.

We write from the perspective of a Black feminist, Black Girlhood Studies scholar, and English professor (Perro), and a social worker, counselor, and parent (Nelson). We write as witnesses to the education system in Louisiana and people who understand the ways lived experiences impact educational outcomes. As advocates for equity and access in education, we invest in discussing transformative practices that can alter the futures of Black children. We explore viral injustices of #FreeGrace, Ka'Mauri Harrison, and Isaiah Elliot to illuminate how skewed treatment of Black students and convoluted policies contribute to the rage that punctuates public responses to disciplinary practices informed by systemic oppression.

Since the inception of the pandemic, news headlines filled with Black students facing punitive consequences ranging from Zoom suspensions to juvenile detention trended on social media. New issues generated new punishments patterned after pre-pandemic policies. Black students continued experiencing criminalization from behind their computer screens. In several cases, punishments distorted the realities of learning from home. Belsha (2020) notes that guardians and advocates raised concerns about discipline and mishandling of misbehavior. Guardians of Indigenous, Black, and disabled students worried that punishments during Covid-19 would mirror the disproportionate punishments of face-to-face instruction (despite schools indicating that they would provide more social and emotional support during the pandemic) (2020). As the pandemic progressed, the reactions of instructors and administrators to minor infractions confirmed guardians' and advocates' fears.

In Sacramento, a school revoked a nine-year-old Black girl's email privileges after she allegedly "bombarded" the district's technology support department with emails (Klein, 2020). As the pandemic dangers escalated, so did the punishments for students struggling to navigate online learning. To address low participation in online classes, instead of thinking about solutions and consulting students and their caregivers about best practices, school districts attempted to curtail truancy in virtual spaces by intensifying standing policies (Hornsby, 2021, p. 18). The flawed logic of punishing students who miss class by providing punitive consequences that include missing class shows an inattentiveness to student needs and a lack of consideration of the digital divide. In April 2021, a viral tweet recounted events leading up to a Black fourth grader's Zoom detention after accusations of being distracted in class. Despite nearly a year's worth of examples, many administrators and teachers struggled to envision effective ways to support students of color and students with disabilities in online settings. Many teachers and administrators still failed to acknowledge stressors impacting learning. These educators illuminate the problems with pandemic pedagogy, online classroom management, and discipline strategies as a whole. In these situations, the subjectivities of disciplinarians were favored over the subjectivities of the students. The teachers and administrators did not consider the implications or their impracticality of the punishments. As incidents of Zoom violations rise and become publicized, it is clear that distance learning did not distance educators and school resource officers from convoluted policies and abusive practices. Boys with toy guns in their homes faced suspensions and criminal charges; their narratives eerily intertwined with the story of Tamir Rice. Though these boys were not murdered, they were policed and positioned as threats. Black girls continued to face pushout for misunderstood behaviors; their narratives entwined with tropes of Black girlhood and a host of girls brutalized by police.

These Zoom punishments illuminate the institutional violence that propels the Black Lives Matter Movement and permeates beyond the institution's walls. The violence often filters students, particularly girls, through what Monique Morris (2016) frames as school-to-confinement pathways in *Pushout: The Criminalization of Black Girls in Schools*. Police presence on school grounds, police interventions during virtual learning, unwritten and inflexible policies, and strong similarities between prison and school operations require abolitionist thinking and activist impulses so that schools do not facilitate entry into the prison system. In addition to addressing and combating the school-to-confinement pathways, it is vital to engage Erika Meiners' (2011) notion of the school-to-prison nexus, which includes policies, ideologies, and practices that contribute to these pathways (p. 548). With this nexus comes the increased likelihood of Black students with disciplinary records that alter the trajectory of their lives. False narratives that lead to pathologizing Black students' behavior also accompany the nexus. Bettina Love (2019) articulates that "both prisons and schools create a narrative of public outrage and fear that dark bodies need saving from themselves" (p. 10). This public outrage, made even more visible on social media, operates on a spectrum. There are people outraged by the behavior of Black students, but not by the stimuli that trigger the behavior. There are also people outraged by the narratives that generate unwarranted fears. Sue J. Kim (2013) frames outrage as a result of collectively agreed upon values; the outrage generates action (p. 177). During the pandemic, much of the outrage supported Black students. Activists, abolitionists, and organizers continued to show that it is not themselves from which Black people need saving. Through research, policy advocacy, and social media activism, supporters of Black children worked to dismantle oppressive notions about Black youth while dismantling the systems that harm them. The nexus of people, protests, and online petitions illuminate ways the "virtual revolution" and its precursors yield the tools for abolitionist approaches to post-pandemic education.

Out of the (Virtual Learning) Revolution: Frameworks for Abolitionist Practices

Two decades ago, Delores P. Aldridge and Carlene Young edited *Out of the Revolution: The Development of Africana Studies* (2000). This fundamental Black Studies text emphasizes the power of the public and their contributions to the field's development. Aldridge and Young illuminate that the Black Studies Movement "forced the American society to be aware that [B]lack people were no longer willing to accept their subordinate and subservient positions without challenging the system that continued oppression" (p. 3). Just as the 1960s Civil Rights and Black Power

Movements ushered in new fields of study, the current revolution and the explosion of social media—in conjunction with the pandemic—presents possibilities for re-envisioning education and disciplinary actions in tangible ways. The present challenges to the system lean toward abolition. In schools, this can take the form of abolishing school resource offers and replacing them with therapists and interventionists trained in de-escalation. It can also manifest through social and emotional learning that is "critical, healing centered, reciprocal in nature, culturally transformative, and dialogical" (Abolitionist Teaching Network, 2020). Abolition in education seeks to transform the culture of education. It centers not only on conversations about injustice but also on actions to combat injustice. It aims to heal Black students and demonstrate that they matter.

The present virtual revolution, #BlackLivesMatter, contributes to the evolution of education in myriad ways. Mirroring past eras, "The demand for representation at all levels of governments, guarantees of civil rights, access to educational institutions, economic opportunity, and social equality [are] the clarion calls of the day" (Aldridge and Young, 2000, p. 4). Abolitionist work moves beyond access to education, pushing for the radical transformation of the institution while centering the identities and histories of historically excluded students. Like Black Studies, emergent disciplines (e.g., Black Girlhood Studies and Resistance Studies) and intersecting movements and protests (e.g., BLM, abolitionist movements, and #Free-Grace marches) reemphasize Black people's challenges to oppressive systems and offer pathways to liberatory consciousness. The movements and disciplines heighten awareness and incite action while holding governmental bodies accountable. Since its inception, the Black Lives Matter Movement prompted race-conscious policies and increased organizing around alternatives to policing. The movement, generated by the criminalization and murder of Trayvon Martin, gained more momentum with the murder of another Black teen, Mike Brown. The boys' stories, etched in public memory through hashtags, mobilized people to advocate for social justice. The global movement amplified initiatives for systemic change. By "Mobilizing through social media, organizing around police brutality, anti–Black racism, blatant racism, and seeking for justice to be recognized where justice has been denied, the movement has gained in scope and attention beyond police brutality" (Howard, 2016 p. 101). #BlackLivesMatter's broad reach illuminates the intersecting matters impacting Black people's safety, health, and well-being. With the mobilizing of people in support of students struggling in online classes, the present arc of protests against injustice returns us to discussions of the dangers faced by Black youth in schools.

Critiques of the education system increase as knowledge of the persistent criminalization of Black youth is made more accessible. In the last decade, digital counterpublics made instances of harsh treatment of Black youth by school resource officers and police go viral (e.g., Aurora PD, Coral Springs PD, McKinney, and Spring Valley). Social media users intervene in conversations, turning their anger into actions in concert with organizers. They aid in generating the pillars of liberatory consciousness. The viral nature of the stories creates hashtag activism that allows students, guardians, accomplices, and agitators to "make identity-based cultural and political demands" (Jackson et al. 2020, p. xxv). Calls for abolition, rooted in cultural experiences and knowledge, require that we "reframe our material and ideological investments in locking people up" (Meiners & Winn, 2010, p. 274). These demands, connected to lived experiences, increase with upsurges in antiracist resistance. Additionally, they are supported by qualitative and quantitative research. Scholars theorize about the mythology of Black girl criminality (Crenshaw, Ocen, & Nanda 2015, Morris 2015, National Black Women's Institute 2019, and Winn 2019) and the school-to-prison pipeline (Meiners & Winn 2010 & 2012 and Morris 2012), presenting narratives and evaluating government data. The Department of Education data reveals that Black girls are six times more likely to be suspended than their white counterparts, and Black boys are three times more likely to be suspended than their white counterparts. Expulsion and excessive force rates also present race and gender disparities (Department of Education, 2018). Though school-to-confinement pathways and their impacts are not new phenomena, the Federal Office of Civil Rights recently began biennial reports of adverse student disciplinary outcomes by race (Gopalan and Nelson, p. 1, 2019). The data reveals what history shows: over-policing of Black students. Social media and scholarly conversations precede pandemic learning. Still, the criminalization of Black students in virtual spaces proves that even in isolation, ideologies that pervade and buttress the system disproportionately impact Black youth. Social media users now attach #BlackLivesMatter to denials of rights that address a broad scope of experiences. As Black lives are memorialized and recognized through hashtags, digital counterpublics also illuminate the narratives of criminalized Black children facing structural violence in online learning spaces.

Giving Grace, Freeing Grace, and Policing During a Pandemic: Criminalization of Black Youth

Stay-at-home orders slowed Black youths' entrance into the juvenile facilities, but disciplinary actions for virtual classroom violations continued to reveal the policing of Black children. Decisions regarding discipline during virtual learning sparked national outrage and intensified debates about abolition. Shifts from face-to-face instruction to virtual learning demonstrated the exigency of shifts in narratives and protocols regarding discipline and school resource officers (SROs). The shifts in the learning environment reveal the need for policies that acknowledge the traumas accompanying the rush to remote education. Vinson and Waldman (2020) note, "Stay at home orders also affected the behaviour of adolescents and law enforcement officer contact; however, such orders were not universal and, when present, were usually shorter in duration than school closures. Additionally, during the early days of the pandemic, there was more judicious use of detention given health concerns" (p. 799). As the pandemic progressed and adults accepted the "new normal," there was often an expectation for children to follow suit. Though behaviors naturally shifted under the duress of the pandemic, several viral stories surrounding the disciplining of Black students show that the behaviors and perceptions of many disciplinarians did not.

In May 2020, a Pontiac, Michigan, teen, referenced in news stories by her middle name, Grace, was deemed a "threat to [the] community" and ordered to a juvenile detention center for failure to complete remote schoolwork (Cohen, 2020a). Grace's story, chronicled by reporter Jodi Cohen across a series of *ProPublica* articles, illuminated her harsh treatment and the need for abolishing zero-tolerance policies. It also exposed the nation to an example of the relationship between employing punitive disciplinary measures and recurring patterns of criminal supervision and incarceration present in scholarship (Crenshaw, Ocen, & Nanda, 2015, p. 5). Grace's pre-pandemic offenses led to disregarding her current circumstances. Prior incidents resulted in Grace's probation. The terms of the probation included a "GPS tether, regular check-ins with a court caseworker, counseling, no phone and the use of the school laptop for educational purposes only. Grace also was required to do her schoolwork" (Cohen 2020a). These policing practices mirror problematic practices attached to adult crimes and extend beyond reasonable and productive correctives.

Pre-Covid disciplinary action against Grace was not rehabilitative and did not create space for self-reflection and healing. The conditions of her probation set her up for failure and trauma, and as a result of not doing her homework (violating probation), she was sent to a juvenile facility. The counterintuitive, counterproductive decision is read as increasingly hasty and harmful in a pandemic. Cohen wrote, "attorneys and advocates in Michigan and elsewhere say they are unaware of any other case involving the detention of a child for failing to meet academic requirements after schools closed to help stop the spread of COVID-19"

(Cohen, 2020a). During a pandemic saturated with anxiety, uncertainty, and stress, her caseworker and the presiding judge deprioritized her mental and physical health. Grace's teacher asserted that she was "not out of alignment with most of my other students," yet the judge presented her as a danger and delivered consequences that endangered her life. (Cohen 2020a). Her case illustrates how educational spaces intersect with the juvenile justice system and deny Black girls' rights—while presenting them as threats when their behaviors are misunderstood and misrepresented. Because Grace had previous offenses, including theft and assault, the judge (who employed zero-tolerance policies) weaponized her discipline record and used it to justify her removal from her home. Grace's experience goes against abolitionist education practices that reject the school-to-confinement pathways and zero-tolerance policies (Love, 2019, p. 11). Zero-tolerance policies rely on punishment and fear instead of accountability (Morris, 2015, p. 71). They allow for silencing of student voices. The silencing and surveilling becomes a threat to Black students' survival and success. The policies limit responses to unique instances and justify removing students from classrooms, and in Grace's case, her home, if behaviors are coded as deviant. Though Grace violated her probation and was out of compliance with the zero-tolerance policy, the judge's decision to uphold the policy disregarded compounded traumas and public health threats.

Consideration of Zoom fatigue and the rapidly changing status of Covid-19 should underscore decisions surrounding students; these considerations should expand as students return to classrooms. Acknowledgment of compounded traumas and oppression should aid in constructing reimagined teaching and policies. In Grace's case, Attention Deficit Hyperactivity Disorder (ADHD) and a mood disorder heightened fatigue and distractions. She was also one of few Black girls in the school. She resides in a county where only 15 percent of youth are Black, but 42 percent of the cases in juvenile court in 2020 involved Black children (Cohen, 2020b). Factors like the racial demographic of the school possibly impacted her behavior before the pandemic. Additionally, the judge did not give Grace's disability proper considerations. Her mother asserted that her instructor did not follow the Individualized Education Plan (IEP). Her IEP afforded extended time on assignments and clarity check-ins (Cohen, 2020a). Choosing to place Grace in a juvenile facility affirms Sarah Hinger's assertions that students of color with disabilities are disproportionately ushered into the criminal justice system for "behavior that may warrant supportive interventions or a trip to the principal's office, not a criminal record" (2017). During virtual learning, emotional and academic support for Grace could have altered the outcome.

policies but has yet to reverse their decision on Ka'Mauri's suspension (though they reduced his suspension following the act's passing) or acknowledge the inflexibility of the policy. Though a written document of virtual policies exists, the gun policy that led to Harrison's suspension is merely replicated in the document. Still, the Ka'Mauri Harrison Act creates a pathway for abolition to reimagine the system and offer alternatives to suspension and expulsion.

Like Grace and Isaiah, Ka'Mauri's story was retold and retweeted through social media. The (social) media presence of the story put pressure on administrators to reverse their decisions. A school board member, Mark Morgan, asserted that the media blitz is novel and credits Covid-19 for the sensation. He pointed to the fact that (news) media has never been present in court for appeals noting, "And the only reason that that happened is because of Covid because we're in a virtual world" (Monteverde, 2020). The virtual world includes online activists spreading Ka'Mauri's story, giving it a national platform. Concerned citizens respond to injustices such as these; they generate conversations about abolition and acknowledging the humanity of Black youth. A Change.Org petition presently has 27,005 signatures (Supreme Shabazz, 2019). The author calls Ka'Mauri's situation "an obvious case of emotional abuse" (Supreme Shabazz, 2019). The public sides with Ka'Mauri and is making interventions on his behalf in the virtual and material world. Beyond support from citizens, Ka'Mauri gained support from the ACLU of Louisiana. ACLU of Louisiana executive director, Alanah Odoms, asserted "Ka'Mauri Harrison's suspension from school was an excessive and unjustified punishment that reflects the deeply rooted racism that criminalizes Black students and fuels the school-to-prison pipeline" (Odoms, 2020). She notes that because education is a fundamental right and suspension and expulsion do harm, they should be last resorts (Odoms, 2020). Odoms statement moves people closer consideration of abolishing practices that deny students the right to education. It also carves space for those unfamiliar with abolition to push beyond this "last resort" and engage abolitionist thinkers. Odoms' statement and Ka'Mauri's story also encourage exploration of the harm resulting from suspension and expulsion, encouraging them to seek and speak about alternatives.

The community support for Grace, Isaiah, and Ka'Mauri shows the power of collective outrage to elicit change. Each child's experience shows the flaws in the education system and demonstrates the concerted effort that it will take to reimagine education. The examples indicate that these are not isolated events; they are connected through systemic racism and false narratives of Black youth. The presented cases drive calls to action for policy changes on all levels. For adultified, criminalized Black students, we must give them grace. Their stories teach us about how to proceed in education and discipline beyond the virus.

Conclusion: Beyond Viruses and Viral Injustices

A global public health threat (re)activated resistance work to solve a nationwide crisis that impacts the quality of education. Though conspiracy theorists call the Covid-19 pandemic a "plandemic," the rush to remote learning illuminates the lack of planning in terms of creating healthy and safe learning spaces beyond considerations of public health. Learning conditions quickly changed, but this carved an opportunity for radical shifts in education. These radical shifts call for co-conspirators at all levels and listening to the voices of historically excluded students. In *Out of the Revolution* (2000), Young articulates that Black Studies have VOICE. Implementation of VOICE in education V(isibility in academia and community) O(rganization: structural and intragroup resources) I(nformation: research, dissemination, and effective networking) C(ommunity linkages: with responsibility, interaction, and reciprocity) E(ducation: scholarship and training) (Aldridge and Young p. 8), creates pathways for abolitionist practices. If co-conspirators apply VOICE to secondary education, they can mitigate pushout and cater to the needs of Black youth and develop activist classrooms.

- *Visibility in academia and community*: As noted by Love and Jiggetts (2019), awareness is a staple of generating liberatory consciousness. Visibility enhances awareness. We must make the problems in education visible at all levels of education and to all individuals impacted. Through all mediums (e.g., research, policies, social media, news, documentaries, and classroom conversations), advocates should continue to make people aware of Black students' issues.
- Centering scholarship that focuses on shifting the narratives of Black children increases the visibility in academia and doing anti-oppressive research and collaborations with communities can heighten awareness in the communities. We must also combat the erasure of Black students' experiences, amplify their voices, and make space for them to tell their stories. By making issues impacting students visible, co-conspirators can build trust with Black students and the community. It is essential to address and redress administrators' overlooking biases, anti-blackness, trauma, and disabilities when administering punishments. As students nationwide experience compounded traumas of isolation,

the continuing implosion of the nation, and fights against police brutality, they face challenges that impact their abilities to perform academically. Carefully acknowledging those traumas through policies and pedagogy can guide us to abolitionist practices.

- *Organization: structural and intragroup resources*: Co-conspirators can seek funding and develop programming, projects, and pedagogical toolkits in collaboration with the community. With calls to defund the police, districts can reallocate funds to hire social workers and facilitate training for the school administrators handling student behavioral issues without law enforcement intervention. Toolkits can be repositories of information that present alternative intervention strategies and ways for parents and teachers to advocate for Black students. These kits can also include empowerment tools for students to advocate for themselves. Providing resources for the next generation of leaders, scholars, and activists can generate conversations and comprehension of the context of lived experiences of Black students. Affinity groups can offer space for students to strategize and commiserate. Developing organizations—non-profit or academic—can mobilize more people and generate resources.

- *Information: research, dissemination, and effective networking*: Meiners and Winn (2010) address the need for a scholarship centering the relationship between education and incarceration. The research disrupts "an ongoing legacy of structural disinvestment" (p. 273). Make research on pushout and Black youth accessible, conduct qualitative and quantitative research on pushout, and allow Black children to participate in and contribute to the research. Teach about phenomena that increase school-to-confinement pathways and utilize citational practices that amplify abolitionists and Black scholars (e.g., #citeaSista and #CiteBlackWomen). Create coalitions and abolitionist networks that disseminate information through teach-ins, forums, conferences, reports, and internet media.

- *Community linkages: with responsibility, interaction, and reciprocity*: Considering Love's and Jiggetts' call for allyship/accountability, co-conspiratorship should extend beyond the classroom. People in the community can be resources and advocates. Schools (secondary and higher-education) should create partnerships and opportunities for service-learning and community engagement ways that carves space to do abolitionist work. Community linkages can expose students to community leaders, organizers, and people in their communities who advocate for them. These connections can also encourage students to become those leaders and organizers. Students should have access to mentoring programs and peer groups of students with shared experiences. Studies have shown "the power and influence of support systems (like the family) in relation to the abilities of participants to cope with their, often, ridiculed and marginalized statuses within the race, class, gender matrix of domination (Collins, 2000)" (Weissinger, Mack, & Watson, 2017, p. 72). Beyond familial support, students must have advocates within the structure. Coalition building and collaboration can aid in putting pressure on policymakers: Vinson and Waldman (2020) suggest collaboration between local school and judicial systems, healthcare providers, and school-justice partnerships to reduce justice system referrals and address the structure (p. 800). Abolitionist educators and youth advocates should push for policies that aid criminalized students in and beyond the pandemic.

- *Education: scholarship and training*: Education about education should shift. Instructors should prepare to unlearn problematic practices and reimagine the system. Teachers should read the work of abolitionists and consider ways to apply their practices to education. Present and post-pandemic education should focus on reconstructing the system to "focus on nurturing the whole child, balancing cognitive with socioemotional skills development and ensuring that all children have access to the conditions and resources that enhance learning and development" (García & Weiss 2020, p. 3). In learning to teach, the training should include race-conscious, trauma-informed pedagogy and acknowledgment of the racist roots of education. Teachers and administrators should analyze and interpret data on racial disparities in discipline practices and understand the history of over-policing students of color. In teaching, instructors should consider critical emotional praxis which addresses "issues of structural inequalities and aims at cultivating a sense of transformative agency (both individual and collective) to advance peacebuilding" (Zembylas, 2015, p. 4). Every school should implement proper staffing and training. Having social workers who are appropriately trained in mental health and working with children who have IEPs, and abolishing school resource officers can significantly change the culture of viewing students with disabilities as criminals. Social workers should play a more active role in assessing children with mental or behavioral health issues. Social workers experienced in working with this population and trained in de-escalation techniques to prevent suspensions and arrests of children, can work directly with children and prepare the school administration to deal with issues properly. We must teach, learn, and administer under the elements of liberatory consciousness. We must be aware of and make our students aware of narrative discrepancies and race and gender bias. Teachers must hold those in power accountable as "Systems do not perpetuate themselves; they are supported, maintained, perpetuated by the actions of people and groups of people who typically act automatically on the basis of their socialization" [Love and Jiggetts 2019, p. xix].

With VOICE, we can consider new tools for teaching, learning, and advocacy. There are a plethora of ways to enter the conversation about supporting Black youth. VOICE acknowledges the grassroots activism that Bettina Love (2019) notes is integral to abolitionist teaching that includes work inside and outside school. People in education can lead the charge for change in coalition with the community and students. At this critical juncture in history, it is necessary to make radical changes. Without these changes, "institutions can heap the shame of stigma back onto the victims by holding ideologies that are unsupportive, isolating, and otherwise empowering to the perpetrator" (Weissinger & Brown, 2017 p 80). We can consider Audre Lorde's ideas from "Learning from the 60s" and apply them to this present moment: "We are making the future as well as bonding to survive the enormous pressure of the present, and that is what it means to be a part of history" (Lorde, 1984 p. 144). In a year characterized by viruses and depathologizing and decriminalizing blackness, we must shift the narrative and the system, decenter whiteness, and be active agents in anti-oppression. Changing the culture of criminality surrounding students of color and changing their schools is a communal effort.

Beyond VOICE, schools should choose to disengage from systems of policing. Presently, school resource officers play active roles in discipline procedures, and in recent years police presence on school grounds increased. With the increased presence of officers on campuses comes an increase in arrests of students and the increased potential for police brutality. The patterns of policing students are vastly disproportionate for Black and Brown public school students (Irwin, Davidson, and Hall-Sanchez, 2013). Though there is no concrete data on policing and pandemic virtual learning, as seen in national headlines and trending topics online, students are still surveilled and disciplined from behind computer screens. Before the apex of the Black Lives Matter Movement and protests against police brutality, "Twenty-seven percent of elementary schools, 39% of middle schools, and 49% of high schools ... employ[ed] SROs or other security guards" (Centers for Disease Control, 2014). Abolitionist efforts can be seen through Monique Morris' commentary about returning to in-class learning "Now that students are returning to school after having collectively experienced the Covid-19 pandemic, which disproportionately impacted communities of color, it is important to cultivate learning environments that are nurturing and responsive to trauma" (Bragg, 2021). Policies activated and animated by the present movements often focus on the removal of police from schools. The uprising in response to police violence and senseless murders of Black people generated outrage and moves toward legislation that protects Black people. Schools in California and Minnesota cut budgets to SROs and abolished police presence on campuses. Oakland Unified School District Board of Education passed George Floyd Resolution to Eliminate the Oakland Schools Police Department. The resolution condemns police violence and connects the matrix of domination to the ways it is mirrored in school systems. The resolution explicitly cites the murder of George Floyd and acknowledges how the present school system supports school-to-prison nexus. Removing police presence is a step toward reimagining school systems. In addition to abolishing police presence and replacing them with peacekeepers and people trained to work with children, Oakland Unified also proposes implicit bias training for all employees (*George Floyd Resolution to Eliminate the Oakland Schools Police Department Oakland Unified School District Board of Education*). As school districts make national news for defunding police, the landscape is primed for envisioning abolitionist schools and an abolitionist society. Policies and legislation that arise out of movements and the pandemic will have lasting impacts on the future of education and the future of Black students.

The present moment implores that educators and administrators recognize their roles in perpetuating or dismantling institutional racism. It also requires acknowledging that education is steeped in racism, from the school-to-prison pipeline to the ivory tower metaphor, racism and classism underscore the United States' educational system. Many institutions founded on white supremacy and named after white supremacists (un)intentionally honor those legacies through policies and norms rooted in white supremacist ideologies. Despite inclusion efforts and calls for anti-racist dialogues, "institutions deflect, misdirect, and interfere with social justice goals" (Love & Jiggetts, 2019, p. xxi). Deflection and misdirection severely impact Black students, as it often results in downplaying their realities and emotions while pathologizing any behavior viewed as deviant or defiant. These interferences affect Black children's learning and create hostile environments. Norms that do not consider all markers of identity or acknowledge shifting cultural climates inhibit students' progress and advancement toward an equitable system. When these norms are presented in discipline practices, they threaten the livelihood and freedom of Black children. Engaging abolitionist work can demarginalize Black students and move us toward preventing isolation and incarceration.

REFERENCES

Abolitionist Teaching Network (2020). *Guide for racial justice and abolitionist social and emotional learning.* https://img1.wsimg.com/blobby/go/8d4b8aa7-b12e-4df8-9836-081a29841523/downloads/ATN%20Guide%20to%20Racial%20and%20Restorative%20Justice%20in.pdf?ver=1618588819301.
Aldridge, D.P., & Young, C. (2000). *Out of the revolution: The development of Africana studies.* Lexington.
Asmar, M.(2020, June 11). *Denver school board votes to phase police out of schools.* Chalkbeat. https://co.chalkbeat.org/2020/6/11/21288866/denver-school-board-votes-remove-police-from-schools.
Belsha, K. (2020, August 21). New rules, more trauma fuel worries of a coming school discipline crisis. Chalkbeat. https://www.chalkbeat.org/2020/8/21/21396481/virtual-suspensionsmasks-school-discipline-crisis-coronavirus.
Centers for Disease Control. (2014). *School health policies and program study (SHPPS).* Centers for Disease Control. http://www.cdc.gov/healthyYouth/shpps.index.htm.
Cohen, J.S. (2020a, July 14). *A teenager didn't do her online schoolwork. So a judge sent her to juvenile detention.* ProPublica. https://www.propublica.org/article/a-teenager-didnt-do-her-online-schoolwork-so-a-judge-sent-her-to-juvenile-detention.
Cohen, J.S. (2020b, July 31). *Grace, Black teen jailed for not doing her online coursework, is released.* ProPublica. https://www.propublica.org/article/grace-black-teen-jailed-for-not-doing-her-online-coursework-is-released.
Crenshaw, K., Ocen, P., & Nanda, J. (2015). *Black girls matter: Pushed out, overpoliced, and underprotected.* African American Policy Forum.
Crockett, J. (2020, September 24). *WDSU investigates 9-year-old Jefferson Parish virtual student suspended for on-campus weapons violation.* WDSU. http://www.wdsu.com.
Cussans, J. (2011). *The paradoxes of protest pedagogy in a "research culture."* The Free School. https://freefreeschool.wordpress.com/.
Evans, S.Y., Domingue. A.D., and Mitchell, T.D. (2019). Introduction: Black women's educational philosophies and social justice values of the 94 percent. In *Black women and social justice education: Legacies and lessons* (pp.1–20). SUNY Press.
Deadrick, L. (2020, August 2). Support grows to #FreeGrace and rings needed attention to disparities Black girls face in school systems. *The San Diego Tribune.* https://www.sandiegouniontribune.com/columnists/story/2020-08-02/support-grows-to-freegrace-and-brings-needed-attention-to-disparities-black-girls-face-in-school-systems?fbclid=IwAR2rLHH3vo7vsGgOfozAbd0QpHQV3dqJ00DoqNyC0L4GBKD0bAxZCtRIugc.
Deliso, M & Gherbremedhin, S. (2021, January 30). *Florida teen body-slammed by school resource officer "traumatized," family says.* ABC News. https://abcnews.go.com/US/florida-teen-body-slammed-school-resource-officer-traumatized/story?id=75582344.
Ending PUSHOUT Act of 2019. H.R. 5325. 116th Cong (2019). https://www.congress.gov/bill/116th-congress/house-bill/5325/text?r=1&s=1.
Families and Friends of Louisiana's Incarcerated Children and National Economic and Social Rights Initiative. (2010). *Pushed out: Harsh discipline in Louisiana schools denies the right to education: A focus on the Recovery School District in New Orleans.* Dignity and Rights. https://dignityandrights.org/wp-content/uploads/2019/11/Pushed-Out.pdf\.

García, E. & Weiss, E. (2020, September 20). *COVID-19 and student performance, equity, and U.S. education policy*. Economic Policy Institute. https://www.epi.org/publication/the-consequences-of-the-COVID-19-pandemic-for-education-performance-and-equity-in-the-united-stateswhat-can-we-learn-from-pre-pandemic-research-to-inform-relief-recoveryand-rebuilding/.

George Floyd Resolution to Eliminate the Oakland Schools Police Department Oakland Unified School District Board of Education, RESOLUTION NO. 1920-0260. https://ousd.legistar.com/LegislationDetail.aspx?ID=4564122&GUID=C591BB69-6054-4DCC-8548-69AA1623E643&Options=&Search=.

Gliha, L.J. (2020). El Paso County 12-year-old speaks about suspension for briefly showing toy gun in Zoom class. KDVR. https://kdvr.com/news/problem-solvers/el-paso-county-12-year-old-speaks-about-suspension-for-briefly-showing-toy-gun-in-zoom-class/.

Gopalan, M. & Nelson, A.A. (2019, April 23). Understanding the racial discipline gap in schools. *AERA Open, 5*(2). http://journals.sagepub.com.

Hinger, S. (2017, November 17). *Police assault on Black students in Kentucky sparks calls for reform*. ACLU. https://www.aclu.org/blog/racial-justice/race-and-criminal-justice/police-assault-black-students-kentucky-sparks-calls.

Hornsby, E. (2021). #FreeGrace and the racialized surveillance state of COVID-19 learning. *Journal of Underrepresented & Minority Progress, 5*(Special Issue), 13–26.

Howard, J. (2021). Toy guns: Black mixed-race boys and the desire to play. *Taboo: The Journal of Culture and Education, 20*(1), 2.

Howard, T.C. (2016). Why black lives (and minds) matter: Race, freedom schools and the quest for educational equity. *The Journal of Negro Education, 85*(2), 101–113.

Jackson, S.J., Bailey, M., & Welles, B.F. (2020). *#HashtagActivism: Networks of race and gender justice*. MIT Press.

Jefferson Parish Schools. *Policies and Procedures for Parents & Students: 2019–2021.*

Irwin, K., Davidson, J., & Hall-Sanchez, A. (2013). The race to punish in American schools: Class and race predictors of punitive school-crime control. *Critical Criminology, 21*(1), 47–71. doi:10.1007/s10612-012-9171-2.

Ka'Mauri Harrison Act. (2020). HB No. 83. HLS 202ES-177. https://www.legis.la.gov/legis/ViewDocument.aspx?d=1192377&fbclid=IwAR17Qqn9wo7JTxl_Oji43xYlGfR6EaXAg95yaOjH0cBUOsETeuYUM8Dhrx8.

Klein, R. (2020). *The new school suspension: Blocked from online classrooms*. Huffpost. https://www.huffpost.com/entry/school-discipline-remote-learning_n_5f329829c5b64cc99fde4d64.

Lorde, A. (1984). Learning from the 60s. In *Sister Outsider* (pp. 134–144). Crossing Press.

Love, B.L. (2019). *We want to do more than survive: Abolitionist teaching and the pursuit of educational freedom*. Beacon Press.

Love, B.J. & Jiggetts. V.D. (2019). Foreword: Black women rising: Jumping double dutch with a liberatory consciousness. *Black women and social justice education* (xi–xx). SUNY Press.

Low, R. (2020). *12-year-old suspended over toy gun seen in virtual class*. KDVR. https://kdvr.com/news/12-year-old-suspended-over-toy-gun-seen-in-virtual-class/.

Meiners E. & Winn M. (2010). Resisting the school to prison pipeline: the practice to build abolition democracies. *Race Ethnicity and Education, 13*(3), 271–276, DOI: 10.1080/13613324.2010.500832 .

Michigan Liberation. (2020). *Free Grace*. Michigan Liberation. https://miliberation.org/free-grace/.

Monteverde, D. (2020, December 4). *4th grader's suspension for BB gun seen on Zoom call reduced in hearing after namesake legislation*. WWLTV. https://www.wwltv.com/article/news/crime/bb-gun-suspension-zoom-call-reduced/289-3ebd6811-2b38-426d-8219-13a8fcf2c2b9.

Morris, M. (2016). *Pushout: The criminalization of Black girls in schools*. The New Press.

Odoms, A. (2020, September 29). *ACLU of Louisiana condemns suspension of 4th grader Ka'Mauri Harrison for BB gun*. ACLU. https://www.aclu.org/press-releases/aclu-louisiana-condemns-suspension-4th-grader-kamauri-harrison-bb-gun.

Peiser, J. (2020). A Black seventh grader played with a toy gun during a virtual class. His school called the police. *The Washington Post.* https://www.washingtonpost.com/nation/2020/09/08/black-student-suspended-police-toy-gun/.

Richardson, V. (2021, February 8). Louisiana AG backs student suspended over BB gun in virtual class. *Washington Times.* https://www.washingtontimes.com/news/2021/feb/8/kamauri-harrison-student-suspended-bb-gun-virtual-/.

Roberts, F. *Second Jefferson Parish student suspended for BB gun in room during virtual school lesson.* NOLA. https://www.nola.com/news/education/article_a43b1d7e-0f0b-11eb-a753-eb7bb03149f8.html.

Rutherford Institute. *Parental reservation of rights—Remote learning surveillance.* Rutherford Institute. https://www.rutherford.org/files_images/general/2020_Parental_Reservation_of_Rights_Remote_Learning.pdf.

Tracking Coronavirus in Michigan: Latest Map and Case Count. (2020). *New York Times.* https://www.nytimes.com/interactive/2021/us/michigan-covid-cases.html.

U.S. Department of Education. *Guidance concerning state and local responsibilities under the gun-free school act of 1994.*

Vinson, S.Y., & Waldman, R.J. (2020). The pandemic caused the U.S. school-to-prison pipeline: Potential lessons learned. *The Lancet Child & Adolescent Health, 4*(11), 799–800. https://doi.org/10.1016/S2352-4642(20)30306-0.

Weissinger, S.E., & Brown, V. (2017). When no place is safe: Violence against Black youth. In S.E. Weissinger, D.A. Mack, & E. Watson (Eds.), *Violence against Black bodies: An intersectional analysis of how Black lives continue to matter* (pp. 75–89). Taylor & Francis.

Weissinger, S.E., Mack, D.A., & Watson, E. (Eds.). (2017). The space of trauma: Violence to the psyche, body, and home. In In S.E. Weissinger, D.A. Mack, & E. Watson (Eds.), *Violence against Black bodies: An intersectional analysis of how Black lives continue to matter* (pp. 71–73). Taylor & Francis.

Whitmer, G. (2020, March 30). Executive Order No. 2020–29. Michigan Legislature. MI.gov.

Zembylas, M. (2015). *Emotion and traumatic conflict: Reclaiming healing in education.* Oxford University Press.

From Woke to Action

School Counselors' Quest for Educational Equity and Social Justice in the Midst of Systemic Racism and Covid-19

Marsha L. Rutledge *and* Tinisha Parker

School systems across the country are scripting re-entry plans for millions of students. However, the question remains if these re-entry plans will address the many issues plaguing student success. Covid-19 has undoubtedly had a negative impact on how instruction is delivered and how students learn. This global pandemic has scarred our physical, mental, and social-emotional health. Though challenging to address in less stressful times, these factors are now coupled with the tragic deaths of Ahmaud Arbery, Breonna Taylor, George Floyd, and others. Regularly, the everyday concerns and challenges of school counseling are overwhelming. School counselors must now consider the consequence of Covid-19, the current race relations, and its impact on student learning.

According to the Centers for Disease Control and Prevention (CDC), the United States, as of April 8, 2021, has seen over 30,814,955 cases of Covid-19, with a death toll of approximately 557,093 deaths (Centers for Disease Control [CDC], 2020b). These numbers are staggering as they reflect the impact the pandemic has on the country. What is even more alarming is the disproportionate rate at which this virus has impacted people of color, especially African Americans or Black individuals. The CDC reports that African Americans make up 34 percent of the total cases even though they only make up 13 percent of the total population (Fortuna et al., 2020). According to the CDC (2020a), factors such as discrimination, lack of healthcare access, essential worker status, educational and wealth gaps, and less favorable housing conditions increase the risk of racial and ethnic minorities contracting and possibly succumbing to the disease. The

CDC (2020c) further suggests that the rate of hospitalization and death rate due to Covid-19 for Blacks is 2.9 times and 1.9 times higher than the White population. For the Hispanic community, the rates are higher; 3.1 percent and 2.3 percent respectively compared to the White population (CDC, 2021c). In terms of racial and ethnic minority children, the disparity is just as evident. Racial and ethnic minority students account for most children's hospitalizations due to Covid-19 (CDC, 2020d). Pandemic trauma, coupled with societal trauma due to the many incidents of police brutality and racism, has resulted in toxic and stressful environments where students are struggling to thrive. Sadly, this trauma is also evident in the educational system, where students spend most of their time.

Systemic racism, discriminatory practices, and inequitable resources are no stranger to K–12 public education. Social justice and advocacy-minded educators have long sounded the alarm to increase multicultural competence and embed cultural responsiveness into the educational system. This includes curriculum, policies, school climate, and interaction. It has been established that ethnic and minority students, oppressed by stricter disciplinary practices, also suffer increased suspensions, are disproportionately recommended for special services, and underrepresented in gifted and higher-level courses (Bazron et al., 2015; Muniz, 2020). Data regarding student outcomes for ethnic and racial minorities have been documented for several years. The most recent report from the National Center of Education Statistics [NCES] (2020) confirms the gaps between Black and Brown students and their White peers. For example, as recorded in the Fall of 2017, Black and Hispanic students had the highest enrollment in high poverty schools (Hussar et al., 2020). Additionally, they had the highest dropout rates and lower college enrollment rates than their White peers (Hussar et al., 2020). As a result, there is still work to be done. School counselors, who are often at the forefront of advocacy efforts for Black and Brown students, must be equipped to do this work. It is no longer enough to be aware of the issue, it is time to address the issue. Now is the time for school counselors to transition from being "woke" to action.

Currently "woke" is a contemporary term used to describe social awareness. In this case, "woke" refers to the awareness of systemic inequities that challenge people of color. From Woke to Action: School Counselors' Quest for Educational Equity and Social Justice Amidst Systemic Racism and Covid-19 means that school counselors are not just aware of social issues such as the inequities resulting from systemic racism and Covid-19, but that they are equipped to actively advocate for minoritized students with the goal of systemic change. Therefore, this essay is written to highlight the call to action for educators, specifically school counselors to move from awareness to action.

As the re-imagining of schools, academic processes, and in-class experiences are being discussed across America because of Covid-19, this is the time to begin dismantling inequities and systemic policies and procedures that have negatively affected Black students and Brown students. Understanding the complexity of the intersection between Covid-19 and current racial tension, educators are challenged to implement social justice and advocacy. We further suggest that school counselors enact change by taking a proactive approach to working with students after traumatic incidents have occurred. In this instance, the trauma caused by Covid-19, in addition to past and current racial tensions.

Covid-19

Covid-19 affects the Black community at a disproportionate rate compared to other groups. As a result, Black students are experiencing the adverse effects of Covid-19 more than their peers. However, the impact of Covid-19 cannot be discussed without the added context of systemic racism, as the two are inextricably linked. Covid-19 is a severe viral pandemic that has wreaked havoc across the globe and our nation. Still, Covid-19 alone is not the issue. The inequitable conditions that exist and are sustained within our nation's anchoring institutions contribute to the negative outcomes of Black youth, particularly those in lower-income communities (Pirtle, 2020). The marginalization of Black people found within the core institutions of healthcare, housing, the economic system, and education play a significant role in the increased deleterious impact Covid-19 has on the Black community and Black students (Slay, 2020).

Impact on Black Students

Covid-19 has impacted all students, but it has disproportionately impacted our Black students. Inequities in systems like health care, employment, and education access have a confounding effect on the already existing biases in education for Black students (Egede & Walker, 2020). Black students and students of color face many challenges when attempting to engage in learning during Covid-19. These challenges include but are not limited to increased exposure to traumatic experiences that are typically identified and treated through the mental health supports provided by schools (Phelps & Sperry, 2020). In addition, the disproportionate loss of adult family members to Covid-19, lack of resources and access to virtual instruction (Garcia et al., 2020), and the adultification of students forced to take on adult responsibilities to help support their families during the pandemic all contribute to decreased academic success and an increased need for mental health supports for students of color. All of these factors have a direct impact on the ability of Black students to connect to important instruction and needed support (Dorn et al., 2020). School counselors and educators, in general, need to be aware of the added burden on Black students and implement ways to provide additional support.

Lack of access to health care, increased comorbidities, and the Black community's death rates increase loss and stressful experiences in Black families (Egede & Walker, 2020). The data is clear; Covid-19 disproportionately affects the Black community as a result of inequitable health care practices, housing, employment, and education (CDC, 2020a). As a result, Black students have a substantial and immediate need for social and emotional support as many racial and ethnic minority students are grieving the loss of loved ones due to Covid-19 and/or lack of home life stability due to the virus (Fontuna et al., 2020). The increase in these negative experiences is happening as school systems struggle to provide critical fundamental educational components, not to mention the increased need for social and emotional services. According to a survey of 130 countries conducted by The World Health Organization (2020), 72 percent of adolescents experienced disruptions to their mental health services due to Covid-19. In the U.S., many Black students receive services through the school system. However, counselors and other support personnel struggle to provide grief assistance, stress relief activities, and critical wrap-around services amid school closures resulting in limited to no virtual access to students (Phelps & Sperry, 2020).

Additionally, many of our Black students have parents who work in industries that have been deemed "essential" like food, retail, service, health and transportation, which have limited work-from-home opportunities, increasing their potential exposures to Covid-19 (Garcia et al., 2020). Out of financial necessity, these families continue to work to provide for their families. On the other hand, some of these same industries have seen significant layoffs or cutbacks in the labor force reducing or eliminating the financial stability that existed in some minority communities, creating unbalanced, and insufficient home environments for our Black students (Chowkwanyun & Reed, 2020). Due to this pandemic, a significant number of families will have filed for unemployment across the nation. The Pew Research center reported that at the end of the 4th quarter of 2020, 4 out of 10 unemployed workers were out of work for more than 6 months and that Black unemployed workers have a higher long-term unemployment rate of 38 percent (Bennett, 2021). The instability and uncertainty that accompanies unemployment give rise to homelessness and resource deficits in families who can no longer afford food, basic necessities, school supplies, transportation, internet service, or virtual learning devices. Currently, The United States Interagency on Homelessness (2020) reports that over 1.5 million public school students faced homelessness during the pandemic increasing the likelihood of challenges these students experienced. In addition, the economic disparities in our country indicate that students of color make up a disproportionate percentage of our homeless youth, confounding the negative impact of Covid-19 and existing disparities and challenges within communities of color (Fortuna et al., 2020). The lack of basic necessities and educational resources makes it difficult for Black students to engage in schooling and for school officials to effectively support students most in need (Phelps and Sperry, 2020).

Black students whose parents work in essential employment sectors, considered critical to the nation's infrastructure, are doing so amid the pandemic. Many of these parents have to make the stressful decision between keeping their jobs or potentially exposing themselves, and their families, to a dangerous virus that is killing Black people more than any other group (CDC, 2020a). As a result of the increased stress on Black parents, Black students are less likely to have their social and emotional needs met and are more likely to experience more responsibility as a result of the household strain (Fortuna et al., 2020). This phenomenon is called adultification and is not new to the Black community. It has been written about in previous years, particularly concerning Black girls who assume many adult roles and responsibilities despite being children and needing parental support themselves (Epstein et al., 2017). With limited capacity to manage these responsibilities, schooling becomes secondary to these students' household and caregiver responsibilities, and they fall behind in their schoolwork.

The barriers and negative consequences our Black students experience more than their peers speak to the urgent need for school counselors and educators to be aware of their Black students' circumstances and the need for creative solutions and interventions to support Black students. Educators, in general, specifically school counselors, must draw upon innovation and imagination to develop interventions and best practices that reach beyond the barriers of Covid-19 if Black students are to learn and succeed in this challenging time.

Call to Action: Educational Communities

Issues, created and exacerbated by Covid-19, are complex. They require a multi-tiered approach by communities and schools to fully attend to student needs and mitigate the negative impact experienced by Black students. As a result, Black students need additional social-emotional support due to the many barriers Covid-19 imposes (Phelps & Sperry, 2020). The barriers to learning include the lack or loss of essential resources, limited access to virtual instruction, and increased home responsibilities. In understanding this, schools must take a thorough look at all available resources as well as the role each employee plays in supporting our Black students.

One of the most important recognitions that a school can make, to support their Black students, is to acknowledge that our current health and social environments are significantly taxing on Black families in ways not experienced by others. In many cases, the emotional grind that burdens the Black community is weighted further by the disbelief or the explaining away of their circumstances by White individuals, diminishing the actual lived experience of Black people (Chowkwanyun & Reed, 2020). Educators, counselors specifically, should become familiar with how Covid-19 deepens the gap in resources and access to education for Black students and how the increased loss of life due to Covid-19 increases the need for social and emotional support. This means actively reading and seeking information that illustrates these facts and looking at how this reality impacts students in the counselor's own school. School officials may determine that this task is not to be left to the interest of individuals. Instead, they create required shared learning opportunities or professional development for educators that foster engaging action conversations about how to best support the Black students in their school. A professional learning series, including presentations, readings, and panels designed to develop empathy and action, can include topics such as equity versus equality, social justice in education, implicit/unconscious bias, understanding microaggressions, and restorative practices. Providing inclusive catalogs of professional development allow school staff to engage in dialogue and learn about the impact of societal issues that negatively impact Black students while also providing opportunities to develop action plans and solutions to mitigate these consequences for your students are all helpful in moving from woke to action (The School Superintendents Association [AASA], 2020).

Call to School Counselors

School counselors are trained to remove education barriers for all students (American School Counselor Association [ASCA], 2020) and draw from several theoretical orientations and counseling techniques to implement comprehensive school counseling programs to support their students. They have extensive training in the concepts of equity, equality, social justice, implicit/unconscious bias, microaggressions, and restorative practices. School counselors can also be a support to administration in these areas by co-creating and facilitating staff presentations. Training and awareness are important to the work of removing barriers to education for students of color, but it cannot stop there. Indeed, school counselors have to be "woke" to the systemic issues that stymie students of color. However, awareness, or being "woke" is not enough, school counselors must be committed to action. They must consistently work to identify barriers to success for racial and ethnic minority students as well as evaluate their own actions for bias that may reinforce processes or systems that disadvantage these same students (Tate, 2021). In order to advocate for all students, school counselors must ensure that each student has equitable access to learning opportunities and the necessary skill development for school success (ASCA, 2020). In doing so, counselors must advocate for students in need, effectively, by being well versed in the barriers to success that negatively impact disadvantaged students. A clear understanding of the issues, strategy, and intentionality is paramount in securing appropriate support and resources. It is paramount for counselors to identify students' specific needs regarding basic access to devices, internet connectivity, or transportation as well as to understand their home life. Knowing whether your student is taking care of younger siblings, is experiencing homeless, is food insufficient, and/or is working a job to help support the family is essential when collaborating with teachers and administration on the needed supports and will help school counselors move from awareness of the situation, "woke," to appropriate and responsive action to best support the student.

School counselors must continue honing their professional skills by participating in counseling specific professional development in counseling techniques, educational trends and comprehensive school counseling practices. This includes learning how to support students in a virtual environment and attending technology-focused professional development. Many students are still not in school buildings and may not be for a while. Therefore, the need for school counselors and educators to communicate with students and parents and work effectively within digital platforms becomes critical.

School counselors also need to be aware of all available resources, including funding from school sources as well as local philanthropic agencies such as faith based organizations, shelters, food banks, and organizations like United Way, Rotary Clubs, Girls and Boys Club, YMCA, Sheltering Arms. It is also advantageous to reach out to local businesses or school partners to see if they are willing and able to support students in various ways. The current pandemic requires that school counselors and educators think outside of the box. For example, if students are not in the building but attending virtually, how are meals provided? It's not the school counselor's responsibility to solve all of the challenges of Covid-19. Still, they should actively work to be a part of the solution by offering suggestions and challenging the status quo. Concerning food uncertainties, can buses be used to drop off items at traditional bus stops during virtual learning? Can students pick up meals at the schools? Can local groups who want to provide food to students be invited to the school for centralized distribution? School counselors could help explore each identified need in the same exploratory way.

School counselors must look at creative and innovative ways to deliver their comprehensive counseling programs in the virtual environment. They will also need to contemplate how their program's in-person delivery will look different due to the health guidelines for Covid-19 (AASA, 2020). Considerations of the concept of safe spaces will need to be explored. How will counseling lessons, rooted in the concept of safe spaces, be received when students may not feel as though they are in a safe space when receiving the lesson? For example, many students are receiving services in their homes with limited privacy or in a public space that offers free internet service. How do school counselors and educators protect students who disclose sensitive information when they are not within the protection of the school building? What is the school counselor's responsibility to mitigate, as much as possible, unintended consequences of safe space violations when services are provided, but students are learning remotely? School counselors must put in place processes and procedures to support, report, and keep our students safe. Virtual grief support rooms, regular communication with students and parents, administrator or social worker well checks, and child services reports need to be included when warranted. Beyond soliciting tangible support from the community, social and emotional support can also be considered. Organizations and individuals who can provide time and emotional support to students are just as important. Some schools have transitioned their mentoring programs to virtual formats and include vetted community members, allowing mentors to continue their support of students virtually. School counselors and educators should actively explore possibilities to maintain social and emotional support already in place for students both in-person and virtually.

The added adult responsibilities placed on some Black students, as a consequence of Covid-19, dramatically impairs their ability to engage in schooling (Epstein et al., 2017). School counselors should develop support plans in collaboration with parents and teachers who consider their circumstances unique. Title I schools can involve their Parent Involvement

Coordinator to support parent educational initiatives, including parent workshops, podcasts, and videos to inform parents of available resources to assist with childcare needs, financial support, and transportation. Counselors can also request and identify specific training needs for parents regarding how to use and navigate the many online tools that teachers are now using for virtual instruction.

School counselors can support Black students suffering the negative impact of Covid-19 by raising awareness and sharing their areas of expertise in critical concepts of equity and social justice with their peers. It is also imperative that they stay keenly aware of how Covid-19 impacts the Black students, and carefully identify their specific needs by pairing them with appropriate support from within the school and the community. These intentional and collaborative practices will help counselors create a network of support during a most challenging time for Black students and their families.

Racial Injustice

Racial injustice is a term that, unfortunately, has a long historical presence within the K–12 educational system. Stemming back to segregation and Brown vs. Board of Education, we have been fighting a system that was not created for the success of Black and Brown students. As a result, we have what is called systemic racism. Systemic racism is when racism and discrimination are masked behind policies, procedures, and practices that perpetuate harm to people of color. The "racial awakening" recently witnessed has caused many past and present acts of racism to be highlighted and magnified. The educational field is no exception. It is critical to our Black and Brown students' success that educators can identify and name those acts of racism that plague our schools and oppress our students.

Society has seen racism play out in the recent murders of George Floyd, Breonna Taylor, Philando Castile, Eric Garner, Michael Brown, Tamir Rice, Trayvon Martin, and countless others who have lost their lives to police brutality. These incidents of racialized trauma are examples of how Black and Brown students experience life. The trauma resulting from these and other experiences impact our children, possibly in ways that we have never seen before (Ang, 2020). It has also permeated educational systems across the country, evident in our schools' existing achievement/opportunity gaps. However, racism expands well beyond the above-named events. As society struggles to navigate and manage the merging crises of racial injustice and the Covid-19 pandemic, we hear the calls and contemplate the premise behind "Black Lives Matter." Yet, as educators, we narrow that focus to declare "Black Students' Lives Matter."

Impact on Black Students

The traumatic impact on our Black students must be recognized and appropriately handled. It has been proven that these crises (racial injustice and Covid-19) are impacting people of color at higher rates than any other population. Educators can refer to Maslow's Hierarchy of Needs and conclude that some of our students are at the bottom of the triangle, having their basic physiological, safety, and belonging needs unmet. When students are faced with racial unrest, educational implications can ensue (Neblett, 2006). McKinsey and Company (2020) after examining the impact of shutdowns due to the pandemic found that students of color were found to be behind their White peers in Math and English upon reopening of schools. In math specifically, "students of color were about three to five months behind in learning; white students were about one to three months behind" (Dorn et al., 2020, para. 3). They also found that 40 percent of African American students and 30 percent of Hispanic students did not have access to online instruction compared to 10 percent of their White peers. Therefore, the community's societal issues often show up in the school thus impacting school climate. As a result, educators need to recognize the privileged vs. marginalized populations served within the building and use this information in determining supportive efforts. Schleicher (2020) offers that due to the pandemic there are great inadequacies reflected in the "supportive environments needed to focus on learning" as well as "the misalignment between resources and needs" (p. 4). Academic success has been associated with whether students feel safe and connected (Fernandez et al., 2019; Voight et al., 2015). Additionally, incidents of racial discrimination have also been found to negatively impact student mental health (Wong et al., 2003), resulting in further academic deficiencies. It is imperative that school systems, educators, and school counselors proactively address their racial and ethnic minority students' experiences during the current social climate to mitigate some of the negative impacts on academic achievement.

Call to Action: Educational Communities

The educational community is a critical component needed in assisting our students and it is "therefore urgent to intervene immediately to support vulnerable students" (Dorn et al., 2020 p. 8). Administrators and educators are tasked with having hard conversations centered on racism, discrimination, and academic divide among their student populations. They are being held accountable for their instructional practices and factors such as school climate, student engagement, and cultural responsiveness among faculty and students. Educational communities have tagged their reopening strategies with labels such as re-imagine, re-engaging, and re-inventing. These terms symbolize or suggest that change is needed and that possibly change is coming. However, as educators, we have to make sure that we are addressing the issues that need re-imagining. One such problem is the plight of the Black student. To re-imagine this topic, administrations must examine how the current system negatively impacts students of color. In doing so, educational communities should also inventory the resources, programs, and individuals available to support students of color. The school counselor is one of the vital resources in this effort.

Call to Action: School Counselors

According to the American School Counselor Association (ASCA), the school counselor's role is to improve outcomes for ALL students by implementing a comprehensive school counseling program. If implemented correctly, these programs are "essential for students to achieve optimal personal growth, acquire positive social skills and values, set appropriate career goals and realize their full academic potential to become productive, contributing members of the world community" (ASCA, 2019a, p. 2). In this fight for social justice, school counselors should lead and collaborate with other educational professionals to advocate for minoritized students working towards systemic change. School counselors can lead the charge by ensuring that as the re-imagining of schools, academic processes, and in-class experiences is being discussed across America because of Covid-19, educators begin dismantling inequities and systemic policies and procedures that have negatively affected Black students and Brown students (Rutledge, 2020). According to Atkins and Oglesby (2019), "If you are not actively seeking to interrupt racism, you are contributing to its perpetuation" (Intro, para. 4). Therefore, the call to action for school counselors is for antiracist work that "supports anti-racist policies through their actions and expressed anti-racist ideas" (ASCA, 2021, para. 2).

Merging of the Two Pandemics

As schools begin to fully reopen, the academic year will likely be drastically different than any other school year. Many students may still be faced with learning in a virtual environment. As safety is a priority for students and faculty, virtual learning has been deemed the best option for some families. However, the consequence of this format is called an academic divide. An academic divide is when there is a clear separation between students who have access and those who do not. The current crises that society is experiencing magnify the educational gap between students of color and their White peers. Although virtual learning allows for continuity of instruction, it is only useful if students can access the training. Research has shown that students of color tend to have less access to the technology needed to stay engaged in an online format (Fortuna et al., 2020). These students have also been impacted more by Covid-19 than their counterparts, possibly contributing to decreased engagement. Referring to Maslow's Hierarchy of Student Needs, when students experience traumatic events such as Covid-19 and racial trauma, basic needs are compromised, making it difficult for learning to occur. Increased challenges to academic success further exacerbate the existing achievement/opportunity gap. Educators will be tasked with creating innovative support for students who are impacted by the academic divide.

School Counseling Response

School counselors are tasked with ensuring that all students' needs are met, academically and socially. Their role in supporting students will be more important than ever as the school year progresses. By implementing culturally responsive and comprehensive school counseling programs, counselors can be critical to students' readjustment. School counselors who follow the ASCA National Model framework understand how themes such as leadership, advocacy, collaboration, and systemic change all support culturally responsive school counseling and antiracist work. We believe that this task of meeting all students' needs cannot be accomplished unless school counselors are dedicated to antiracist school counseling and the implementation of culturally responsive programming.

Antiracist School Counseling

American University School of Education defines antiracist school counseling as the reflection of the "mindset, behaviors, and professional practices that address and dismantle racist ideologies, policies, and practices in K–12 schools" (American University, 2020). Dismantling racist ideologies requires identifying the systemic racism found in education, including structural and institutional racism (Elizondo-Urrestarazu, 2020). To be "woke" is to be aware of the type of racism that is at play and being able to systematically address the negative impact that results. Institutional racism is defined as "ways in which institutional policies and practices create different outcomes for different racial groups" (Racial Equity Tools, n.d.). Institutional racism happens within schools by administrators and other policy makers who create, implement, and repeat discriminatory policies and procedures negatively impacting students of color. For example, lack of access to advanced level courses, underrepresentation in gifted programs, overrepresentation in special services, and increased disciplinary infractions against students of color are all instances of racism that show up in education. Structural racism is defined as "the normalization and legitimization of an array of dynamics—historical, cultural, institutional, and interpersonal—that routinely advantage White students while producing cumulative and chronic adverse outcomes for people of color" (Lawrence and Keleher, 2004; Racial Equity Tools, n.d.). Structural racism is the foundation that the educational system is built upon that perpetuates and reinforces discriminatory practices. An example of structural racism can be evidenced in districting and school location and the funding that results as a means to segregate students (Baker et al., 2020; Darling-Hammond, 2007). Segregation in itself is not harmful as research has provided benefits of students receiving instruction from educators who are of the same race (Downer et al., 2016; Gershenson et al., 2021). The racist component is the inadequate or unequal funding that is provided for schools heavily populated with students of color versus their White peers. Systemic racism, although similar to institutional and structural racism, includes social culture (beliefs, values, behaviors, habits) (The Aspen Institute, n.d.). Systemic racism includes the racist attitude and resulting behaviors that educators exhibit towards students of color. This shows up as students of color being "invisible" in the classroom, disproportionate disciplinary infractions, and/or blaming parents for lack of academic progress. Identifying these types of racism within the school system involves examining policies to include discipline, access, and placement. Examining the academic and school climates are also useful in identifying embedded racism. Due to the former and current crises that racial and ethnic minority students face, the need for calling out racist policies and procedures has significantly increased. School Counselors should take advantage of the current momentum and work to eradicate racism from educational systems. Despite knowing the charge, eliminating embedded racism requires getting to the root of the problem and extracting the cause. If not, the behaviors, the beliefs, and the practices that got us here will return or continue to manifest. Antiracist work requires school counselors to exhibit leadership skills that entail a certain risk level. It is noted that this work is not easy and school counselors should recognize the challenges that come with addressing racism and how it is viewed as one of the most difficult roles required of a leader (Greene, 2007). However, despite the challenge, we implore them to do this work.

According to ASCA, school counselors are expected to "specifically address the needs of every student, particularly students of culturally diverse, low social-economic status, and other underserved or underperforming populations" (ASCA, 2005, p. 77 as cited in ASCA, 2015). The role of the school counselor is critical in their ability to advocate for underrepresented populations. Holcomb-McCoy (2007) suggests that school counselors have "an enormous amount of power" that should be constructively used to improve our Black and Brown students' outcomes. Antiracist school counseling begins with great introspection about personal beliefs and values for their students of color, discrimination issues, systemic racism, and inequities. According to ASCA 2021, "The role of the school counselor in ensuring anti-racist practices is to enhance awareness, obtain culturally responsive knowledge and skills, and engage in action through advocacy" (The School Counselor's Role section, para. 4). Additionally, understanding implicit bias is necessary to work with diverse populations. To implement a comprehensive school counseling program that is socially just and supports students of color, school counselors must examine their beliefs about students, culture, education, achievement gaps, systemic racism, and social justice (Holcomb-McCoy, 2007). As shared with school counselors across the country, Rutledge (2020) offers the following starting point:

EDUCATE YOURSELF: Know and understand the historical underpinnings behind racism.

KNOW YOURSELF: Take time for reflection and introspection. Know how this is affecting you. Acknowledge your beliefs and values regarding Black Lives Matter, and recognize the best way to support Black and Brown children.

ACKNOWLEDGE THE ISSUES: Be respectful, thoughtful, and intentional about that acknowledgment, and have a plan to move forward. Lifelong activist Dena Simmons (2019) writes, "When we see racism—whether at the individual or policy level—we must have the courage to act."

NEVER STOP ADVOCATING: This is not a one-time conversation but a series of discussions and interventions leading to change.

Culturally Responsive School Counseling

A viable antiracist school counseling method is viewing the comprehensive school counseling program from a cultural lens and implementing culturally responsive school counseling (Schellenberg & Grothaus, 2009). Culturally responsive school counseling is based on the seminal work of Geneva Gay and Gloria Ladson Billings and their work on culturally relevant and responsive pedagogy. According to Gay (2002), "culturally responsive teaching (CRT) is defined as using the cultural characteristics, experiences, and perspectives of ethnically diverse students as conduits for teaching them more effectively" (p. 106). It is further recognized as an evidence-based method that allows students to better connect school (academics) and home (culture) (Understood, n.d.).

A historical practice in education is that students of color are forced to conform to a westernized view of instruction that has failed to consider the differences in racial and ethnic minority students' learning process. In essence, students of color are forced to adhere to learning processes rooted in views and practices that may be foreign to them, putting their White peers at an educational advantage (Klump & McNeir, 2005). Sowers (2004) refers to a cultural mismatch while others agree that the educational experience of students of color is misaligned with the experiences faced outside of school (Banks, 1991; Dee & Penner, 2016; Gay, 1988). This one-dimensional view has perpetuated academic and opportunity gaps found between students of color and their White peers. The current state of education, as a result of the pandemics (Covid-19 and social injustices), has illuminated not only the existing achievement gaps but the contributing factors. Corwin (2020) suggests that specific factors contributing to achievement gaps are categorized into three categories: school-based factors, classroom factors, and student factors. School factors include negative school culture and climate, as well as policies and procedures that oppress and marginalized students of color. Classroom factors include operating using implicit bias or stereotype threat, lack of awareness and knowledge about interventions specific for ethnic and racial minorities' needs, and lack of appropriate training in CRT practices.

When considering the school counselor's role, CRT principles can be adapted to existing counseling interventions such as individual counseling, group counseling, and core curriculum lessons. Thus, the following principles have been adapted from CRT and applied to school counseling: Positive perspectives on culture and family; Communication of higher expectations; Learning within the context of culture; Student-centered instruction; Culturally mediated instruction; Reshaping the curriculum; School counselor as facilitator (Adapted from Ladson-Billings, 1995; The Education Alliance at Brown University, n.d.)

Additionally, Muniz (2019) offers eight common competencies of culturally responsive educators to include: reflecting on one's cultural lens, recognizing and redressing bias in the system, drawing on student's culture to share curriculum and instruction, bringing real-world issues into the classroom, modeling high expectations for all students, promoting respect for students differences, collaborating with families and the local community, communicating in linguistically and culturally responsive ways. These competencies are strikingly similar to standards and competencies that already exist for school counselors. For example, ASCA (2019b) shares school counselor professional criteria and standards where specifically B-PF 6 references how school counselors should "Demonstrate an understanding of the impact of cultural, social, and environmental influences on student success and opportunities" (p. 2).

Another example can be found in standard B-PF 9, where it states, "Create systemic change through the implementation of a school counseling program" (p. 2). Therefore, it is the position of ASCA that school counselors should work towards cultural responsiveness. Doing so helps promote students' academic, career, and social/emotional success (ASCA, 2015).

Benefits of CRT

Research has confirmed the positive impact that cultural responsiveness has on outcomes for students of color. As cited by Gay (2018), this idea of incorporating culture into the curriculum stems back to the 1970s. Currently, we know that students who experience educational settings that respond to culture have shown enhanced learning and improved academic outcomes (Byrd, 2016; Kalyanpur, 2003), strengthened student connectedness to school (Bazron et al., 2005), and improved behavior (Day & Hairston, 2005; Larson et al., 2018).

According to a study conducted by Dee and Penner (2016), 9th graders, as a result of CRT practices, had increased attendance, GPA, and the total number of credits earned. Muniz (2019) suggests that as much as CRT benefits students, it has a far-reaching impact on educators and school systems as well. Klump and McNeir (2005) highlight other advantages such as a more positive school climate respectful of student culture, connections between student's previous knowledge and academic learning, educators ability to make instruction "more meaningful and relevant to their student's lives," and culture embedded into the curriculum (p. 9). Gay (2018) depicts CRT as "empowering," "validating," and "transformative." When educators can implement the eight competencies related to CRT as outlined by Muniz (2019), not only is it "good teaching" as Ladson-Billings (1995) terms it, it is the best approach for teaching students of color.

Application of CRT to School Counseling

Although the concept of culturally responsive teaching has been noted in the literature for years, what is still missing is the direct application to school counseling. School counselors are expected to be culturally competent, culturally aware, and culturally responsive. However, they aren't taught how to integrate these behaviors into their comprehensive programs. Hammond (2015) offers a "Ready for Rigor" framework of CRT that can be viewed from a school counseling lens with the following components.

Knowledge & Awareness—Knowledge and awareness of culture and understanding the impact it has on student outcomes. Although all counselors take a multiculturalism course as part of their training, it is essential to continue learning beyond the surface awareness of cultural differences. To build meaningful relationships and appropriately support students, school counselors must be aware of their own biases and stereotypes, as well as oppressive societal norms and ways of thinking that negatively impact students.

Partnerships & Relationships—Getting to know your students and colleagues, and connect with your students. It is essential to invite students into the conversation. School counselors should partner with students about their individual needs and what would work best for them. Collaboration and advocacy are vital components as well. In addition to partnering with students, school counselors should build social capital by connecting students with outside resources. These partnerships are valuable in extending the ability to provide much-needed resources to students.

Information Processing—Information processing is the learning method that includes new ways of thinking, behaving, growing, and developing. School counselors should consider how to use culture to assist students in connecting relevant information. School counselors are tasked with ensuring that students complete their programs with specific attitudes, skills, and knowledge that leads them towards successful futures. How that task is achieved is through various interventions (individual counseling, group counseling, classroom lessons) that teach students these necessary skills. These involvements require counselors to take on the role of educator and effectively teach and model appropriate skills and strategies. Culturally responsive education requires counselors to adapt their lessons and interventions to reflect the population being served.

Environment & culture—School counselors can provide a safe and positive school climate that supports student voice and agency. A safe and positive school climate is essential for students to feel welcome and included. School climate has been shown to improve student engagement, resulting in increased overall academic improvement (Konold et al., 2018).

The above framework lends itself to culturally responsive school counseling by taking what is currently being done and intentionally using culture as a vital part of that work. It requires moving beyond celebrating diversity at specific points during the year, to using culture in everyday work. The first step to implementing this framework is to examine existing and future interventions from a cultural lens. Are the language, examples, activities, and processing questions created to account for diverse populations within the setting? Are counselors being intentional about interacting and engaging with all students in the class or the group? Can all students see themselves in the content being addressed? These are a few critical questions to ask when examining interventions. Second, counselors should find ways to integrate cultural responsiveness into their existing comprehensive programs. Some examples of foci include:

- Culturally responsive SEL and curriculum integration
- Interventions that focus on topics related to ethnic and racial minority issues
- School Climate/Relationship Building
- Analyzing and Using data to support interventions
- Identifying and utilizing virtual counseling tips

Lastly, culturally responsive school counseling requires counselors to apply CRT principles to comprehensive school counseling directly. As previously noted, research on how to do this is scarce. Figure 1 offers a visual of CRT principles and examples of direct implications for school counseling. In addition to providing culturally responsive school counseling that includes student's cultural knowledge and experiences, counselors must then ensure that these practices are culturally sustaining throughout not just the school counseling curriculum, but the entire academic curriculum.

Figure 1: CRT Principles Applied to School Counseling

CRT Principles	Implications in School Counseling
Positive perspectives on culture and family	Increase learning opportunities and collaborative experiences Integrate culture within school counseling curriculum
Communication of higher expectations	Operate from a strength-based approach Define success individually Encourage students to set their own goals
Learning within the context of culture	Integrate appropriate cultural examples Provide opportunities for the same cultural and cross-cultural experiences
Student-centered instruction	Create a safe environment where students can take charge of their own learning. Provide student choice
Culturally mediated instruction	Understanding student's learning styles, their strengths, and their beliefs
Reshaping the curriculum	Using diverse resources Using culturally relevant examples Developing learning activities that are more compatible with students' backgrounds
Counselor as facilitator	Develop non-judgmental, trusting relationships Facilitate culturally relevant interventions and programs Assist other educational professionals in CRT work

Note: CRT principles applied to school counseling. Adapted from Applying the Culturally Responsive Pedagogies in Training Culturally Diverse Counseling Students. Y.C. Chiu (2019). Adapted with permission.

School Counselor Self-Care

Working to support students' emotional well-being during social unrest and a global health crisis, over a sustained period, has proven to be a stressor for many school counselors and their fellow educators. Many of our colleagues have experienced burnout symptoms characterized as feelings of being depleted, overextended, and emotionally exhausted, in addition to a sense of decreased productivity and enjoyment of one's work (Morse et al., 2012). The enduring nature of both the health pandemic and social unrest creates an environment that is full of uncertainty. Berinato (2020) explains that the loss of normalcy, fear of economic toll, and the failure to connect on both an individual and societal level manifest themselves as grief. Along with the rest of the world, educators are also grieving the loss of life, financial security, and the ability to engage physically with loved ones in times of need. Nonetheless, school counselors and other educators are working despite these complex emotional experiences. Our work's quality and the quality of our own mental wellness have significance for the students in our care.

As mental health professionals, it is paramount that we take our own mental health seriously and recognize the signs of burnout and mental exhaustion. One of the most critical steps counselors and other educators can take to help mitigate the adverse effects of both pandemics is to engage in self-care practices regularly. Self-care is defined as the intentional actions individuals and organizations engage in to support well-being and reduce stress (Bloomquist et al., 2015). It should be deliberate and attend to several physical, psychological, emotional, spiritual, and professional domains. During these challenging times, school counselors and educators, in general, need to aggressively pay attention to their own well-being. Figure 2 outlines standard practices, techniques, and guidelines to support general, physical, and mental well-being (CDC, 2016).

Figure 2: Self-Care Strategies

Domains	Self-Care Actions
Physical	Move your body and exercise regularly to increase the number of endorphins in your body. You can engage in physical activity outside as well as in your home. Eat well-balanced meals. Nutrition is key to optimal body function
Psychological	Prioritize sleep by getting plenty of rest and developing a sleep routine, and avoiding sleep conditions free from overstimulation and distraction. Avoid excessive alcohol use

Domains	Self-Care Actions
Emotional	Find ways to connect with people who bring you joy and that you trust via phone calls, video conferencing tools, or socially distanced meetings. Take breaks from watching, reading, and listening to social media on controversial topics. Practice mindfulness activities to focus on the here and now.
Spiritual	Find time to practice your faith or spiritual practices. Remind yourself of your core faith-based or spiritual beliefs and reflect on how those principles can help you get through tough times. Seek support from your faith-based organizations you trust.
Professional	Stay as informed as possible on the new rules and changes that occur at your job. Knowing how your workplace is addressing both pandemics helps you understand how to navigate your environment.

Conclusion

The current Covid-19 pandemic, the long-standing social injustices, and the systemic racism that Black and other racial and ethnic minorities have long suffered in our country converged to disproportionately levy negative consequences against Black students. The educational disparities that existed before Covid-19 are widening (The Annie Casey Foundation, 2006). Access to virtual education has proven insufficient for many Black students, and the pandemic's economic hardships created unstable and stressful home environments (Slay, 2020). However, becoming "woke" to these growing disparities, combined with the refusal of the Black community to endure further social injustice and systemic racism, steadies the call for change. School counselors are uniquely trained to answer this call for change. Through the skill of advocacy, school counselors effectively communicate the issues plaguing Black students to stakeholders, garnering support to influence systemic change (Havlik, 2019). Trained to be reflective and introspective, empathizing with those whose experiences differ from their own, school counselors support and lead their peers in understanding the hardships Black and Brown students experience as a result of Covid-19, social injustices, and systemic racism.

School counselors take an intentional and strategic approach to mitigating negative consequences that impede academic success or students' personal well-being. School counselors remain "woke" by assessing the needs of Black and Brown students and providing applicable resources and interventions to support their educational achievement and mental health. This work is not easy and, in fact, can be relatively stress-inducing. School counselors work to bring their colleagues to an understanding of social justice and the need to create equitable practices, policies, and procedures, confirming that all students have access to the essential prerequisites that will ensure their success. While this work may be new to some school counselors, antiracist school counseling is imperative so that the re-imagined education system is truly one that serves and benefits ALL students.

References

American University. (2020, July 29). *Antiracist school counseling: A call to action.* [Webinar] https://www.american.edu/centers/cprs/antiracist-school-counseling-a-call-to-action.cfm.

American School Counselor Association. (2015). *The school counselor and cultural diversity.* American School Counseling Association.

American School Counselor Association. (2019a). *The essential role of high school counselors.* American School Counselor Association.

American School Counselor Association. (2019b). *ASCA school counselor professional standards & competencies.* American School Counselor Association.

American School Counselor Association (2021). *The school counselor and anti-racist practices* [Unpublished Draft]. American School Counselor Association.

Ang, D. (2020). *The effects of police violence on inner-city students.* HKS Working Paper No. RWP20–016. http://dx.doi.org/10.2139/ssrn.3625082.

The Annie E. Casey Foundation. (2006). *Unequal opportunities in education.* [Issue Brief]. Annie E. Casey Foundation. https://www.aecf.org/resources/race-matters-how-race-affects-education-opportunities/.

The Aspen Institute. (n.d.) *Glossary for understanding the dismantling structural racism/Promoting racial equity analysis.* https://www.aspeninstitute.org/wp-content/uploads/files/content/docs/rcc/RCC-Structural-Racism-Glossary.pdf.

Atkins, R., & Oglesby, A. (2018). *Interrupting racism: Equity and social justice in school counseling.* Routledge.

Banks, J.A. (1991–1992). Multicultural education: For freedoms sake. *Educational Leadership, 49*(4), 32–36.

Bazron, B., Osher, D., & Fleischman, S. (2005). Creating culturally responsive schools. *American Educator, 11*(1), 38–47.

Bennett, J. (2021). Long-term unemployment has risen sharply in U.S. amid the pandemic, especially among Asian Americans. Pew Research Center. https://pewrsr.ch/3tbhrzK.

Berinato, S. (2020). That discomfort you're feeling is grief. *Harvard Business Review, 23*(03), 2020.

Bloomquist, K.R., Wood, L., Friedmeyer-Trainor, K., & Kim, H.W. (2015). Self-care and professional quality of life: Predictive factors among MSW practitioners. *Advances in Social Work, 16*(2), 292–311.

Byrd, C.M. (2016). Does culturally relevant teaching work? An examination from student perspectives. *SAGE Open, 6*(3), 1–10. doi.org/10.1177/2158244016660744

Centers for Disease Control. (2016, July 15). *Tips for Better Sleep.* https://www.cdc.gov/sleep/about_sleep/sleep_hygiene.html.

Centers for Disease Control. (2020a, July 24). *Health equity considerations & racial & ethnic minority groups.* https://www.cdc.gov/coronavirus/2019-ncov/community/health-equity/race-ethnicity.html.

Centers for Disease Control. (2020b, August 14). *Hospitalization rates and characteristics of children aged <18 years hospitalized with laboratory-confirmed COVID-19*. [MMWR Early Release]. https://www.cdc.gov/mmwr/volumes/69/wr/pdfs/mm6932e3-H. pdf?fbclid=IwAR3jfNN0W9DInc-Lr_g6Z5As0SXNl0JBAen3Ao1RCkOPn1d5e7xPWn zdi9Q.

Centers for Disease Control. (2020c, August 18). *COVID-19 hospitalization and death by race/ethnicity*. https://www.cdc.gov/coronavirus/2019-ncov/covid-data/investigations-discovery/hospitalization-death-by-race-ethnicity.html.

Center for Disease Control. (2020d, March 10) *Racial and ethnic disparities in COVID-19 incidence by age, sex, and period among persons aged <25 Years - 16 U.S. jurisdictions, January 1 - December 31, 2020*. https://www.cdc.gov/mmwr/volumes/70/wr/mm7011e1. htm?s_cid=mm7011e1_w.

Centers for Disease Control. (n.d.). *COVID data tracker*. Department of Health and Human Services. https://covid.cdc.gov/covid-data-tracker/#datatracker-home.

Chiu, Y.C. (2019, October). *Applying the culturally responsive pedagogies in training culturally diverse counseling students* [Concurrent session]. Association for Counselor Education and Supervision (ACES) Conference, Seattle, WA.

Chowkwanyun, M., & Reed A.L., Jr. (2020). Racial health disparities and COVIS-19—Caution and context. *New England Journal of Medicine*.

Corwin (n.d.) *Common cause of the achievement gap*. Corwin. https://us.corwin. com/en-us/nam/equity-causes-of-achievement-gaps.

Day-Vines, N.L., & Day-Hairston, B.O. (2005). Culturally congruent strategies for addressing the behavioral needs of urban, African American male adolescents. *Professional School Counseling, 8*(3), 236–243.

Dee, T., & Penner, E. (2016). The causal effects of cultural relevance: Evidence from an ethnic studies curriculum. CEPA Working Paper No. 16–01. *Stanford Center for Education Policy Analysis*.

Dorn, E., Hancock, B., Sarakatsannis, J., & Viruleg, E. (2020). *COVID-19 and student learning in the United States: The hurt could last a lifetime*. McKinsey & Company. https://www.mckinsey.com/industries/public-and-social-sector/our-insights/covid-19-and-student-learning-in-the-united-states-the-hurt-could-last-a-lifetime.

Downer, J.T., Goble, P., Myers, S.S., & Pianta, R.C. (2016). Teacher-child racial/ethnic match within pre-kindergarten classrooms and children's early school adjustment. *Early Childhood Research Quarterly, 37*, 26–38.

Education Alliance at Brown University. (n.d.). *Culturally responsive teaching*. Brown University. https://www.brown.edu/academics/education-alliance/teaching-diverse-learners/strategies-0/culturally-responsive-teaching-0.

Egede, L.E., & Walker, R.J. (2020). Structural racism, social risk factors, and COVID-19—A dangerous convergence for Black Americans. *New England Journal of Medicine, 383*(12), e77.

Elizondo-Urrestarazu, J. (2020). *The other pandemic: Systemic racism and its consequences*. European Network of Equality Bodies. https://equineteurope.org/2020/the-other-pandemic-systemic-racism-and-its-consequences/.

Epstein, R., Blake, J., & González, T. (2017). Girlhood interrupted: The erasure of Black girls' childhood. *Available at SSRN 3000695*.

Fernandez, A., Loukas, A., Golaszewski, N.M., Batanova, M., & Pasch, K.E. (2019). Adolescent adjustment problems mediate the association between racial discrimination and school connectedness. *Journal of School Health, 89*(12), 945–952.

Fortuna, L.R., Tolou-Shams, M., Robles-Ramamurthy, B., & Porche, M.V. (2020). Inequity and the disproportionate impact of COVID-19 on communities of color in the United States: The need for a trauma-informed social justice response. *Psychological Trauma: Theory, Research, Practice, and Policy. 12*(5), 443–444. http://dx.doi.org/10.1037/tra0000889.

Garcia, M.A., Homan, P.A., García, C., & Brown, T.H. (2021). The color of COVID-19: Structural racism and the disproportionate impact of the pandemic on older Black and Latinx adults. *The Journals of Gerontology: Series B, 76*(3), e75-e80. doi:10.1093/geronb/ gbaa114.

Gay, G. (1988). Designing relevant curricula for diverse learners. *Education and urban society, 20*(4), 327–340.

Gay, G. (2002). Preparing for culturally responsive teaching. *Journal of Teacher Education, 53*(2), 106–116.

Gay, G. (2018). *Culturally responsive teaching: Theory, research, and practice.* Teachers College Press.

Gershenson, S., Hart, C.M., Hyman, J., Lindsay, C., & Papageorge, N.W. (2021). *The long-run impacts of same-race teachers* (No. w25254). National Bureau of Economic Research.

Greene, M.P. (2007). Beyond diversity and multiculturalism: Towards the development of anti-racist institutions and leaders. *Journal for Nonprofit Management, 11*(1), 9–17.

Hammond, Z. (2014). *Culturally responsive teaching and the brain: Promoting authentic engagement and rigor among culturally and linguistically diverse students.* Corwin Press.

Havlik, S.A., Malott, K., Yee, T., DeRosato, M., & Crawford, E. (2019). School counselor training in professional advocacy: The role of the counselor educator. *Journal of Counselor Leadership and Advocacy, 6*(1), 71–85.

Holcomb-McCoy, C. (2007). *School counseling to close the achievement gap: A social justice framework for success.* Sage Publications.

Hussar, B., Zhang, J., Hein, S., Wang, K., Roberts, A., Cui, J., Smith, M., Bullock Mann, F., Barmer, A., and Dilig, R. (2020). *The condition of education 2020* (NCES 2020–144). U.S. Department of Education.

Kalyanpur, M. (2003). A challenge to professionals: Developing cultural reciprocity with culturally diverse families. *Focal Point, 7*(1), 1–6.

Klump, J., & McNeir, G. (2005). *Culturally responsive practices for student success: A regional sampler.* Northwest Regional Educational Laboratory NWREL.

Konold, T., Cornell, D., Jia, Y., & Malone, M. (2018). School climate, student engagement, and academic achievement: A latent variable, multilevel multi-informant examination. *Aera Open, 4*(4), 2332858418815661.

Krouse, H.J. (2020). COVID-19 and the widening gap in health inequity. *Otolaryngology–Head and Neck Surgery, 163*(1), 65–66.

Ladson-Billings, G. (1995). But that's just good teaching! The case for culturally relevant pedagogy. *Theory into Practice, 34*(3), 159–165.

Larson, K.E., Pas, E.T., Bradshaw, C.P., Rosenberg, M.S., & Day-Vines, N.L. (2018). Examining how proactive management and culturally responsive teaching relate to student behavior: Implications for measurement and practice. *School Psychology Review, 47*(2), 153–166.

Lawrence, K., & Keleher, T. (2004, November). *Chronic disparity: Strong and pervasive evidence of racial inequalities: Poverty outcomes: Structural racism.* Race and Public Policy Conference.

Morse, G., Salyers, M.P., Rollins, A.L., Monroe-DeVita, M., & Pfahler, C. (2012). Burnout in mental health services: A review of the problem and its remediation. *Administration and Policy in Mental Health and Mental Health Services Research, 39*(5), 341–352.

Muniz, J. (2019). *Culturally responsive teaching: A reflection guide.*[Policy Paper] New America. https://www.newamerica.org/education-policy/policy-papers/culturally-responsive-teaching-competencies/.

National Association of the Advancement of Colored People (n.d.). *Coronavirus impact on students and education systems.* NAACP. https://naacp.org/coronavirus/coronavirus-impact-on-students-and-education-systems/.

Neblett E.W., Jr., Philip, C.L., Cogburn, C.D., & Sellers, R.M. (2006). African American adolescents' discrimination experiences and academic achievement: Racial socialization as a cultural compensatory and protective factor. *Journal of Black Psychology, 32*(2), 199–218.

Nelson, J.R., Hall, B.S., Anderson, J.L., Birtles, C., & Hemming, L. (2018). Self-compassion as self-care: A simple and effective tool for counselor educators and counseling students. *Journal of Creativity in Mental Health, 13*(1), 121–133.

Phelps, C., & Sperry, L.L. (2020). Children and the COVID-19 pandemic. *Psychological Trauma: Theory, Research, Practice, and Policy, 12*(S1), S73.

Pirtle, W.N.L. (2020). Racial capitalism: A fundamental cause of novel coronavirus

(COVID-19) pandemic inequities in the United States. *Health Education & Behavior,* 47(4), 504–508.

Poteat, T., Millett, G., Nelson, L.E., & Beyrer, C. (2020). Understanding COVID-19 risks and vulnerabilities among Black communities in America: The lethal force of syndemics. *Annals of Epidemiology, 47,* 1–3.

Purdue University (n.d.). *Critical race theory (1970s-present).* https://owl.purdue.edu/owl/subject_specific_writing/writing_in_literature/literary_theory_and_schools_of_criticism/critical_race_theory.html.

Race Equity Tools (n.d.). Racial Equity Tools Glossary. Retrieved April 13, 2021, from https://www.racialequitytools.org/glossary.

Reichert, S. (2020, April 7). *Self-care tips during the COVID-19 pandemic.* Mayo Clinic. https://www.mayoclinichealthsystem.org/hometown-health/speaking-of-health/self-care-tips-during-the-covid-19-pandemic.

Rutledge, M.L. (2020, July/August). A change is gonna come. *ASCA School Counselor.* https://www.ascaschoolcounselor-digital.org/ascaschoolcounselor/july_august_2020/MobilePagedArticle.action?articleId=1601128#articleId1601128.

Schellenberg, R., & Grothaus, T. (2009) Promoting cultural responsiveness and closing the achievement gap with standards blending. *Professional School Counseling 12,* 440–457. doi:10.5330/PSC.n.2010-12.440.

Schleicher, A. (2020) *The impact of COVID-19 on education—Insights from education at a glance 2020.* Organisation for Economic Co-operation and Development. www.oecd.org/ education/education-at-a-glance-19991487.htm.

The School Superintendents Association (2020, May 29). *Resolution in support of safe, healthy, and district-specific reopening process informed by the centers for disease control and prevention guidelines.* AASA. http://aasacentral.org/wp-content/uploads/2020/05/AASA-Resolution-in-Support-of-a-Safe-Healthy-and-District-Specific-Reopening-Process.pdf.

The School Superintendents Association (n.d.). *AASA COVID-19 recovery task force guidelines for reopening schools: An opportunity to transform public education.* AASA. http://aasacentral.org/wp-content/uploads/2020/06/AASA-COVID-19-Recovery-Task-Force-Guiding-Principals-and-Action-Steps-for-Reopening-Schools.pdf.

Simmons, D. (2019). How to be an antiracist educator. *Education Update, 61*(10).

Slay, Bre-Ann. (2020). *COVID-19 will intensify education inequities for black students.* Diverse Issues in Higher Education. https://diverseeducation.com/article/177796/.

Sowers, J. (2004). *Creating a community of learners: Solving the puzzle of classroom management.* Northwest Regional Educational Laboratory.

Tate, E. (2021). *School counselors have implicit bias. Some are ready to address it.* EdSurge. https://www.edsurge.com/amp/news/2021-04-06-school-counselors-have-implicit-bias-some-are-ready-to-address-it?utm_campaign=site&utm_content=-share-46&__twitter_impression=true&fbclid=IwAR0a4giIJ8ERaEHjUJv_X1qLpopMZ8bg9cp6t_dxc44n3euBSvZvNpeYITE.

Tello, M. (2020, April 16). *6 self-care steps for a pandemic—Always important, now essential.* Harvard Health. https://www.health.harvard.edu/blog/6-self-care-steps-for-a-pandemic-always-important-now-essential-2020041619563.

Understood. (n.d.). *Culturally responsive teaching: What you need to know.* Understood. https://www.understood.org/en/school-learning/for-educators/universal-design-for-learning/what-is-culturally-responsive-teaching.

United States Interagency Council on Homelessness. (2020, March 16). *Supporting children and youth experiencing homelessness during the COVID-19 outbreak: Questions to consider.* USICH. https://www.usich.gov/tools-for-action/supporting-children-and-youth-experiencing-homelessness-during-the-covid-19-outbreak-questions-to-consider.

Van Dyke M.E., Mendoza M.C., Li W., Parker E.M., Belay, B., Davis, E.M., Quint, J.J., Penman-Aguilar, A., & Clare, K.E. (2021). *Racial and ethnic disparities in COVID-19 incidence by age, sex, and period among persons aged <25 Years—16 U.S. jurisdictions, January 1–December 31, 2020.* [MMWR Morb Mortal Wkly Report] 70:382–388. DOI: http://dx.doi.org/10.15585/mmwr.mm7011el.

Voight, A., Hanson, T., O'Malley, M., & Adekanye, L. (2015). The racial school climate gap: Within-school disparities in students' experiences of safety, support, and connectedness. *American Journal of Community Psychology, 56*(3–4), 252–267.

Wong, C.A., Eccles, J.S., & Sameroff, A. (2003). The influence of ethnic discrimination and ethnic identification on African American adolescents' school and socioemotional adjustment. *Journal of Personality, 71*(6), 1197–1232.

World Health Organization (2020, October 5). *COVID-19 disrupting mental health services in most countries, WHO survey* [News release]. WHO. https://www.who.int/news-room/detail/05-10-2020-covid-19-disrupting-mental-health-services-in-most-countries-who-survey.

Dismantling Disproportionality in Special Education Through Antiracist Practices

DENA D. SLANDA, LINDSEY M. PIKE, LÉA HERBERT, ERIC B. WELLS, *and* CANDACE PELT

> Do not get lost in a sea of despair. Be hopeful, be optimistic. Our struggle is not the struggle of a day, a week, a month, or a year, it is the struggle of a lifetime. Never, ever be afraid to make some noise and get in good trouble, necessary trouble.
> —Lewis, 2018

Educational achievement is a transformative equalizer and pathway to economic mobility, social empowerment, and improved quality of life. However, structural elements, including systemic racism and federal and state policies, prevent access and opportunity in education, especially for Culturally, Linguistically, Ethnically, Economically, Academically, and Racially[1] (CLEEAR) diverse students (Blanch, 2016). Students from CLEEAR diverse backgrounds are disproportionately identified as eligible for special education (USDOE, 2020a). Contributing to these concerns are: (a) the overwhelming whiteness of the teaching cadre, which does not reflect an increasingly diverse student population, and (b) the failure of education policy to deliver equity for CLEEAR diverse students. The general education system is not designed to meet the individual needs of an increasingly diverse student population and does not provide the actionable items required to include all students. Further, special education requires equitable access to the general curriculum for students identified as having disabilities who require specially designed programming; yet, it has historically resulted in limited access, reduced achievement, and stigmatizing labels with lasting implications.

The annual report to Congress on the implementation of the *Individuals with Disabilities Education Act* (IDEA) consistently highlights disproportionality leading to reduced opportunity and outcomes for students from CLEEAR diverse backgrounds. Disproportionality is "among the most significant and intransigent problems in the field of special education" (Skiba et al., 2005, p. 130). Persistent inequities are particularly evident in special education referral, evaluation, and placement. More recently, Covid-19 further exposed inequities in access to education and inherent subjectivity in the identification process in special education for the largest IDEA disability category, specific learning disability, which comprises nearly half of the students served under IDEA (USDOE, 2020a).

Some solutions, including culturally responsive pedagogy and multi-tiered systems of support (MTSS), have not sustainably or significantly reduced disproportionality. However, by addressing implicit teacher bias and cultural marginalization, antiracist teaching practices and education policies offer promising options for reducing subjectivity in special education identification. Antiracism is a positive approach that requires actively promoting racial equity by identifying and eliminating racism in systems, policies, practices, and procedures (Kendi, 2019). Yet, the field of education has only begun to define antiracist teaching. Much work remains to infuse antiracist teaching practices into inclusive classroom settings. Such a vision requires a universally applicable framework that enables the disruption, dismantling, and transformation of the current educational system into a system that promotes educational justice.

Part I: Defining Disproportionality and Acknowledging Its Implications

Disproportionality: Over- and Under-Representation in Special Education

The commonly accepted definition of disproportionality in the context of special education refers to both the over- and under-identification of students from sociodemographic groups that systems have historically marginalized for special education placement (Barrio, 2017; Sullivan & Osher, 2019; Thorius et al., 2019). Disproportionality results from the practice of identifying students from socially, racially, ethnically, linguistically, or culturally diverse backgrounds as having a disability with greater frequency than their white peers (Sullivan & Proctor, 2016). Disproportionality can be determined by using composition, risk index, or risk ratio calculations (Anastasiou et al., 2011). *Composition* is derived by comparing the number of students in a specific racial or ethnic group identified for special education to the overall number of students in that racial or ethnic group. *Risk index* refers to the percentage of a given group served in special education. *Risk ratio* is a calculation that denotes the relative level of risk for a specific group as compared to a reference population.

The Annual Report to Congress on the Implementation of IDEA includes risk index and risk ratio (RR). For ages 6 through 21 across all disability categories, American Indian or Alaska Native students (RR 1.6), Black or African American students (RR 1.4), Hispanic/Latino students (RR 1.1), and Native Hawaiian or Other Pacific Islander students (RR 1.5) were more likely to be served under IDEA than were students in all other racial/ethnic groups combined (USDOE, 2020a). During the 2018–2019 school year, Black or African American students comprised 13.8 percent of the total population of students ages 6 to 21, but accounted for 17.89 percent of students with disabilities (USDOE, 2020b). Further, Black or African American students were more likely to be identified with intellectual disability and emotional disturbance and less likely to be identified with speech or language impairment or autism than all students with disabilities (USDOE, 2020b). In fact, data from the Office for Civil Rights reveals that Black or African American students have been overrepresented in the IDEA categories of intellectual disability and emotional disturbance every year since 1968 (Proctor et al., 2012).

Disproportionality exists not only across racial categories, but also impacts students with cultural and linguistic diversity as evidenced by the number of English Learners (EL) placed in special education (Harry & Klingner, 2006; USDOE, 2020a). Similar to the experiences of their Black or African American peers, ELs are most often placed in subjective disability categories such as specific learning disability (SLD) where there is no required psychoeducational evaluation or clear standardization of placement (Barrio, 2017). The IDEA (2004) cited studies that "have documented apparent discrepancies in the levels of referral and placement of limited English proficient children in special education" (Section 601[C][11][B], IDEA). Further, IDEA (2004) emphasized that "more minority children continue to be served in special education than would be expected from the percentage of minority children in the general school population" (Section 601[C][12][B], IDEA).

Though disproportionality is a generally accepted phenomenon, confirmed by the federal Office of Special Education Programs (USDOE, 2017; Posny, 2007), some researchers have sought to dismiss this reality (e.g., Morgan et al., 2015; Shifrer et al., 2011) and argue that white students are the true victims of disproportionality (e.g., Morgan et al., 2017; Morgan et al., 2020). Other researchers have acknowledged the existence of

the digital divide disproportionately impacted students who are Black or African American, Hispanic/Latino, living in rural areas, and/or navigating poverty (Lake & Mikori, 2020).

As the pandemic continued its stronghold on the nation, inequities persisted. During a time when the most vulnerable students needed protections and safeguards, some education professionals were concerned about whether they would be able to meet IDEA requirements for eligibility, placement, and service, and advocated for the flexibility of such protections. For example, the Council of Administrators of Special Education (CASE) and National Association of State Directors of Special Education (NASDSE) (2020) sent a joint letter to Congress requesting flexibility of IDEA provisions given a number of compliance issues they faced in providing accessibility and accommodations during school closings (Slanda & Martin, 2021). In their joint letter, CASE and NASDSE requested flexibilities in three main areas: (a) timelines related to evaluation, annual Individualized Education Program reviews, transition from Part C to Part B, and complaint responses; (b) procedures related to documentation of a free appropriate public education, IEP meetings and reporting, and data collection, and (c) fiscal management. Educating and evaluating children while adhering to safeguards for students already identified as having a disability became a critical challenge and forced some schools to shutter completely for the remainder of the 2019–2020 school year.

In response, the USDOE clarified that federal accessibility laws (e.g., IDEA, Section 504 of the Rehabilitation Act, Title II of the American with Disabilities Act) should not be used to prevent schools from choosing to offer distance learning opportunities to all students, including students with disabilities (USDOE, 2020c). Further, the USDOE stressed the importance that schools continue to offer a free appropriate public education (FAPE) to all students, including specialized instruction and related services. Without any specific regulatory guidance, the schools could offer services and instruction virtually, online, or telephonically and emphasized the need for parents, educators, and administrators to collaboratively and creatively meet the needs of students for intervention and instruction. Unfortunately, many schools and districts struggled to provide FAPE for their students, especially those with high intensity needs, leaving some students with less support than they had prior to the Covid-19 pandemic (Knox et al., 2021; Lee, 2020).

As the 2020–2021 school year approached, districts across the nation developed and implemented blueprints for returning to the classroom (Knox et al., 2021). State autonomy in designing the response to Covid-19 within schools led to significant variations. For example, in some states (e.g., Florida, Georgia), caregivers were able to select their preferred instructional model (face-to-face, hybrid, and virtual) beginning in August 2020. However, caregivers in other states (e.g., California, New York) were only able to select virtual schooling as the state struggled to reopen schools due to the high number of infections and associated deaths. The Center for Economic and Social Research (CESR) surveyed caregivers at the start of the 2020–2021 school year. At that time, 39 percent of parents favored fully remote learning and 44 percent wanted a mix of some in person and some online learning (CESR, 2021). One year later in March 2021, 56 percent of caregivers surveyed reported their children were still engaged in online learning platforms (either fully online or hybrid) (CESR, 2021). The variety of school delivery options impacted all students, but especially students from CLEEAR diverse backgrounds.

Identification for Special Education: Referral, Evaluation, and Eligibility and Placement

Considering the historic disproportionate referral and placement of CLEEAR diverse students into special education, understanding the processes of referral and placement provides useful insight into disproportionality prevention. Steps within the special education referral and placement process include (a) the referral process, (b) psychoeducational evaluation and interpretation of assessment results, and (c) eligibility and placement decisions. Federal legislation mandates, such as the IDEA-embedded child find requirement, attempt to provide safeguards within the special education process, but subjectivity throughout the process continues to result in disproportionality. To address this issue, it is critical for each step of the process to be examined and potential sites for bias identified and addressed.

The Referral Process

The initiation of the referral process is a critical first step in the path to overrepresentation of CLEEAR diverse children in special education. Children enter school with a wide range of abilities, skill sets, and behavior patterns which are shaped by their *pre* school experiences including family and cultural norms (Fish, 2016). When these norms are not consistent with the established norms of the dominant culture, teachers begin to categorize and classify students based on perceived academic skills (low or high achieving) and behaviors (or misbehaviors) (Fish, 2016). At the discretion of the teacher, children who are suspected to deviate from the *norm* are often referred to special education (Fish, 2016). This process provides room for subjectivity in the classroom teacher's determination about whether a student's achievement or behavior requires specially designed programming (Graves & Mitchell, 2011). The teacher's determination, including its inherent subjectivity, is a crucial component of the process, as students referred for special education by teachers are confirmed and labeled as having a disability at rates between 73 percent and 90 percent (Fish, 2016; Harry & Klingner, 2006).

Because placement in special education begins with teacher perception and referral, it is critical to note that teacher perception and treatment of students differs based on student race and ethnicity (Fish, 2016). Teachers' race-based assumptions may influence their decision to refer students for special education testing. Data shows approximately 79 percent of public school teachers in the U.S. are white (National Center for Educational Statistics [NCES], 2020b), in stark contrast to the 52 percent (and growing) of students of color they serve (de Brey et al., 2019).

Psychoeducational Evaluation and Interpretation of Assessment Results

Upon entering the school system, students are measured, assessed, and evaluated using instruments developed and implemented by educators at various levels, including school psychologists, who are responsible for administering psychoeducational evaluations. Data indicates that over 90 percent of school psychologists in the U.S. are white females (Castillo et al., 2013; Proctor & Romano, 2018). Much like the predominantly white teaching cadre, this presents a disconnect between school psychologists and the students they serve. Despite attempts by the National Association of School Psychologists (NASP) to reduce disproportionality in their profession and effectively address systemic inequities in schools, implicit bias remains prevalent (NASP, 2017). Implicit bias is the unexamined beliefs or associations one has about a group; these biases can impact their subsequent evaluation of that group (NASP, 2017). School psychologists are vulnerable to implicit bias which can influence subjective decisions during the evaluation process and through interpretation of assessment results. This potential is especially concerning given the shift in some states to eliminate or even prohibit the use of intelligence testing after the 2004 reauthorization of IDEA (Graves & Mitchell, 2011).

The shift away from intelligence testing for placement in special education categories such as SLD has been attributed to the inherent bias in the assessments towards Black or African American students in particular (*Larry P. v. Riles*, 1979; *Marshall et al. v. Georgia*, 1984/1985; *PASE v. Hannon*, 1980; Proctor et al., 2012). To reduce bias in eligibility determination, federal legislation (e.g., IDEA, 2004) required the use of a multi-tiered system of supports (MTSS) framework, known at the time as Response to Intervention (RTI; Fuchs & Vaughn, 2012). The MTSS framework is a three-tiered structure for providing instruction and intervention using evidence-based and research-validated methods which increase in intensity in response to the individual needs of the student (Slanda, 2017; Slanda & Little, 2020). The MTSS framework, discussed in detail later in this essay, was also developed as an alternative to intelligence testing and a proactive and responsive way to identify students for services within the SLD category (IDEA, 2004; Hartlep & Ellis, 2012; Proctor et al., 2012). Although MTSS was developed to reduce subjectivity and bias, the system is inherently subjective, especially when not implemented in a culturally responsive manner (Proctor et al., 2012).

The overreliance on systems such as MTSS can equally increase the subjectivity and potentially contribute to the overrepresentation of CLEEAR diverse students in special education (Graves & Mitchell, 2011; Proctor et al., 2012). According to data from the USDOE (2020a), SLD is the largest category served under IDEA (38.2 percent of students with disabilities) and is the "most prevalent … disability category for almost every racial/ethnic group" (p. xxvi). Nearly half of students with disabilities from ethnic minority groups are labeled SLD (American Indian/Alaskan Native–45 percent, Black or African American–45 percent, Hispanic/Latino–45 percent, Native Hawaiian or Other Pacific Islander–50 percent) (USDOE, 2020a).

Eligibility and Placement

Whether using standardized measures or an MTSS model, the decision-making process that leads to determination for special education services and placement decisions is based on ambiguous and subjective regulations (Sadeh & Sullivan, 2017; Sullivan et al., 2017). Since their inception, these regulations, including the definitions and protocols for determination and placement in special education, have been left intentionally vague (Anastasiou et al., 2011). The vagueness allows for educators to inappropriately include, rather than exclude, students from special education (Anastasiou et al., 2011). With the language open for interpretation, states and districts have determined their own threshold for qualification and set their own parameters to guide the process. School psychologists and other education professionals exercise their own professional, often implicitly biased, decision-making regarding special education eligibility and placement (NASP, 2017).

Even when eligibility decisions are made using a multidisciplinary team approach, the subjectivity remains, especially when considering the discretionary disability categories in which CLEEAR diverse students are most disproportionately placed (e.g., Emotional Disturbance [ED], Intellectual Disability [ID], SLD) (Sullivan et al., 2019). Black and Native American students face a greater risk of not only being identified for special education in general, but of being identified for a discretionary disability category as opposed to a category more closely tied to a medical diagnosis (Ahram et al., 2011; Shealey et al., 2011). For example, federal guidance for identification for emotional disturbance requires the student exhibits "an inability to maintain satisfactory interpersonal relationships with peers and teachers" (34 § C.F.R. 300.8[c][4]). Such guidance provides room for interpretation (e.g., who determines satisfactory behavior?) and allows for cultural perception of behavior (Sullivan & Sadeh, 2014; Sullivan et al., 2019).

Acknowledging Implications of Disproportionality

The overrepresentation of CLEEAR diverse students in special education has several implications. Research findings signify ongoing oppression and negative treatment of students at the intersection of race and disability, given the "deficit-based framings of disability, reliance on whiteness, and English as the norm for developmental benchmarks" (Thorius et al, 2019, p. 157). CLEEAR diverse students who are placed in special education face twice the discrimination—first by systems of oppression tied to race, language, or ethnicity and again by systems of oppression tied to disability (Albrecht et al., 2012). Recognizing the intersectional oppression experienced by this cross section of students and identifying the specific consequences they face from systems are key to reducing disproportionality and dismantling the systems producing it.

Once identified, students with disabilities from diverse backgrounds are placed in more restrictive environments and remain in special education longer than their white peers (USDOE, 2020b). Students at the intersection of race and disability, especially those with ED, experience greater expulsion rates and are stereotyped as being more difficult to educate (Fenning & Rose, 2007; Stoutjesdijk et al., 2012). This prejudice results in limited access to the general education curriculum, stunted academic gains, and reduced postsecondary outcome opportunities (Brown et al., 2019; Sullivan & Proctor, 2016). The trajectory for CLEEAR diverse students with special education labels includes segregation from their peers in PreK–12, underrepresentation in higher education as compared to their white peers with the same disability label (Reid & Knight, 2006; Thorius et al., 2019), and, in some cases, a funneling into the school-to-prison pipeline (Mahon-Reynolds & Parker, 2016; Thorius et al., 2019). Students without disabilities who are inappropriately identified for special education encounter these same barriers and incur the additional damage of misplaced stigmatization and ineffective special education services (Sullivan & Proctor, 2016). Albrecht and colleagues (2012) emphasize the connection between placement and equity, stating "discrimination is manifested in inequitable treatment in segregated and unequal schools and in the disproportionate risk of receiving inadequate and inappropriate special education services as a result of systemic problems in general education" (p. 14).

Inequity in education and opportunity for students labeled with disabilities becomes starkly visible in high school graduation rates. Almost 30 percent of students served by IDEA do not graduate with a regular diploma. Just over 17 percent of students with disabilities drop out of high school (USDOE, 2020a)—a rate more than three times the national average of 5.3 percent (NCES, 2020). The statistics are even bleaker for Black or African American students with disabilities. Black or African American students with disabilities are more likely to drop out and less likely to graduate with a regular diploma than *all* other students with disabilities (USDOE, 2020b). When disaggregated by specific disability category, students with emotional disturbance (ED), a category often determined by teacher-led referral and data, experience dropout rates near 30 percent, higher than any other IDEA category (USDOE, 2020a). As mentioned earlier, Black or African American students and Native American students are 1 to 2 times more likely to be labeled with ED than their white peers (USDOE, 2020a). With each intersectional identity, the probability of graduation for a Black or Brown student with a disability diminishes.

Part II: Efforts to Reduce Disproportionality in Special Education

Efforts to reduce disproportionality in special education have included (a) systemic reform initiatives initiated through legislation and (b) enhancements to teacher education programs. To address disproportionality directly, politicians, advocates, and other educators have successfully lobbied for the revision and strengthening of federal legislation. Legislative reform has brought about enhanced identification policies and procedures, such as the MTSS framework which provides proactive and early intervention in academics and behavior for students with high-intensity needs. Additionally, legislation has led to reform in teacher preparation to ensure educators at all levels are entering the field more

complexity of needs of their children. The nation's educational systems' responses to Covid-19 impacted students and their families in a variety of ways (Chatterjee, 2020; Rundle et al., 2020).

Recent evidence demonstrates that the Covid-19 virus disproportionately impacted CLEEAR diverse communities compared to white communities (Laurencin & McClinton, 2020). During the early onset of the pandemic, educational disparities were exacerbated along racial, ethnic, and socioeconomic status lines due to lack of access to learning resources essential to online and remote learning, such as reliable high-speed internet connection and digital devices (Rauf, 2020). High bandwidth use greatly affected the efficiency of technological devices (Herold & Kurtz, 2020), and difficulties adjusting to remote learning were compounded by adults' unfamiliarity with course content and role overload for parents juggling occupational demands and remote learning demands for their students (Gallagher & Egger, 2020). Despite the concerted efforts made by districts to improve access through district-internet service provider partnerships, limited access continued to disproportionately impact various communities. Ultimately, the federal government has the onus and responsibility to close the digital divide (Herold & Kurtz, 2020). Disparities were not limited to digital device and internet access, but extended to access to dedicated teachers who engaged in providing continued learning experiences (Dorn et al., 2020). In a survey conducted by the EdWeek Research Center, data exposed that the percentage of teachers in under-resourced schools delivering instruction during the pandemic was 22 points lower than the number of teachers delivering instruction in high-income schools (Herold & Kurtz, 2020).

It is predicted that learning loss will be the greatest for CLEEAR diverse communities, specifically Black, Hispanic, and low-income students (Dorn et al., 2020). These learning losses have the potential to be misconstrued as disabilities rather than the result of interrupted learning, which could lead to inappropriate referrals to special education and further the impact of disproportionality. Educational interruptions from Covid-19 also have the potential to increase dropout rates, further widening the opportunity gap by an estimated 15 percent to 20 percent (Dorn et al., 2020). Additionally, Masonbrink and Hurley (2020) caution that extended school closures have the potential to lead to lower test scores, reduced educational attainment, and eventually, decreased earning potential.

Educator-Based Reforms: Enacting Change in Teacher Preparation Programs

In addition to legislative and policy-based efforts, researchers and policy-makers have also turned their attention to educator-based reforms to reduce the overrepresentation and identification of CLEEAR diverse students in special education. Educator-based reforms have implications for teacher preparation programs that are responsible for ensuring teachers leave with the knowledge, skills, and dispositions to work with increasingly diverse students. To address disproportionality, teacher preparation programs have (a) infused competencies related to culturally responsive teaching practices and (b) equipped teachers with practical knowledge and skills related to universal design for learning (UDL).

Culturally Responsive Teaching Practices

School demographics continue to shift, reflecting a multicultural and multidimensional nation. Between 2000 and 2017, the number of white students in public schools decreased from 61 percent to 48 percent and the number of Hispanic/Latino students increased from 16 percent to 27 percent (NCES, 2020a) illustrating these shifting demographics. By contrast, the demographics of the 3.5 million public school teachers nationwide have remained static with 79 percent being white (NCES, 2020b). Data related to the demographics of educators at all levels (e.g., principals, counselors, school psychologists) reflect similar trends in racial composition, highlighting the critical need for educators who are better prepared to engage in the complex and nuanced process of educating CLEEAR diverse students and communities (Kieran & Anderson, 2018).

Students enter schools with varied background knowledge and assorted experiences which affect learning and, ultimately, achievement outcomes. In an effort to mitigate the impact of the disconnect between student and educator demographics, educators must know how to leverage students' cultures, prior experiences, and learning preferences to promote a safe, respectful, and responsive learning environment that leads to improved student outcomes (Gay, 2002; Ladson-Billings, 1994[a]; Ladson-Billings, 1994 [b]; Ladson-Billings, 1994 [c]; Ladson-Billings, 1995; Ladson-Billings & Tate, 1995). Culturally responsive teaching (CRT) potentially provides a meaningful approach to educating students from diverse backgrounds (Gunn et al., 2020; Lewis et al, 2017; Siwatu, 2007) and a method for reducing inappropriate referrals for special education. CRT uses "the cultural knowledge, prior experiences, frames of reference, and performance styles of ethnically diverse students to make learning encounters more relevant to and effective for them" (Gay, 2010, p. 31). CRT acknowledges that academic standards must be contextualized within the lived experiences of students (Gay, 2002). Through CRT, educators engage students and empower them to feel connected to their learning environment and to the content (Abacioglu et al., 2019). Such engagement could lead to improved student outcomes (Abaciouglu et al., 2019; Gay, 2002; Gay, 2010) and reduced special education placement. Culturally responsive educators not only consider the unique needs and beliefs of their students, they examine their own beliefs and explore personal bias (Bennett, 2012).

Weaknesses in CRT in Addressing Disproportionality

However, for disproportionality to be impacted by CRT, educators require explicit preparation in culturally relevant pedagogy (CRP) to implement CRT practices that are both inclusive and meet the varied needs of an increasingly diverse population of students (Barnes, 2006; Frye et al., 2010; Gay, 2002; Siwatu, 2011). Educator preparation programs must provide sustained skill development across multiple courses with embedded opportunities to practice acquired knowledge in authentic settings. CRT practices should be infused throughout course syllabi, course content, and resources (Siwatu, 2007) rather than being offered as a one-time stand-alone course. CRT requires educators to develop their ability to: (a) include ethnic, racial, and cultural diversity in classroom curricula; (b) develop knowledge and cultivate value related to cultural diversity, (c) foster a safe classroom culture built on relationships and trust, (d) increase communication responsive to cultural needs of diverse students, (e) deliver instruction that recognizes students' unique learning needs, and (f) hold all students to high expectations (Gay, 2002). If teacher preparation programs do not establish a prioritized and pervasive presence for CRT, it often becomes a footnote or an add-on that has little sustained impact on the teacher practices and systemic patterns that create disproportionality for CLEEAR diverse students with disabilities.

Also fundamental to CRT is the personal commitment of the educator. Educators must acknowledge their own cultural identity and examine and reflect on their own beliefs, student interactions, and instructional practices (Shealey et al., 2011). Shealey and colleagues (2011) stressed the importance of CRT in reducing disproportionality, but also recognized barriers to CRT effectiveness, including negative educator attitudes, failure to understand the intersectionality of race and disability, and inability or unwillingness to reflect on their own beliefs related to ethnicity and diversity. Ladson-Billings (2004) argued educators often fall short of engaging in meaningful reflection. Without such reflection, educators limit their understanding of CRT and often reduce cultural responsiveness to celebrating holidays or eating ethnic foods in disconnected or stereotypical ways (Civitillo et al., 2019). Such activities fail to promote equity or recognize the value inherent in the student's culture.

Differentiation and Practices Grounded
in Universal Design for Learning

Traditional instructional delivery of curriculum content treats all students as a homogenous group, a narrow approach which does not account for the variability of learning needs found in a diverse classroom (Crevecoeur, 2016). Standardized instructional techniques fail to engage students and do not address the variability of learning needs in a diverse classroom. Declining to address diversity in learning results in educators who confuse variability for disability (Gay, 2002; Kieran & Anderson, 2018). Providing equitable access to the general education curriculum requires differentiated instruction that is responsive to the needs of students. Universal design for learning (UDL) has been offered by researchers as a foundation to proactively remove barriers to learning, differentiate instruction, and meet the needs of a wide range of learners through diversified instructional strategies and materials (Basham et al., 2010; Pisha & Coyne, 2001). Federal legislation (Higher Education Opportunity Act of 2008) has recognized UDL as a "scientifically valid framework for guiding educational practice" that "maintains high achievement expectations for all students, including students with disabilities" (USDOE, 2010).

Developed by Meyer and Rose (1998), UDL is a proactive instructional approach that includes three guiding principles: (a) multiple means of engagement, (b) multiple means of representation, and (c) multiple means of action and expression (CAST.org, 2020). The first guiding principle, *multiple means of engagement*, emphasizes how teachers should use a variety of ways to engage learners. Multiple means of engagement accounts for variability in the way learners engage with content and in what motivates their learning (Hall et al., 2015; Rose & Meyer, 2006). The second guiding principle, *multiple means of representation*, pushes teachers to use a variety of methods and mediums to present content. Providing multiple means of representation reduces student frustration because if they did not understand the information in one modality, they will have the opportunity to understand it in another (Johnson-Harris & Mundschenk, 2014). The third guiding principle, *multiple means of action and expression*, provides students with options for responding to and expressing what they have learned in ways that are meaningful to them. Students are able to maximize their strengths and take ownership over their learning when they are provided with options for how to demonstrate their knowledge.

Designing and delivering instruction within the UDL framework addresses disproportionality by removing barriers to learning often experienced by CLEEAR diverse students. The UDL framework allows teachers to proactively provide all students with equal opportunities to learn by valuing the diversity all learners bring to the educational experience (James, 2018). UDL allows educators to consider the curricula, assessments, and instructional practices in ways that are responsive to students with diverse cultural and linguistic needs (Crevecoeur, 2016). Similar to CRT practices, UDL makes learning relevant and is responsive to the learners' experiences and background knowledge. Much like culturally responsive educators, educators who adhere to UDL principles place value on instructional approaches that foster student engagement and learning (Kieran & Anderson, 2018).

Falling Short: How UDL Fails to Address Disproportionality

The principles of UDL provide a potential pathway to equity and access to the curriculum. Despite the promising emerging research on the effects of UDL on disproportionality, barriers limit its implementation. Teachers are typically responsible for 20 or more students at any given time. Designing individualized instruction that meets the needs of such a large pool of students can be a daunting task (Lindner et al., 2019). This challenge is especially difficult when districts require teachers to follow curriculum maps that limit the time they can spend on teaching specific skills or units. The need to personalize instruction for multiple learners can be further complicated by limited resources available to teachers for facilitating instructional strategies (Stavrou & Koutselini, 2016). Additionally, some accountability measures require teachers to be evaluated on their ability to improve student outcomes for all learners, while standards are becoming increasingly demanding and rigorous (Brimijoin, 2005).

Part III: Dismantling Disproportionality Through Antiracism: A Pathway Forward

> To love all children, we must struggle together to create the schools we are taught to believe are impossible: Schools built on justice, joy, love, and anti-racism.—Love, 2019

The history of disproportionality in special education and the largely unsuccessful attempts to resolve the issue over the years suggest there is something fundamental left unaddressed in previous measures. The authors posit that because legislation like IDEA and ESSA and frameworks such as MTSS and CRT do not explicitly name and set out how to address implicit bias and its root of racism, these systems have failed to effect real change. Therefore, intentional, proactive, and systemic antiracist education practices must be employed at all levels to effectively dismantle disproportionality in special education (Welton et al., 2018). Antiracist teaching, like antiracism as a whole, is a positive, multifaceted approach that requires actively promoting racial equity by identifying and eliminating racism in systems, policies, practices, and procedures (Kendi, 2019). It is imperative to move our schools and our culture from a "non-racist" stance to antiracist practice. As discussed by King and Chandler (2016), non-racist curriculum and pedagogy reduce racism to a microanalysis of the individual and to overt, immoral, and prejudiced behaviors, while antiracism explains how racism is manifested in various spaces, makes the social construct of race visible, and is an active rejection of the institutional and structural aspects of race and racism. This essay proposes antiracism as the key approach to reducing disproportionality in special education, especially in light of the disproportionate impact of Covid-19.

A Path Forward in Addressing Disproportionality During and After Covid-19

Covid-19 demanded innovation to support CLEEAR diverse students. Understanding Covid-response efforts can benefit special educators, but it is also important to use such acute intervention as innovative starting points for long-term investments. One example of sustainable intervention comes from NASP. The organization has made efforts to deconstruct inequitable and discriminatory realities in relation to diverse students regarding special education referral, evaluation, and determination (NASP, 2020b). Specifically, efforts have been made to create resources for remote instruction, strengthening parenting practices, and free virtual professional development series (NASP, 2020b). Additionally, researchers have called for mitigating Covid-19 evaluation halts and increased training for remote administration of the *Wechsler Intelligence Scale for Children*, Fifth Edition (Wright, 2020). Improving avenues for antiracist teaching and disproportionality prevention has far-reaching implications for fostering healthy social emotional faculties among students and families.

During a recent professional presentation, education expert Larry Walker emphasized to school leaders, "We need more Covid trained practitioners" (Walker, 2020, n.p.). More specifically, Walker stated that Covid-conscious leaders need to consider inclusive education equity systems, antiracist teaching practices, and adaptive family and guardian

When school leaders at every level commit to the cause and necessity of equitable multicultural school ecologies (Annamma & Morrison, 2018), CLEEAR diverse students are understood and valued, teachers are culturally competent, and minoritized students are less likely to be mislabeled for special education. By increasing the knowledge and value for nondominant cultures, those responsible for evaluating students for disabilities are able to better distinguish between incidences of cultural difference and academic need (Johnson et al., 2017). Understanding of and respect for cultural diversity can help protect against biased determination of disability and unnecessary placement outside of the general education classroom for CLEEAR diverse students (Rowe & Francis, 2020).

Privilege and Prioritize CLEEAR Diverse Student Voice and Representation

It is not enough to provide access to or acknowledge the presence of CLEEAR diverse students and communities that systems have marginalized within education. Antiracist educational leaders prioritize the access, participation, and sustained feedback of individuals and groups from multiple perspectives, especially those who are often silenced (Kozleski & Smith, 2009). Educational leaders committed to antiracism ensure CLEEAR diverse students are visible and celebrated within all school settings to demonstrate value, respect, and representation (Fritzgerald, 2020). Students, families, teachers, administrators, and community members from backgrounds of color are engaged in policy-making, decision-making, and critical reviews to disrupt inequitable business as usual (Artiles & Kozleski, 2007, 2016; Penuel, 2019). Highlighting and following the lead of CLEEAR diverse professionals, students, and families ensures antiracist policies and changes are made with input from all stakeholders and increases the effectiveness and sustainability of these changes in schools (Barajas-López & Ishimaru, 2020; Kozleski et al., 2020).

Including people from communities of color in educational decision-making, especially as it relates to special education, creates a safeguard against disproportionality for CLEEAR diverse students. To advance antiracist efforts in education, people from CLEEAR diverse backgrounds should be actively recruited to pursue careers as teachers, administrators, school psychologists, and special education professionals to promote equitable representation and contribution (Welton et al., 2018) throughout the special education process and programs. Affirming a school culture of representation and respect for CLEEAR diverse individuals at all levels of the education system ensures multiple perspectives, experiences, and knowledge underpin a system of appropriate identification, evaluation, and placement of CLEEAR diverse students within special education (Cioè-Peña, 2020, Rowe & Francis, 2020).

Ensure Equitable Opportunity for All Students

To address disproportionality, the long-held belief in the "achievement gap" for CLEEAR diverse students must be replaced with an understanding of how the education system creates *opportunity* gaps for this student population. The narrative must move away from placing the inherent deficit within students (Venzant & Chambers, 2009) and towards a perspective which acknowledges the deficit lies within the system itself—a deficit that dis-serves CLEEAR diverse students and families (Boykin & Noguera, 2011; Ladson-Billings, 2006; Venzant & Chambers, 2009). At the root of equitable opportunity is the clear connection between teacher expectancy and student achievement, especially for CLEEAR diverse students (Andrews & Gutwein, 2017; Atwater, 2008; Liou et al., 2016). Teachers categorize students' intellectual potential based on social identities and communicate, both indirectly and overtly, varied expectations for students (Liou et al., 2016). If teachers expect less of particular students, opportunities for academic exploration, enrichment, and enhancement are less likely to be offered to those students (Shifrer et al., 2013). As Darling-Hammond (2017) pointed out, "thinking curriculums" focused on 21st century learning and skills are typically reserved for those students on advanced tracks. These tracks rarely serve students of color. As discussed earlier, the underrepresentation of CLEEAR diverse students within gifted and talented programs is just one such example (Ford et al., 2014; Morgan, 2019). Similarly, when students perceive low expectations from their teachers, through language or actions, their self-esteem and self-efficacy decline and their achievement follows suit (Gregory & Korth, 2016; Marsh & Noguera, 2018). Antiracist educational leaders ensure that high expectations are established for CLEEAR diverse students and that they are given the same challenges and opportunities to succeed and exceed. School environments that are committed to antiracism recognize and honor CLEEAR diverse students at the same rates, in the same ways, and for the same variety of reasons as white students (Fritzgerald, 2020).

Working towards equitable opportunity in schools ensures CLEEAR diverse students encounter rich, dynamic educational experiences that enhance their potential for academic growth. By providing *all* students with diverse and innovative ways to learn and perform that are developed from multiple perspectives, CLEEAR diverse students will have the opportunity to achieve more (Fritzgerald, 2020). Raising expectations, promoting equity in opportunity, and providing multiple means of achievement can create educational environments that truly support the growth and diversity of all learners (Fritzgerald, 2020). This will result in fewer inappropriate special education referrals, labels, and placements.

Evaluate Disciplinary Practices

A widespread, long-standing problem of overrepresentation of CLEEAR diverse students in disciplinary practices exists (Losen, 2018; Nowicki, 2018) and leads to inappropriate referral for special education services, especially within the category of ED (Sullivan, 2017). Higher suspension and expulsion rates for CLEEAR diverse students (Whitford et al., 2016) is particularly concerning, given the long-lasting impacts of exclusionary discipline on student placement in special education, achievement, academic tracking, social relationships, and career outcomes (DeMatthews et al., 2020; Losen, 2018). When CLEEAR diverse students with disabilities are inappropriately withdrawn from class, their rights to a free appropriate public education (FAPE) are impacted.

To address this issue, antiracist educational leaders must shift towards a culture of responsiveness and restorative justice. The OSEP National Technical Assistance Center for Positive Behavioral Intervention Systems Disproportionality Workgroup recommends seven key features to include in school discipline policy to address disproportionality: (a) specific commitment to equity, (b) family partnerships in policy development, (c) focus on implementing positive, proactive behavior support practices, (d) clear, objective discipline procedures, (e) removal or reduction of exclusionary practices, (f) graduated discipline systems with instructional alternatives to exclusion, and (g) procedures with accountability for equitable student outcomes (Green et al., 2015). These features must take on an antiracist and social justice approach by removing zero-tolerance policies and implementing restorative justice-based and similarly grounded practices (Welton et al., 2018). It is also critical for teacher preparation programs to incorporate courses and experiences in restorative justice practices and equity safeguards into teacher education (Mills & Ballantyne, 2016). The vast majority of teachers in U.S. schools are white, making it imperative for pre-service teachers to be taught to be reflective on how they perceive disciplinary approaches for CLEEAR diverse students and the practices in K–12 schools that lead to stigmatization and disproportionality in discipline for these students (Bryan, 2017). Teacher educators must engage in professional learning around restorative justice practices, think critically about the role bias may play in common contemporary disciplinary and classroom management practice, and extend this learning into what is taught to pre-service teachers in preparation programs (Souto-Manning & Stillman, 2020). By incorporating restorative justice-based disciplinary programs, infusing restorative justice concepts throughout school culture, and ensuring reflection and accountability of practice for educators, educational leaders reduce disproportionality and its detrimental consequences for CLEEAR diverse students with disabilities. It is essential for antiracist teachers, teacher educators, and educational leaders to consider bias and continuously and critically analyze disciplinary systems and practices which result in documentation, referral, evaluation, and placement in special education (Green et al., 2019; Gregory et al., 2017; Welton et al., 2018).

Promote Education for Social Justice

It is essential to ensure all students are seen in the full expansiveness of their human dignity and valued for all of their social identities throughout their educational experiences. An education that realizes this aspiration for an individual student ensures that the student receives equitable content, experience, and opportunity given their unique intersectional social identity, the strengths and assets they bring to their education, and their educational needs. An equitable education system does that for all students. To become an equitable education system, the system must become intentionally antiracist.

As part of antiracist education practices, education should be seen as a method and means for advancing social justice. Teachers and other educational leaders committed to antiracist education should view providing equitable education as an act of social justice, and simultaneously teach and model concepts of social justice to the students they educate (Darling-Hammond, 2017). Principles of multicultural education and social justice education can be combined in the classroom to reinforce and enhance one another in a way that teaches multiculturalism and social justice while modeling it (Cho, 2017).

Educational leaders are key in creating school ecologies which embody social justice principles and practices to transform education for CLEEAR diverse students (Annamma & Morrison, 2018; Darling-Hammond et al., 2016). Antiracist educators recognize their role as social justice activists and seek to instill these same values and practices within their students and school community (Welton et al., 2018). They model advocacy, self-advocacy, and the protection of rights for all students, especially those who are CLEEAR diverse. Similarly, it is crucial for teacher educators to instill the perspective of teaching as social justice

multiple case study. *Teaching and Teacher Education, 77,* 341–351. https://doi. org/10.1016/j.tate.2018.11.002.

Codrington, J., & Fairchild, H.H. (2012). Special education and the mis-education of African American children: A call to action. *The Association of Black Psychologists.* http://www.abpsi.org/pdf/SpecialEdPositionPaper021312.pdf.

Collins, K.M., Connor, D., Ferri, B., Gallagher, D., & Samson, J.F. (2016). Dangerous assumptions and unspoken limitations: A disability studies in education response to Morgan, Farkas, Hillemeier, Mattison, Maczuga, Li, and Cook (2015). *Multiple Voices for Ethnically Diverse Exceptional Learners, 16*(1), 4–16. https://doi.org/10.5555/2158-396X.16.1.4.

Cooc, N. (2018) Examining the underrepresentation of Asian Americans in special education: New trends from California school districts. *Exceptionality, 26*(1), 1–19, DOI: 10.1080/09362835.2016.1216847.

Cooc, N. (2019). Disparities in the enrollment and timing of special education for Asian American and Pacific Islander students. *The Journal of Special Education, 53*(3), 177–190. https://doi.org/10.1177/0022466919839029.

Cook, B.G., & Cook, S.C. (2013). Unraveling evidence-based practices in special education. *The Journal of Special Education, 47*(2), 71–82.

Council of Parent Attorneys and Advocates Inc. v. Elizabeth (Betsy) DeVos, Secretary of Education; Johnny W. Collet, Assistant Secretary for Special Education and Rehabilitative Services; U.S. Department of Education, Civil Action No. 18-cv-1636 (TSC), U.S. District Court for the District of Columbia (March 8, 2019). https://ecf.dcd.uscourts.gov/cgi-bin/show_public_doc?2018cv1636-31.

Crevecoeur, Y.C. (2016). Using the universal design for learning framework as a mitigating factor to reduce disproportionality in special education. In B. Ogunkola & S. Blackman (Eds.), *Transforming learning: International perspectives* (pp. 130–156). Cambridge.

Darling-Hammond, L. (2011). Testing, No Child Left Behind, and educational equity. In L.M. Stulberg & S.L. Weinberg (Eds.), *Diversity in American Higher Education: Toward a More Comprehensive Approach* (pp. 36–47). Routledge.

Darling-Hammond, L. (2017). Teaching for social justice: Resources, relationships, and anti-racist practice. *Multicultural Perspectives, 19*(3), 133–138.

Darling-Hammond, L., Ramos-Beban, N., Altamirano, R.P., & Hyler, M.E. (2016). *Be the change: Reinventing school for student success.* Teachers College Press. https://doi.org/10.1080/15210960.2017.1335039.

de Brey, C., Musu, L., McFarland, J., Wilkinson-Flicker, S., Diliberti, M., Zhang, A., Branstetter, C., & Wang, X. (2019). *Status and Trends in the Education of Racial and Ethnic Groups 2018.* NCES 2019-038. National Center for Education Statistics. https://nces.ed.gov/pubsearch/pubsinfo.asp?pubid=2019038.

Dee, T.S., & Penner, E.K. (2017). The causal effects of cultural relevance: Evidence from an ethnic studies curriculum. *American Educational Research Journal, 54*(1), 127–166. https://doi.org/10.3102/0002831216677002.

DeMatthews, D. (2015). Making sense of social justice leadership: A case study of a principal's experiences to create a more inclusive school. *Leadership and Policy in Schools, 14*(2), 139–166.

Dorn, E., Hancock, B., and Sarakatsannis, J. (2020). COVID-19 and student learning in the United States: The hurt could last a lifetime. *McKinsey & Company, 3.* https://www.mckinsey.com/industries/public-sector/ourinsights/covid-19-and-student-learning-in-the-united-states-the-hurt-could-last-a-lifetime.

Dunn, L.M. (1968). Special education for the mildly retarded—Is much of it justifiable? *Exceptional children, 35*(1), 5–22. https://doi.org/10.1177/001440296803500101.

Education for All Handicapped Act of 1975. 20 U.S.C. & 1401 et. seq (1975).

Education Week. (2020, May 6). Map: Coronavirus and school closures. *Education Week.* https://www.edweek.org/ew/section/multimedia/map-coronavirus-and-school-closures.html.

Evans, A.E. (2007). School leaders and their sensemaking about race and demographic change. *Educational Administration Quarterly, 43*(2), 159–188. https://doi.org/10.1177/0013161X06294575.

Every Student Succeeds Act, 20 U.S.C. § 6301 (2015). https://www.congress.gov/bill/114th-congress/senate-bill/1177.

Fairlie, R., & Loyalka, P. (2020). Schooling and COVID-19: Lessons from recent research on EdTech. *Science of Learning, 5*(1), 1–2. https://doi.org/10.1038/s41539-020-00072-6.

Farkas, G., Morgan, P.L., Hillemeier, M.M., Mitchell, C., & Woods, A.D. (2020). District level achievement gaps explain Black and Hispanic overrepresentation in special education. *Exceptional Children, 86*(4), 374–392. https://doi.org/10.1177/0014402919893695.

Farmer, R.L., McGill, R.J., Dombrowski, S.C., McClain, M.B., Harris, B., Lockwood, A., … Benson, N.F. (2020). Tele-assessment with children and adolescents during the coronavirus (COVID-19) pandemic and beyond practice and policy implications. *Professional Psychology: Research and Practice, 51*(5), 477–487. https://doi.org/10.31234/osf.io/2py3j.

Feng, L., & Sass, T.R. (2013). What makes special-education teachers special? Teacher training and achievement of students with disabilities. *Economics of Education Review, 36*, 122–134. https://doi.org/10.1016/j.econedurev.2013.06.006.

Fenning, P., & Rose, J. (2007). Overrepresentation of African American students in exclusionary discipline the role of school policy. *Urban Education, 42*(6), 536–559.

Ferri, B.A., & Connor, D.J. (2005). Tools of exclusion: Race, disability, and (re)segregated education. *Teachers College Record, 107*(3), 453–474. http://educ625spring2011.pbworks.com/f/Tools+of+Exclusion.pdf.

Fish, R.E. (2016). The racialized construction of exceptionality: Experimental evidence of race/ethnicity effects on teachers' interventions. *Social Science Research, 62*, 317–334. https://doi.org/10.1016/j.ssresearch.2016.08.007.

Ford, D.Y., Marsh, L.T., Blakely, J., & Amos, S.O. (2014). Missing in action: African American males in gifted education. In Fred Bonner (Ed.), *Building on resilience: Models and frameworks of Black male success across the P-20 pipeline* (pp. 62–74). Stylus Publishing, LLC. https://doi.org/10.1353/csd.2014.0085.

Ford, D.Y., & Russo, C.J. (2016). Historical and legal overview of special education overrepresentation: Access and equity denied. *Multiple Voices for Ethnically Diverse Exceptional Learners, 16*(1), 50–57. https://doi.org/10.5555/2158-396X.16.1.50.

Fritzgerald, A. (2020). *Antiracism and universal design for learning: Building expressways to success.* CAST Professional Publishing.

Frye, B., Button, L., Kelly, C., & Button, G. (2010). Preservice teachers' self-perceptions and attitudes toward culturally responsive teaching. *Journal of Praxis in Multicultural Education, 5*(1), 5. https://doi.org/10.9741/2161-2978.102.

Fuchs, L.S., & Fuchs, D. (2007). A model for implementing responsiveness to intervention. *Teaching Exceptional Children, 39*(5), 14–20. https://doi.org/10.1177/004005990703900503.

Fuchs, L.S., & Vaughn, S. (2012). Responsiveness-to-intervention: A decade later. *Journal of Learning Disabilities, 45*(3), 195–203. https://doi.org/10.1177/0022219412442150.

Furrer, C., & Skinner, E. (2003). Sense of relatedness as a factor in children's academic engagement and performance. *Journal of Educational Psychology, 95*(1), 148–162. https://doi.org/10.1037/0022-0663.95.1.148.

Fusarelli, L.D. (2004). The potential impact of the No Child Left Behind Act on equity and diversity in American education. *Educational Policy, 18*(1), 71–94.

Gable, R.A. & Hendrickson, J.M. (2004). Teaching all the students: A mandate for educators. In J.S. Choate (Ed.), *Successful inclusive teaching: Proven ways to detect and correct special needs* (4th Ed.) (pp. 2–17). Pearson.

Gallagher, R., & Egger, H.L. (2020). *School's out: A parents' guide for meeting the challenge during the COVID-19 pandemic.* NYU Langone Health. https://nyulangone.org/news/schools-out-parents-guide-meeting-challenge-during-covid-19-pandemic.

Gay, G. (2002). Preparing for culturally responsive teaching. *Journal of Teacher Education, 53*(2), 106–116. https://doi.org/10.1177/0022487102053002003.

Gay, G. (2010). *Culturally responsive teaching: Theory, research, and practice* (2nd ed). Teachers College Press.

Goings, R.B., & Ford, D.Y. (2018). Investigating the intersection of poverty and race in gifted education journals: A 15-year analysis. *Gifted Child Quarterly, 62*(1), 25–36. https://doi.org/10.1177/0016986217737618.

Graves, S., & Mitchell, A. (2011). Is the moratorium over? African American psychology professionals' views on intelligence testing in response to changes to federal policy. *Journal of Black Psychology, 37*(4), 407–425. https://doi.org/10.1177/0095798410394177.

Graves, S.L., & Nichols, K.D. (2016). Learning Disabilities. In A.M. Breland-Noble, C.S. Al-Mateen, & N.N. Singh (Eds.), *Handbook of mental health in African American youth* (pp. 261–270). Springer.

Green, A.L., Cohen, D.R., & Stormont, M. (2019). Addressing and preventing disproportionality in exclusionary discipline practices for students of color with disabilities. *Intervention in School and Clinic, 54*(4), 241–245. https://doi.org/10.1177/1053451218782437.

Green, A., Nese, R.N.T., McIntosh, K., Nishioka, V., Eliason, B., & Canizal Delabra, A. (2015). *Key elements of policies to address discipline disproportionality: A guide for district and school teams.* Center on Positive Behavioral Interventions and Support, University of Oregon. www.pbis.org.

Gregory, A., & Korth, J. (2016). Teacher-student relationships and behavioral engagement in the classroom. In K.R. Wentzel, & G.B. Ramani (Eds.), *Handbook of social influences in school contexts: Social-emotional, motivation, and cognitive outcomes* (pp. 178–191). Routledge.

Gregory, A., Skiba, R.J., & Mediratta, K. (2017). Eliminating disparities in school discipline: A framework for intervention. *Review of Research in Education, 41*(1), 253–278. https://doi.org/10.3102/0091732X17690499.

Guisbond, L., & Neill, M. (2004). Failing our children: No Child Left Behind undermines quality and equity in education. *The Clearing House: A Journal of Educational Strategies, Issues and Ideas, 78*(1), 12–16.

Gunn, A.A., Bennett, S.V., Alley, K.M., Barrera IV, E.S., Cantrell, S.C., Moore, L., & Welsh, J.L. (2020). Revisiting culturally responsive teaching practices for early childhood preservice teachers. *Journal of Early Childhood Teacher Education*, 1–16. https://doi.org/10.1080/10901027.2020.1735586.

Haager, D. (2007). Promises and cautions regarding using response to intervention with English language learners. *Learning Disability Quarterly, 30*, 213–218. https://doi.org/10.2307/30035565.

Hall, T.E., Cohen, N., Vue, G., & Ganley, P. (2015). Addressing learning disabilities with UDL and technology: Strategic reader. *Learning Disability Quarterly, 38*(2), 72–83.

Harris, D.M. (2012). Postscript: Urban schools, accountability, and equity: Insights regarding NCLB and reform. *Education and Urban Society, 44*(2), 203–210. https://doi.org/10.1177/0731948714544375.

Harry, B., & Klingner, J.K. (2006). The special education referral and decision-making process for English language learners: Child study team meetings and staffings. *Teachers College Record, 108*, 2247–2281. https://nepc.colorado.edu/publication/special-education-referral-and-decision-making-process-english-language-learners-child-s.

Hartlep, N.D., & Ellis, A.L. (2012). Just what is response to intervention and what's it doing in a nice field like education? A critical race theory examination of response to intervention. *Counterpoints, 425*, 87–108. https://www.jstor.org/stable/42981792.

Hattie, J. (2012). *Visible learning for teachers: Maximizing impact on learning.* Routledge.

Heller, K.A. (1982). *Placing children in special education: Equity through valid educational practices. Final report.* National Academy Press.

Herold, B., & Kurtz, H.Y. (2020, May 11). Teachers work an hour less per day during COVID-19: 8 key EdWeek survey findings. *Education Week.* https://www.edweek.org/ew/articles/2020/05/11/teachers-work-an-hour-less-per-day.html.

Hunter, R.C., & Bartee, R. (2003). The achievement gap: Issues of competition, class, and race. *Education and Urban Society, 35*(2), 151–160.

Hursh, D. (2007). Exacerbating inequality: The failed promise of the No Child Left Behind Act. *Race Ethnicity and Education, 10*(3), 295–308.

Individuals with Disabilities Education Act (IDEA). (2004). 20 U.S.C.§1401(34).

Izvorski, I., Mahajan, S., Moorty, L. and Vincelette, G. (2020, April 20). *A policy framework for mitigating the economic impact of COVID-19.* Brookings. https://www.brookings. edu/blog/future-development/2020/04/20/a-policy-framework-for-mitigating-the-economic-impact-of-covid-19/.

James, K. (2018). Universal design for learning (UDL) as a structure for culturally responsive practice. *Northwest Journal of Teacher Education, 13*(1), 4. https://doi.org/10.15760/nwjte.2018.13.1.4.

Johnson, J.L., Bahr, M.W., & Navarro, V.L. (2017). School psychology and cultural competence: Room to grow? *Educational Policy, 33*(7), 951–976. https://doi.org/10.1177/0895904817741542.

Johnson-Harris, K.M., & Mundschenk, N.A. (2014). Working effectively with students with EBD in a general education classroom: The case for universal design for learning. *The Clearing House: A Journal of Educational Strategies, Issues and Ideas, 87*(4), 168–174. https://doi.org/10.1080/00098655.2014.897927.

Kauffman, J.M., & Anastasiou, D. (2018). Nomear e manter: Dois requisitos básicos para uma educação especial viável e vibrante [Naming and maintaining: Two basic requirements for viable and vibrant special education]. *Educação Inclusiva & Necessidades Educacionais Especiais [Inclusive education and special needs],* 35À54.

Kauffman, J.M., & Anastasiou, D. (2019). On cultural politics in special education: Is much of it justifiable? *Journal of Disability Policy Studies, 30*(2), 78–90.

Kendi, I.X. (2019). *How to be an antiracist.* One World.

Khalifa, M.A. (2018). *Culturally responsive school leadership.* Harvard Education Press.

Kieran, L., & Anderson, C. (2018). Connecting universal design for learning with culturally responsive teaching. *Education and Urban Society, 51*(9), 1202–1216. https://doi.org/10.1177/0013124518785012.

Kim, J.S., & Sunderman, G.L. (2005). Measuring academic proficiency under the No Child Left Behind Act: Implications for educational equity. *Educational Researcher, 34*(8), 3–13.

King, L.J., & Chandler, P.T. (2016). From non-racism to anti-racism in social studies teacher education: Social studies and racial pedagogical content knowledge. In A.R. Crowe & A. Cuenca (Eds.), *Rethinking social studies teacher education in the twenty-first century* (pp. 3–21). Springer. https://doi.org/10.1007/978-3-319-22939-3_1.

Knotek, S. (2003). Bias in problem solving and the social process of student study teams: A qualitative investigation. *Journal of Special Education, 37,* 2–14. https://doi.org/10.1177/0022466903037001 0101.

Knox, R., Slanda, D.D., & Little, M.E. (2021). *Supporting educators in the implementation of intensive interventions in a virtual setting* [Proceedings]. Society for Information Technology and Teacher Education 32nd International Conference.

Kozleski, E.B. & Smith, A. (2009). The complexities of systems change in creating equity for students with disabilities in urban schools. *Urban Education, 44*(4), 427–451. https://doi.org/10.1177/0042085909337595.

Kozleski, E.B., Stepaniuk, I., & Proffitt, W. (2020). Leading through a critical lens: The application of DisCrit in framing, implementing and improving equity driven, educational systems for all students. *Journal of Educational Administration, 58*(5). https://doi.org/10.1108/JEA-12-2019-0220.

Kulkarni, S.S. (2020). *Racial and ethnic disproportionality in special education programs.* Oxford Research Encyclopedia of Education. https://doi.org/10.1093/acrefore/9780190264093.013.1242.

Ladson-Billings, G. (1994a). What we can learn from multicultural education research. *Educational Leadership, 51*(8), 22–26. https://eric.ed.gov/?id=EJ508261.

Ladson-Billings, G. (1994b). Who will teach our children: Preparing teachers to successfully teach African American students? In E.R. Hollins, J.E. King, & W.C. Hayman (Eds.), *Teaching diverse populations: Formulating a knowledge base* (pp. 129–142). SUNY Press.

Ladson-Billings, G. (1994c). *Dreamkeepers: Successful teachers of African American children.* Jossey-Bass. Publishers.

Ladson-Billings, G. (1995). But that's just good teaching! The case for culturally relevant pedagogy. *Theory Into Practice, 34*(3), 159–165. https://doi.org/10.1080/004058495 09543675.

Ladson-Billings, G. (2004). *Crossing over to Canaan: The journey of new teachers in diverse classrooms.* John Wiley & Sons.

Ladson-Billings, G. (2006). From the achievement gap to the education debt: Understanding achievement in U.S. schools. *Educational Researcher, 35*(7), 3–12. https://doi.org/10.3102/0013189X035007003.

Ladson-Billings, G., & Tate, W.F. (1995). Toward a critical race theory of education. *Teachers College Record, 97*(1), 47–68.

Lake, R., & Makori, A. (2020). *The digital divide among students during COVID-19: Who has access? Who doesn't?* Center on Reinventing Public Education [CRPE]. https://www.crpe.org/about-us/crpe.

Larry P. v. Riles (1979, 1984, 1986). 343 F. Supp. 1306 (N.D. Cal. 1972) (preliminary injunction). aff'd 502 F. 2d 963 (9th cir. 1974); 495 F. Supp. 926 (N.D. Cal. 1979) (decision on merits) aff'd (9th Cir. no. 80–427 Jan. 23, 1984). Order modifying judgment, G71–2270 RFP, September 25, 1986.

Laurencin, C., & McClinton, A. (2020). The COVID-19 pandemic: A call to action to identify and address racial and ethnic disparities. *Journal of Racial and Ethnic Health Disparities,7*(3), 398–402. https://doi.org/10.1007/s40615-020-00756-0.

Leonardo, Z. (2007). The war on schools: NCLB, nation creation and the educational construction of whiteness. *Race Ethnicity and Education, 10*(3), 261–278.

Lewis Chiu, C., Sayman, D., Carrero, K.M., Gibbon, T., Zolkoski, S.M., & Lusk, M.E. (2017). Developing culturally competent preservice teachers. *Multicultural Perspectives, 19*(1), 47–52. https://doi.org/10.1080/15210960.2017.1267515.

Lewis, T.J., McIntosh, K., Simonsen, B., Mitchell, B.S., & Hatton, H.L. (2017). School-wide systems of positive behavior support: Implications for students at risk and with emotional/behavioral disorders. *AERA Open, 3*(2), 2332858417711428. https://doi.org/10.1177/2332858417711428.

Lindner, K.T., Alnahdi, G.H., Wahl, S., & Schwab, S. (2019). Perceived differentiation and personalization teaching approaches in inclusive classrooms: Perspectives of students and teachers. *Frontiers in Education, 4.* https://doi.org/10.3389/feduc.2019.00058.

Liou, D.D., Marsh, T.E., & Antrop-Gonzalez, R. (2016). The spatiality of schooling: A quest for equitable classrooms and high expectations for low-income students of color. *Inter-Actions: UCLA Journal of Education and Information Studies, 12*(2). https://escholarship.org/uc/item/4mn4927d.

Losen, D.J. (2018). *Disabling punishment: The need for remedies to the disparate loss of instruction experienced by black students with disabilities.* The Center for Civil Rights Remedies. https://today.law.harvard.edu/wp-content/uploads/2018/04/disabling-punishment-report-.pdf.

Love, B. (2019, March 18). Dear white teachers: You can't love your black students if you don't know them. *Education Week, 38,* 26. https://www.edweek.org/ew/articles/2019/03/20/dear-white-teachers-you-cant-love-your.html.

Lustick, H. (2017). Making discipline relevant: Toward a theory of culturally responsive positive schoolwide discipline. *Race Ethnicity and Education, 20*(5), 681–695. https://doi.org/10.1080/13613324.2016.1150828.

Mahon-Reynolds, C., & Parker, L. (2016). The overrepresentation of students of color with learning disabilities: How "working identify" plays a role in the school-to-prison pipeline. In D.J. Connor, B.A. Ferri, & S.A. Ananamma (Eds.), *DisCrit: Disability studies and critical race theory in education* (pp. 145–156). Teachers College Press.

Marsh, L.T.S., & Noguera, P.A. (2018). Beyond stigma and stereotypes: An ethnographic study on the effects of school-imposed Labeling on black males in an urban charter school. *The Urban Review, 3,* 447. https://doi.org/10.1007/s11256-017-0441-x.

Marshall et al. v. Georgia (U.S. District Court for the S.D. of Georgia, CV482–233, June 28, 1984), aff'd (11th Cir. No. 84–8771 Oct. 29, 1985).

Masonbrink, A.R., & Hurley, E. (2020). Advocating for children during the COVID-19 school closures. *Pediatrics, 146*(3). https://doi.org/10.1542/peds.2020-1440.

Matsumura, L.C., & Wang, E. (2014). Principals' sensemaking of coaching for ambitious reading instruction in a high-stakes accountability policy environment. *Education Policy Analysis Archives, 22*(51), 1–37. https://doi.org/10.14507/epaa.v22n51.2014.

Mayfield, V. (2020). *Cultural competence now: 56 exercises to help educators understand and challenge bias, racism, and privilege.* ASCD.

McKown, C, & Weinstein, R.S. (2008). Teacher expectations, classroom context, and the achievement gap. *Journal of School Psychology, 46*, 235–261. https://doi.org/10.1016/j.jsp.2007.05.001.

Meek, S.., Gordon, L. Allen, R., McIntosh, K., Smith, C., Gilliam, W. Hemmeter. M. Dl., & Catherine, E. (2020). Equity and COVID-19: Considering equity in the transition back to school and early childhood programs: Policy recommendations for Congress. *Children's Equity Project.* https://childandfamilysuccess.asu.edu/sites/default/files/2020-09/Covid%20Equity%20Brief.pdf.

Mills, C., & Ballantyne, J. (2016). Social justice and teacher education: A systematic review of empirical work in the field. *Journal of Teacher Education, 67*(4), 263–276. https://doi.org/10.1177/0022487116660152.

Morgan, H. (2019). The lack of minority students in gifted education: Hiring more exemplary teachers of color can alleviate the problem. *The Clearing House: A Journal of Educational Strategies, Issues and Ideas, 92*(4–5), 156–162. https://doi.org/10.1080/00098655.2019.1645635.

Morgan, P.L., Farkas, G., Hillemeier, M.M., & Maczuga, S. (2017). Replicated evidence of racial and ethnic disparities in disability identification in US schools. *Educational Researcher, 46*(6), 305–322. https://doi.org/10.3102/0013189X17726282.

Morgan, P.L., Farkas, G., Hillemeier, M.M., Mattison, R., Maczuga, S., Li, H., & Cook, M. (2015). Minorities are disproportionately underrepresented in special education: Longitudinal evidence across five disability conditions. *Educational Researcher, 44*(5), 278–292. https://doi.org/10.3102/0013189x15591157.

Morgan, P.L., Woods, A.D., Wang, Y., Hillemeier, M.M., Farkas, G., & Mitchell, C. (2020). Are schools in the US south using special education to segregate students by race? *Exceptional Children, 86*(3), 255–275. https://doi.org/10.1177/0014402919868486.

Murawski, W.W., & Hughes, C.E. (2009). Response to intervention, collaboration, and co-teaching: A logical combination for successful systemic change. *Preventing School Failure, 53*(4), 267–277. https://doi.org/10.3200/PSFL.53.4.267-277.

National Association of School Psychologists. (2017). *Implicit bias: A foundation for school psychologists* [handout].

National Association of School Psychologists. (2020a). *Telehealth: Virtual service delivery updated recommendations.* NASP. https://www.nasponline.org/resources-andpublications/resources-and-podcasts/covid-19-resource-center/special-education-resources/telehealth-virtual-service-deliveryupdated-recommendations.

National Association of School Psychologists. (2020b). *Strategies for supporting teachers delivering remote instruction.* NASP. https://www.nasponline.org/resources-and-publications/resources-and-podcasts/covid-19-resource-center/webinar-series/strategies-for-supporting-teachers-delivering-remote-instruction.

National Center for Learning Disabilities, & National Association of School Psychologists. (2020). *Navigating special education evaluations for specific learning disabilities (SLD) amid the COVID-19 pandemic.* https://www.ncld.org/wp-content/uploads/2020/11/Navigating-Special-Education-Evaluations-for-Specific-Learning-Disabilities-SLD-Amid-the-COVID-19-Pandemic.pdf.

National Center of Education Statistics [NCES]. (2020a). *The condition of education 2020: Characteristics of public school teachers.* (NCES 2020144). https://nces.ed.gov/programs/coe/indicator_clr.asp.

National Center of Education Statistics [NCES]. (2020b). *The condition of education 2020: Racial/ethnic enrollment in public schools.* (NCES 2020144). https://nces.ed.gov/programs/coe/indicator_cge.asp.

National Education Association. (2020). *The digital divide and homework gap in your state: NEA's digital equity report details the digital divide in each state and provides policy recommendations to help close it.* NEA. https://www.nea.org/resource-library/digital-divide-and-homework-gap-your-state.

National Public Radio. (2020, March 17). *Poll Shows partisan differences over how seriously people are taking coronavirus.* NPR. https://www.npr.org/2020/03/17/817354092/poll-shows-partisan-differences-over-how-seriously-people-are-taking-coronavirus.

Neill, M., Guisbond, L., & Schaeffer, B. (2004). Failing our children. How No Child Left Behind undermines quality and equity in education. An accountability model that supports school improvement. *National Center for Fair & Open Testing (FairTest).*

No Child Left Behind Act of 2001, Pub. L. 107–110 (2001). http://www.ed.gov/policy/elsec/leg/esea02/107-110.pdf.

Nowicki, J.M. (2018). K–12 Education: Discipline disparities for black students, boys, and students with disabilities. Report to Congressional Requesters. GAO-18–258. *US Government Accountability Office.* https://files.eric.ed.gov/fulltext/ED590845.pdf.

Owens, A., & Sunderman, G.L. (2006). *School accountability under NCLB: Aid or obstacle for measuring racial equity?* The Civil Rights Project at Harvard University.

Penuel, W.R. (2019). Co-design as infrastructuring with attention to power: building collective capacity for equitable teaching and learning through design-based implementation research. In Pieters, J., Voogt, J. and Roblin, N.P. (Eds), *Collaborative curriculum design for sustainable innovation and teacher learning* (pp. 387–401). Springer. https://doi.org/10.1007%2F978-3-030-20062-6_21.

Pisha, B. & Coyne, P. (2001). Smart from the start: The promise of universal design for learning. *Remedial and Special Education, 22*(4), 197–203.

Posny, A. (2007, April 24). Disproportionality of racial and ethnic groups in special education. https://www2.ed.gov/policy/speced/guid/idea/memosdcltrs/osep07-09disproportionalityofracialandethnicgroupsinspecialeducation.pdf.

Prasse, D. (1980). *PASE v. Hannon. NASP Communique, 9*(3), 3.

Prasse, D.P. (2006). Legal supports for problem-solving systems. *Remedial and Special Education, 27*(1), 7–15.

Proctor, S.L., Graves S.L., Jr., & Esch, R.C. (2012). Assessing African American students for specific learning disabilities: The promises and perils of response to intervention. *The Journal of Negro Education, 81*(3), 268–282. https://doi.org/10.7709/jnegroeducation.81.3.0268.

Proctor, S.L., & Romano, M. (2016). School psychology recruitment research characteristics and implications for increasing racial and ethnic diversity. *School Psychology Quarterly, 31*(3), 311.

Pullen, P.C., & Cash, D.B. (2011). Reading. In J.M. Kauffman, & D.P. Hallahan (Eds.), *Handbook of special education* (pp. 409–421). Routledge.

Rauf, D.S. (2020, April). Coronavirus squeezes supply of Chromebooks, iPads, and other digital learning devices. *Education Week.* https://www.edweek.org/ew/articles/2020/04/01/coronavirus-squeezes-supply-of-chromebooks-ipads-and.html.

Reid, D.K., & Knight, M.G. (2006). Disability justifies exclusion of minority students: A critical history grounded in disability studies. *Educational Researcher, 35*(6), 18–23.

Rivkin, S.G., Hanushek, E.A., & Kain, J.F. (2005). Teachers, schools, and academic achievement. *Econometrica, 73*, 417–458.

Rose, D.H., & Meyer, A. (2006). *A practical reader in universal design for learning.* Harvard Education Press.

Rowe, D.A., & Francis, G.L. (2020). Reflective thinking: Considering the intersection of microcultures in IEP planning and implementation. *TEACHING Exceptional Children, 53*(1), 4–6. https://doi.org/10.1177/0040059920952007.

Rundle, A.G., Park, Y., Herbstman, J.B., Kinsey, E.W., & Wang, Y.C. (2020). COVID-19 related school closing and risk of weight gain among children. *Obesity, 28*, 1008–1009.

Sadeh, S., & Sullivan, A.L. (2017). Ethical and legal landmines: Causal inference in special education decisions. *Psychology in the Schools, 54*(9), 1134–1147.

Sharkey, P., & Elwert, F. (2011). The legacy of disadvantage: Multigenerational neighborhood effects on cognitive ability. *The American Journal of Sociology, 116*(6), 1934–1981. http://dx.doi.org/10.1086/660009.

Shealey, M.W., McHatton, P.A., & Wilson, V. (2011). Moving beyond disproportionality: The role of culturally responsive teaching in special education. *Teaching Education, 22*(4), 377–396. DOI: 10.1080/10476210.2011.591376.

Shifrer, D., Callahan, R.M., & Muller, C. (2013). Equity or marginalization? The high school course-taking of students labeled with a learning disability. *American Educational Research Journal, 50*(4), 656–682. https://doi.org/10.3102/0002831213479439.

Shifrer, D., Muller, C., & Callahan, R. (2011). Disproportionality and learning disabilities: Parsing apart race, socioeconomic status, and language. *Journal of Learning Disabilities, 44*(3), 246–257. https://doi.org/10.1177/0022219410374236.

Simmons, D. (2020, June 22). *The trauma we don't see.* ASCD Education. http://www.ascd. org/publications/educational-leadership/may20/vol77/num08/The-Trauma-We-Don't-See.aspx.

Siwatu, K.O. (2007). Preservice teachers' culturally responsive teaching self-efficacy and outcome expectancy beliefs. *Teaching and Teacher Education, 23*(7), 1086–1101.

Siwatu, K.O. (2011). Preservice teachers' culturally responsive teaching self-efficacy-forming experiences: A mixed methods study. *The Journal of Educational Research, 104*(5), 360–369.

Skiba, R.J., Poloni-Staudinger, L., Simmons, A.B., Renae Feggins-Azziz, L., & Chung, C.G. (2005). Unproven links: Can poverty explain ethnic disproportionality in special education? *The Journal of Special Education, 39*(3), 130–144.

Slanda, D. (2017). Role ambiguity: Defining the elusive role of the special education teacher who works in inclusive settings. *Electronic Theses and Dissertations.* https://stars.library.ucf.edu/etd/5563.

Slanda, D.D., & Little, M.E. (2018). Exceptional education is pecial. In G.E. Hall, L.F. Quinn, & D.M. Gollnick (Eds.), *The Wiley handbook of teaching and learning.* John Wiley & Sons.

Slanda, D.D., & Little, M.E. (2020). Enhancing teacher preparation for inclusive programming. *SRATE Journal 29*(2).

Snyder, T.D., & Dillow, S.A. (2015). *Digest of education statistics 2013* (NCES 2015–011). U.S. Department of Education. https://doi.org/10.1177/00224669050390030101.

Souto-Manning, M., & Stillman, J. (2020). In the pursuit of transformative justice in the education of teacher educators. *The New Educator, 16*(1). https://doi.org/10.1080/15476 88X.2019.1698871.

Stavrou, T.E., & Koutselini, M. (2016). Differentiation of teaching and learning: The teachers' perspective. *Universal Journal of Educational Research, 4*(11), 2581–2588.

Stoiber, K.C. (2014). A comprehensive framework for multitiered systems of support in school psychology. In P.L. Harrison & A. Thomas (Eds.), *Best practices in school psychology: Data-based and collaborative decision making* (pp. 41–70). National Association of School Psychologists.

Stoutjesdijk, R., Scholte, E.M., & Swaab, H. (2012). Special needs characteristics of children with emotional and behavioral disorders that affect inclusion in regular education. *Journal of Emotional and Behavioral Disorders, 20*(2), 92–104.

Sullivan, A.L. (2017). Wading through quicksand: Making sense of minority disproportionality in identification of emotional disturbance. *Behavioral Disorders, 43*(1), 244–252. https://doi.org/10.1177/0198742917732360.

Sullivan, A.L., Kohli, N., Farnsworth, E.M., Sadeh, S., & Jones, L. (2017). Longitudinal models of reading achievement of students with learning disabilities and without disabilities. *School Psychology Quarterly, 32*(3), 336.

Sullivan, A.L., & Osher, D. (2019). IDEA's double bind: A synthesis of disproportionality policy interpretations. *Exceptional Children, 85*(4), 395–412.

Sullivan, A.L., & Proctor, S.L. (2016). The shield or the sword? Revisiting the debate on racial disproportionality in special education and implications for school psychologists. *School Psychology Forum, 10*(3).

Sullivan, A.L., Sadeh, S., & Houri, A.K. (2019). Are school psychologists' special education NCES eligibility decisions reliable and unbiased? A multi-study experimental investigation. *Journal of School Psychology, 77*, 90–109.

Thorius, K.A. (2019). Facilitating encounters with special education's cloak of benevolence in professional learning to eliminate racial disproportionality in special education. *International Journal of Qualitative Studies in Education, 32*(3), 323–340.

Thorius, K.A., Moore, T.S., & Coomer, M.N. (2019). We can do better: Critically reframing special education research and practice at the intersections of disability and cultural and linguistic diversity for young children. *Advances in Special Education,* 157–171. doi:1 0.1108/s0270-401320190000034010.

Thorius, K.A.K., & Maxcy, B.D. (2015). Critical practice analysis of special education policy: An RTI example. *Remedial and Special Education, 36*(2), 116–124.

Tracey, C.A., Sunderman, G.L., & Orfield, G. (2005). *Changing NCLB district accountability standards: Implications for racial equity.* SPPS Bulletin.

UNESCO. (2020). *290 million students out of school due to COVID-19: UNESCO releases first global numbers and mobilizes response.* UNESCO. https://en.unesco.org/news/290-million-students-out-school-due-covid-19-unesco-releases-first-global-numbers-and-mobilizes.

U.S. Department of Education (2010). *Higher Education Opportunity* Act –2008. U.S. Department of Education.

U.S. Department of Education, Office of Special Education and Rehabilitative Services, & Office of Special Education Programs. (2017). *IDEA Part B regulations, significant disproportionality* (Equity in IDEA). 81 Fed. Reg. 92376 (Dec. 19, 2016), 34 CFR 300. https://sites.ed.gov/idea/files/significant-disproportionality-qa-03-08-17.pdf.

U.S. Department of Education (USDOE). (2020a). *41st annual report to Congress on the implementation of the Individuals with Disabilities Education Act, 2019.* USDOE. https://sites.ed.gov/idea/files/41st-arc-for-idea.pdf.

U.S. Department of Education (USDOE). (2020b). *OSEP fast facts: Black or African American children with disabilities.* USDOE. https://sites.ed.gov/idea/osep-fast-facts-black-or-african-american-children-with-disabilities-20/.

U.S. Department of Education (USDOE). (2020c). *Urging states to continue educating students with disabilities, Secretary DeVos publishes new resource on accessibility and distance learning options.* USDOE. https://www.ed.gov/news/press-releases/urging-states-continue-educating-students-disabilities-secretary-devos-publishes-new-resource-accessibility-and-distance-learning-options.

Utt, J., & Tochluk, S. (2020). White teacher, know thyself: Improving anti-racist praxis through racial identity development. *Urban Education, 55*(1), 125–152. https://doi.org/10.1177/0042085916648741.

Vaughn, S., & Fuchs, L.S. (2003). Redefining learning disabilities as inadequate response to instruction: The promise and potential problems. *Learning Disabilities Research & Practice, 18*(3), 137–146.

Venzant-Chambers, T.T. (2009). The "receivement gap": School tracking policies and the fallacy of the "achievement gap." *The Journal of Negro Education, 78*(4), 417–431.

Walker, L. (2020). *Dismantling Systems That Negatively Impact Black Student's Well Being* [Keynote]. Supporting High Needs Populations/Urban Education Special Interest Group, September 2020, University of Central Florida, Orlando, Florida.

Welton, A.D., Owens, D.R., & Zamani-Gallaher, E.M. (2018). Anti-racist change: A conceptual framework for educational institutions to take systemic action. *Teachers College Record, 120*(14).

West, J.E., & Whitby, P.J.S. (2008). Federal policy and the education of students with disabilities: Progress and the path forward. *Focus on Exceptional Children, 41*(3).

Whitford, D.K., & Carrero, K.M. (2019). Divergent discourse in disproportionality research: A response to Kauffman and Anastasiou (2019). *Journal of Disability Policy Studies, 30*(2), 91–104.

Whitford, D.K., Katsiyannis, A., & Counts, J. (2016). Discriminatory discipline: Trends and issues. *NASSP Bulletin, 100*(2), 117–135. https://doi.org/10.1177/0192636516677340.

World Health Organization (WHO). (2020). *Coronavirus disease 2019 (COVID-19) Situation Report–84.*

Wright, A.J. (2020). Equivalence of remote, digital administration and traditional, in-person administration of the Wechsler Intelligence Scale for Children, Fifth Edition (WISC-V). *Psychological Assessment, 32*(9), 809–817. doi:10.1037/pas0000939.

Yell, M.L., Katsiyannis, A., & Bradley, M.R. (2011). The Individuals with Disabilities Education Act: The evolution of special education law. In J.M. Kauffman, & D.P. Hallahan (Eds.), *Handbook of special education* (pp. 61–76). Routledge.

Yell, M.L., Rogers, D., & Rogers, E.L. (1998). The legal history of special education: What a long, strange trip it's been! *Remedial and Special Education, 19*(4), 219–228.

Re-Imagining Racial Liberation Within the Applied Theatre Classroom and Beyond

Amanda Masterpaul

I can live within my entirety.
—Student of Color

[Applied theatre] taught me to seek out opportunities to question the systems under which we live ... [and] has emphasized community care and has encouraged radical thinking; imagination of a world where we are always electing to advocate for each other.
—White Student

I am able to embrace my wholeness.
—Student of Color

Imagine

Dare to dream.

As children, we are taught to dream, to imagine with abandon, expansion, and wild curiosity. As we age and become faced with societal benchmarks, we encounter prescribed measures of success which limit and restrict our natural inclination to dream. Patriarchy, homophobia, transphobia, anti-blackness, white supremacy culture, and racial capitalism are well-positioned to suppress and diminish our capacity to dream; and, for marginalized bodies, there are higher stakes associated with the outcomes of unmet dreams. The compounded weight of systemic oppression can numb any playfulness of childhood with a fear of devastating risk and failure and resign dreaming and imagination to hopelessness. And yet, if we want to be free, we must realize dreaming as essential and foundational work. Through dreaming, we stoke the desire for a reimagined and deeply felt socio-political change. We have permission to imagine our best-case scenarios. We have a mutual ownership to dream and to co-author a future good with precious, lasting purpose.

The Applied Theatre classroom invites this vision. Through Applied Theatre, we amplify the voices of underestimated communities and ideas and work to interrupt multiple axes of oppression. It is further directed at improving the livability of communities through performance and activism that is life-affirming, generative, and sustaining. Applied Theatre practices are grounded in an antiracist, anti-oppressive, intersectional, and liberatory ethic. In order for these principles to be actualized, it must be community-informed and grounded in reciprocal wholeness and dignity.

Theatre of the Oppressed and the wider umbrella of applied theatre has a rich legacy. These practices unite people through performance, conscious dialogue, and interactive playmaking. Applied Theatre and Theatre of the Oppressed are pleasurable, thought-provoking, and humanity centered. These practices are intended to be in solidarity with impacted communities, focused on interrupting interlocking systems of oppression and replacing them with bold visions of communities embedded in personal and collective care. Theatre of the Oppressed and Applied Theatre offers an aesthetic space where reality can be re-imagined and practiced. Applied Theatre can amplify and bolster social justice movements. It supports communities to identify the root of their oppression, leading them to articulate their goals and demands, so as to achieve liberation. And much like activism, these performances require community organization, improvisation, community care, and radical imagination.

Within the Applied Theatre classroom, and similarly with social justice work, learning is experienced through dialogic, experiential, and transformative practice. For these reasons, Applied Theatre is a humanizing pedagogy which upholds political and social efficacy. In this essay, I will focus on how techniques used in the fields of Applied Theatre and Theatre of the Oppressed engage an embodied methodology for challenging and transforming the society that engenders those oppressions, encouraging minoritized students within the classroom and beyond to cultivate a brave space for mobilizing their confident, civically courageous voices.

Analyze

Examine first, dream next.

Beth E. Ritchie (2012) describes a violence matrix illustrating multitiered experiences of Black violence on an everyday basis. She states,

"Surrounding the violence matrix is the tangled web of structural disadvantages, institutionalized racism, gender domination, class exploitation, heteropatriarchy, and other forms of oppression that lock the abuse of Black women in place. Responses need to be developed that take all of the forms of abuse and all of the spheres within which injustice occurs into account" (Ritchie, 2012, p. 133). College campuses are a microcosm mirroring a national landscape saturated in the political, social, and economic demands for minoritized communities to experience justice, dignity, and equity. Higher education expects students of color to perform and advance within structurally unequal environments while simultaneously enduring the internalized and multi-layered traumas of state-sanctioned violence and civil unrest. In the wake of continued brutalization and public dehumanization of Black and brown bodies, students of color are all too familiar with a compounded pattern of disease, suffering, marginalization, discrimination, and assault as an everyday lived experience. In response to Covid-19, the U.S. witnessed intensified, politicized, racist rhetoric towards the AAPI (Asian Americans and Pacific Islander) community. Organizations such as Stop AAPI Hate reported an increase of one hundred and fifty percent in hate crimes within the past year. The horrific Atlanta shooting of eight people, six of them Asian women, in March 2021, further revealed the deep-rooted patterns of oppression embedded in racialized sexism, misogyny, and white supremacy. Similarly, the Latino/a/x communities have endured a continued and sustained assault on their lives through immigration enforcement, detention, familial separation, and incarceration. Immigration detention escalated into a humanitarian crisis when news erupted that children were being separated from their families, left unfed and uncared for at the border. The targeted attacks upon the Black community, AAPI community, and Latino/a/x communities reveal a compounded brutalization and dehumanization of racially minoritized people.

On predominantly white campuses (PWI), students of color face polarizing and seemingly unsafe conditions. Within academia, administration can be resistant in challenging racism and white supremacy culture while also reluctant to outwardly define policies or plans as antiracist. As a result, students of color may experience distrust and alienation with the university. Therefore, minoritized students simultaneously experience and examine racialized inequity on campus as a lived civics project. A Black femme student in an Applied Theatre class spoke to the emotional labor involved in having to directly confront anti-blackness on campus while simultaneously showing, presenting, and explaining blackness their peers and to their professors. As a byproduct of white supremacist education, BIPOC students feel as though their experience, knowledge, and contribution are an afterthought, rather than an educational priority. In reality, the experiential knowledge of BIPOC students is vital for understanding how racialized subordination functions within education, and furthermore, provides empirical evidence informing how academia can center race more consciously, authentically and holistically.

Popularized by higher educational institutions, Diversity, Equity, and Inclusion initiatives have arisen as an answer to effecting positive change on college campuses. Diversity-focused strategic plans offer a promise of inclusivity and cultural competency through strategically placed offices of a Diversity, Equity, and Inclusion division; all while campuses still face scrutiny for racially insensitive and racist practices and policies. Cultural inclusivity educator, Dena Samuels, suggests, "Given the reality of racial inequality, the discrepancy in the perceptions of White people and Black people regarding educational equity highlights the inability of White people to acknowledge the racial inequalities that exist in the U.S. educational system" (2014, p. 13). Diversity approaches face critique in that they embrace and emphasize differences while overlooking and neglecting structural barriers and inequities.

Pivoting from concentrating on diversity towards focusing on equity positions universities to examine the ways in which white supremacy culture operates within the institution. White supremacy culture has been historically situated, and is an institutionally perpetuated system of exploitation and oppression for the purpose of establishing, preserving, and defending wealth, power, and privilege. Academic spaces can interrogate the ways in which paternalism, perfectionism, individualism, and either/or thinking are reproduced as manifestations of white supremacy culture. Collegiate administrators and educators must recognize that challenging white supremacist education is not a uniform outcome to achieve with a checked box or with expectations of perfectionism. hooks (2003) asserts that educators are reluctant to openly address, challenge, and confront the ways in which white supremacist thinking influences and impacts every aspect of the educational experience. Talking explicitly about race within a university setting can be seen as a threat and, thus, cause social exclusion, division, and defensiveness. Sometimes these discussions become filtered—censored and gaslit—by those in power to uphold the status quo. However, ignited by George Floyd's brutal death and a continued national outcry for racial justice, antiracism garnered mainstream attention. Antiracist movements not only emphasized antiracist policy changes for Black people, but also exposed the necessity to address the harsh acceleration of Asian hate crimes incited by racist vitriol with the Coronavirus pandemic.

Antiracism relies upon self-reflection and invites disclosure, active listening, and repair. In addition, antiracism is not solely theoretical; rather, antiracism is a praxis for "one who is supporting an antiracist policy through their actions or expressing an antiracist idea" (Kendi, 2019, p. 13). When one is not explicitly and pointedly antiracist, they are producing and complicit with racist pedagogy and outcomes. Furthermore, when entering a critical conversation about antiracism with a homogeneous group, shouldn't whiteness be addressed first? There is an urgency for academia to reckon with racialized inequality and white supremacy culture as a functionality of collegiate space. Anti-blackness is at the center of racist pedagogy; therefore, educators committed to antiracism are called to seize opportunities which challenge assumptions and question how standards are enforced, contributing to patterns with significant, material impact.

As a collegiate educator of Applied Theatre, I practice radical transparency. I share with students that I identify as a white, cis-female, bisexual, intersectional feminist and the reason why I share these identities is because my most immediate and urgent work is in how I uproot systems of conditioned power within myself. How am I embodying and modeling an active process of unlearning racialized dominance and white supremacy culture? I am acutely aware of my positionality as a member of a racially dominant group and the weight my whiteness holds within higher educational spaces. Far too often, white, well-meaning, female educators inadvertently cause harm through self-prescribed good intentions; and when challenged upon their conduct, they resist self-inquiry and self-interrogation. As a white educator, I resist classifying myself as an ally, but rather as an ever-evolving project committed to anti-oppressive culture. I am someone who is bound to make missteps and to fail, and yet, my conviction remains unwavering. hooks (2003) states, "When black people/people of color fully embrace the reality that white people who choose to do so can be anti-racist to the core of their being then we can draw these folks to us. Their commitment to anti-racism does not mean they never make mistakes, that they never buy into race privilege, or that they never enact racial domination in daily life. What it does mean is that when they make a mistake they are able to face it and make needed repair" (p. 61). Acknowledgment, reflexivity, and personal admission are conditions of an antiracist politic (Kendi, 2019).

As a humanizing pedagogy, Applied Theatre supports minoritized students and instructors to nurture their ethical and social citizenship. Participation in Applied Theatre encourages social cohesion and fosters intercultural understanding while inspiring students to take control of their lives and become activated as citizens (Jeannotte, 2003). Students of dominant cultural groups can be transformed by challenging systems of oppression and by bonding with students of color in the struggle for racial justice. By empowering students of color who experience intergenerational trauma on PWI campuses, an Applied Theatre classroom becomes a place of healing and revolutionary voice-making through performance and critical practice. By integrating these principles within the classroom, everyone can embody and create a community of care based on communal contribution and significance.

Practice

Dreaming is revolutionary.

According to a 2002 study conducted by the National Endowment for the Arts, participation in the arts leads to a higher investment of civic engagement, volunteerism, and non-arts community involvement. As a result, cultural participation leads to higher degrees of community participation. Civically-conscious arts-based models, such as Applied Theatre, can increase and galvanize students' involvement in local issues and efforts.

Applied Theatre does not have a singular defining characteristic, rather, it is used as an umbrella term for theater and performance, which seeks to make an impact and difference within peoples' lives. Generally, Applied Theatre takes place within non-traditional settings and is performed by artists and non-artists alike who have a vested interest and stake with the issue being addressed by the community. The content for Applied Theatre performances is often originally assembled from the direct reflections of everyday lived experience as a means for raising consciousness and generating tactile change. Applied Theatre works to undermine socio-political norms and to "[wake] up the audience to its obligations and responsibilities through its collective imagination" (Prendergast & Saxton, 2009, p. 8). In this way, this work in the classroom—and beyond—emphasizes community building and interaction as means for critical consciousness and social justice.

As a notable representation of Applied Theatre, Theatre of the Oppressed is a theatrical and political practice targeted at promoting social transformation. Theatre of the Oppressed was developed in Brazil during the 1960s and 1970s by cultural and political activist and theater practitioner Augusto Boal. Originating in Brazilian culture, Theatre of the Oppressed epitomized a language of the oppressed, including those racially marginalized. Theatre of the Oppressed is to support political and social emancipation in service of the oppressed so as to transform the society producing those oppressions. Boal (1979) declared, "Theater in itself is not revolutionary, but it is surely a rehearsal for the revolution ... the spectator no longer delegates power to the characters to think or act in his place. The spectator frees himself; he thinks and acts for himself!"

(p. 155). Theatre of the Oppressed includes a number of techniques such as Image Theatre, Forum Theatre, Newspaper Theatre, and Legislative Theatre, to name a few. These techniques are not designed to be mastered, but rather, to be used as a guide for invention, intervention, and imagining. People's stories are presented as a catalyst for analyzing and dismantling the macro-scales of institutionalized oppression and the micro-scales of internalized oppression.

Boal began experimenting with theatrical processes by engaging with audience members as active participants within the scope of the drama. No longer a passive observer, a "spect-actor" is a non-actor who inserts themself into the play in order to re-imagine and re-construct the theatrical scenario to their purpose. Through Theatre of the Oppressed, a spect-actor becomes an engaged and participatory actor within a performance by problematizing and theatricalizing their resolutions and alternatives. A spect-actor has the opportunity to step into the role of the protagonist or a potential ally in order to exercise their visions, wishes, and desires for change through active and embodied role-playing. The spect-actor engages in the story emotionally during the initial performance, taking note of what worked and what didn't work. Once they've formed their solidified understanding of the play and its implications, they take to the stage to improvise their contribution to the script, thus re-imagining, re-creating, and re-shaping the original play.

By placing oneself within the circumstances of the play, a spect-actor can concurrently experience and extrapolate the conditions with which they desire for their lived reality. In addition, embodying the character allows one to empathize, while developing personal and mutual strategies for the benefit of those with whom they are in community. Augusto Boal (2002) proclaims, "Life is expansive, it expands inside our own body, growing and developing, and it also expands in territory, physical and psychological, discovering spaces, forms, ideas, meanings, sensations— this should be done as a dialogue: receiving from others what others have created, giving them the best of our own creation" (p. 2). The process of spect-acting allows one to learn by doing. As a story unfolds, spect-actors are challenged and welcomed into the narrative as real time editors and advocates. Applied Theatre and Theatre of the Oppressed works to invite exploration into not only the struggles of an individual, but more so, to demand examination of the communal struggle. The techniques require participants to identify power dynamics, to strategize ways towards agency, and to activate their own power and voice. By focusing on the collective struggle among spect-actors and actors, people actualize their power in the aesthetic realm to train themselves for enacting their power in everyday lived experiences.

Applied Theatre is inherently "multi": multi-cultural, multi-experiential, and multi-disciplinary. The aim is to make theater *with* community that is facing marginalization, not *for* those who are located within an oppressed, marginalized, or culturally non-dominant group. Intersectionality is a framework for processing the multi-lived, compounded experiences of minoritized people who are experiencing marginalization. Intersectionality, as coined by Kimberle Crenshaw, interrogates the intersections of gender, race, class, and other societal constructs as simultaneously experienced by marginalized communities in relationship to power by "transcend[ing] traditional single-axis horizons" (Cho, Crenshaw, & McCall, 2013, p. 785). Intersectionality establishes the lens through which one can assess power and inequity through various overlapping social categories of identification. Simplistic or singular narratives deprive people of their humanity and power. When a community is generalized, they are disempowered because they cannot exist outside of stereotypes. If representation is connected to the stories we tell, then limiting the spectrum of representation also limits power. One of the integral aspects of Applied Theatre is that it centers participation by and alongside communities experiencing oppression, and subsequently, intersectionality as a functional "prism can inform connections across privilege as well as subordination to better facilitate meaningful collaboration and political action" (Cho, Crenshaw, & McCall, 2013, p. 803). When consciously used, Applied Theatre and Theatre of the Oppressed can employ a praxis approach of intersectionality to "excavate and expose the multilayered structures of power and domination" and "engage the conditions that shape and influence the interpretive lenses through which knowledge is produced and disseminated" (Cho, Crenshaw, & McCall, 2013, p. 804). Performance, in this way, is an avenue for contemplating and discerning transformative alternatives to interpersonal and systematic harm which take into account the fullness and wholeness of peoples' experiences.

There is considerable care and attention necessary with tending to how stories are told and presented within the aesthetic space. One must be cautious in sensationalizing the trauma of the oppressed or marginalized. Applied Theatre works to expose injustice without contributing to its continuation or glorification. As such, there is great responsibility in the depiction and construction of stories directed at freedom. Performance, as a social and political practice, challenges the reproduction of our time, promoting reflexive and dialogic democracy sensitive to "ethics and representation," rather than perpetuating singular narratives reinforcing a stagnant, monolithic, autocratic voice (Madison, 2011, p. 4). Applied Theatre humanizes humanity by leveraging nuanced representations of culturally non-dominant groups. Applied Theatre functions as a living and breathing critique and commentary upon lived experience for the express purpose of disrupting and shifting hegemonic status quo. When and if faced with portrayals of clichés, communities can reflect upon their personal experiences of privilege and disadvantage to question what the performance reveals about systemic oppression.

Dialogue invites communities to build coalitions across differences. Theatre of the Oppressed works to restore such egalitarian dialogue through art as a social and political practice. As the journalist, historian, and Marxist intellectual, Vijay Prashad (2017) claims, "Perhaps the antidote to cynicism is to retain faith in the capacity of human beings to overcome the present. For this it is important to treat the people that one interviews not merely as repositories of information, but also as reservoirs of hope and anticipation" (2017, para. 6). Applied Theatre challenges the notion that the oppressed are non-agents resigned to their place. Instead, ordinary people are capable of extraordinary action by decentralizing power, centering relationships and acknowledging how all are producers of knowledge (Prashad, 2017; Freire 1998). Consistent among antiracist pedagogy and Applied Theatre is the "conviction that change is possible" and that one's "role in the world, is not restricted to a process of only observing what happens but it also involves [one's] intervention as a subject of what happens in the world" (Freire, 1998, p. 72–73). Applied Theatre actively seeks to listen and learn from communities, highlighting their stories of resistance and civic courage to "produce a confident community of struggle" through the lens of theatrical discourse and activism (Prashad, 2017, para. 2). Therefore, Applied Theatre and Theatre of the Oppressed serve as an artistic and dialogic nexus encouraging people to feel, then fight.

Re-Imagine

Dreams are renewed.

"Theatre allows us to converse with our souls—to passionately pursue and discover ways of living with ourselves and others. We are all artists, and theatre is a language. We have no better way to work together, to learn about each other, to heal, and to grow" (Rohd, 1998, p. xix). Applied Theatre seeks to cultivate empathy by re-imagining and re-defining the human experience, and as a result, relationships are transformed. These practices engage diverse communities in ideological struggles which are deeply universal and personal. Theatre of the Oppressed and Applied Theatre are dependent upon the peoples' willingness to continuously re-make and re-shape the world as a means for decolonizing and dismantling systems of oppression. People are brought into the struggle and into the creation; they play a role through performance that is embodied, visceral, and experiential. Applied Theatre requires participatory action, demanding all parties to be driven by a curiosity to critically question the presentation of current realities. This practice is a "rehearsal for revolution," where a reflexive, unfinished, and unpolished performance is designed for contemplation, strategizing, and action. Within the classroom and beyond, Applied Theatre is more than a series of theater games; rather, it is an application of principles and techniques which bridge into the everyday lived experiences of peoples' personal and professional lives as battlegrounds for justice. Students of color who have taken Applied Theatre classes speak to how the techniques gave them permission to "live in [their] entirety" and to "embrace [their] wholeness." Former Applied Theatre students have referred to the classes as "validating," "cultivating and refining what is already inside of [them]," and as "sacred work." Another student of color described Applied Theatre as "uplift[ing]." With a breadth of issues widely and deeply felt among students of color, Applied Theatre can be a space to materialize social, political, and economic acts of personal transformation, collective resistance, and coalition-building.

At the beginning of each semester, all students and I undergo a community agreement process where we co-design parameters for safe, critical, and brave space. Establishing these agreements for community care provides the groundwork for which vulnerability can be cultivated. Vulnerability is instrumental in theatricalizing, actualizing, and interrogating topics of a sensitive nature. Defining community agreements dismantles power structures by building community and providing spoken expectations as to how everyone will work alongside one another. The process begins with a set of questions and students are invited to co-create the conditions of these agreements. Either by writing on post-it notes and displaying them on large sticky paper or by getting into groups and drafting a set of declarations, or by using their bodies to create a physical depiction of select community agreements, the prompts are as follows:

- Prompt 1: How do you want this space to feel so you can creatively and freely express yourself?
- Prompt 2: What specific actions can you take to attain the desired community you want to be in?
- Prompt 3: What are your expectations of others in upholding this space, including the professor?
- Prompt 4: As a community embarking on this process, what do we value?

Following this exercise, students feel emboldened in holding themselves and one another accountable, while also nurturing a space that is representative of their needs and desires. As a communal activity, students explicitly share ownership and responsibility in establishing and sustaining a collective vision which centers mutual understanding and develops relational leadership. By engaging students in this co-creative process, it sets the tone for all future endeavors to follow. If supportive parameters are in place, students can address tough and controversial experiences within the classroom environment. Even within a higher educational institution perpetrating white supremacy culture, a classroom can become a transformative space where everyone vigilantly works to identify racist policy, practices, and microaggressions. Intrinsic to antiracism, allowing for correction and reconciliation of harm is a welcome opportunity for growth and progress. With universities being risk-averse, admitting to fault can seem counterintuitive to risk management; however, all other aspirations for race conscious outcomes will fall short when a legacy of harm is not acknowledged. Students need to know that their lived experiences, their grievances, and their right to safety will not be minimized and trivialized; community agreements can lay that ground work.

As participants in Applied Theatre, students are trained to be intentional, curious, courageous, and empathetic. Community agreements define and reaffirm governing ethics, accountability, transparency, and confidentiality for everyone involved. In the Applied Theatre classroom, there is a mutual agreement that people are there because they want to make a difference. This assumption can provide reassurance to students of color as they realize they and their peers are mutual stakeholders in the work. In Applied Theatre, BIPOC students intermingle and form trusting relationships with students of privilege who care deeply about their well-being, safety, and dignity. As a result, students cultivate empathy, respect, and love for people who look nothing like them. BIPOC students describe the solidarity they felt in Applied Theatre as surpassing the educational space. They were able to expand their understanding of embodied solidarity and the role one plays as a member of multiple communities facing intersecting axes of oppression. By emphasizing antiracist pedagogy as a staple of Applied Theatre, BIPOC students feel prioritized and not as an afterthought within the educational setting.

Applied Theatre is an ecosystem with many roles and facets, including collaboration and partnership, shared leadership and responsibility, and communal envisioning. All of these aspects are symbiotic with activism and social justice. These practices develop competency and appreciation for advocacy while understanding a widespread gravity for social justice. Project-based assignments extending outside of the classroom also fosters experiential learning and localized coalition building. Applied Theatre is a diplomatic way to approach social change and a safe space to practice being an activist without consequences. A white student stated, "Through applied theatre, we can change how we think differently about problems we're facing" because all participants are stakeholders in the process. Specialized critical thinking skills acquired in Applied Theatre can be useful for all aspects of life. Applied Theatre provides a contextual and aesthetic space to analyze social structures so as to recognize and interrupt toxic environments. A Black femme student reflected on their Applied Theatre experience by saying they were able to remove themself from a harmful and discriminatory employment situation; Applied Theatre helped them "know their worth and value." As an act of resistance, this student's remembering of self-worth and embodiment of self-preservation extricated them from an oppressive work environment.

Through this embodied work, students can own their truth by knowing that their experiences are valid. Applied Theatre supports one's ability to learn in their own time and to cultivate ownership of knowledge production as a shared responsibility. More specifically, Theatre of the Oppressed is reliant upon members of culturally non-dominant groups to speak from personal experience. It is important to demonstrate personal connections as a basis for the work, however, emphasis should remain on the societal barriers/obstacles in relationship to those personal experiences. Students explore self-representation by playing characters like them or directly adjacent to them. The self-representation of actors and non-actors fosters autonomy while showcasing stories of personal relevance, resiliency, and urgency. BIPOC students shared how their understanding of the world shifted while simultaneously enduring the effects of the world; they were acutely aware of how they fit into society while experiencing and teaching through Applied Theatre. Students of color used Applied Theatre techniques as a language for expressing their anger, their hurt, their pain, their joy, their passion, and their vision for liberation. With performance as a creative modality, emotions are alchemized into stories of healing the past and dreaming for the future, all while building solidarity with those in relationship. In addition, BIPOC students stated that Applied Theatre mobilized them to form empathetic links with other non-white groups. Personal experiences are the places of which politics are regulated and embodied. By sharing experiences and building relationships with one another in dialogic practice, students witness transformative revelations among people, influencing how they will interact with the world after embodying this newfound knowledge.

Applied Theatre provides opportunities for all students to grapple with matters related to race and gender, alongside various socialized identities. As a theatrical means of analyzing complex intersectional issues, Applied Theatre explicitly names systems of oppression, questions power dynamics, and deconstructs deficit-centered narratives of minoritized people. There is concentrated focus on shaping collective strategy and refining collective knowledge through Applied Theatre performance. It activates a communal desire for creative and innovative ideas to address the material conditions of structural (in)justice on display. As such, one sees themself in and through the work and is able to know more of oneself. White students and students of color gain a deeper understanding in connection to institutional power so as to not feel alienated and disempowered by their positionality within this dynamic.

However, there are considerations for Applied Theatre practice. When specifically working alongside BIPOC students, Queer-identifying students, immigrant students, and disabled students, educators should be cognizant of the risks of trauma-inducing experiences through these practices. As an example, when a student proclaims a statement such as, "It's not just me," the sentiment can reflect an affirmation of community, but may also forge trauma bonding. Trauma bonding could develop through the persistent reinforcement of dangerous, exploitative, or shameful narratives as defining a group of people. Applied Theatre practices need to be healing-centered and trauma-informed so as to offer permission and space for healing as crucial to the work. The process of sharing personal experiences may invite cognitive dissociation as a way of coping with traumatization. BIPOC students may be undergoing trauma while displaying at the same time. It may be conducive and proactive to have counseling resources available and crisis intervention specialists on hand to support an extended community of care for students. Applied Theatre should not be produced to the detriment of self-care and community care. Whether implicitly or explicitly expressed, stewarding collective care is integral to having sustained and deep impact. Healing is a benefit resulting from the work. Within the aesthetic space, there is a layer of protection, through the performative elements, which distance and alleviate some of the emotional labor involved theatrical process. The theatrical process has a compounded nature where it is emotionally taxing while also cathartic and therapeutic. Although Applied Theatre and Theatre of the Oppressed can address racialized harm, it is vital to remember that these practices are to be liberatory-centered so that one can find release and joy in the work. Having rigorous fun and pleasure, while fighting for justice, motivates people to want to show up for the revolution. When done with care and awareness, Applied Theatre can prepare and equip minoritized communities for survival and visions of joy.

Act

Manifest all dreams.
Applied Theatre is an aesthetic space where people live outside of

regulation and can speak for themselves. Furthermore, Applied Theatre belongs with, interacts with, and is interdependent with social justice and activism. Applied Theatre is an effective pedagogical means for unlearning racist ideology and supports racially marginalized students in becoming storytellers and knowledge producers, stewarding a re-imagined reality of their collective making. Ganz (2013) asserts, "By telling personal stories of challenges we have faced, choices we have made, and what we learned from the outcomes, we become more mindful of our own moral resources and, at the same time, share our wisdom so as to inspire others. Because stories enable us to communicate our values not as abstract principles, but as lived experience, they have the power to move others." Applied Theatre generates stories which challenge dominant narratives, amplify silenced or marginalized voices in order to challenge status quo, combat apathy or complacency, and further social efficacy.

The process of Applied Theatre begs people to re-imagine liberation and freedom while also unlearning the impacts of socialization and inter-nalized oppression which resigns minoritized people to disenfranchise-ment. Eve Tuck (2009) calls for merging community survival alongside resistance in a desire-based framework, cautioning people to "consider the long-term repercussions of *thinking of ourselves as broken.*" Communities can fixate on damage-centered examination. Oftentimes, there is an immo-bilizing focus on the oppression which counteractively relegates communi-ties to persistent suffering, while subsequently negating or overlooking the liberation communities so desperately desire. Tuck (2009) inspires educa-tors to highlight survival and resistance as vital in moving away from dehu-manization and closer towards re-humanization. As such, Applied Theatre can restore dignity and power to the people through enacting desire-based theatricalization.

Arts-based practices, Theatre of the Oppressed, and Applied The-atre mobilize performance and collective action as a tool for re-imagining racial liberation. In order to re-imagine racial liberation, students and educators must integrate antiracism as a personal practice. To such means, Applied Theatre is a modality for cross-examining and contextualizing socially normalized ideologies, such as whiteness as a social project and gender as a social construct. Below is a sampling of two poplar Theatre of the Oppressed exercises which use imagery as an opportunity to analyze, critique, and personify racially conscious knowledge production.

Machine of Rhythms

Making a circle, one person enters the circle and begins a sound and movement with their own body that is representative of their interpretation of a given theme. Other students add onto the original person's sound and movement by creating their own sound and movement in relationship. As more people enter, collectively, the students create a rhythmic machine which brings a given theme to life. The machine of rhythms then turns into a combined, connected, responsive, ebbing and flowing live machine.

- Themes: select from an array of large-scale to small-scale themes such as freedom, education, politics, democracy, justice, race relations, etc.
- Freeze the machine at a certain point and have someone step outside the frozen image to discuss what they see, subjectively and objectively.
- Sample movements: dancing to express freedom; standing upright and gesturing with a hand to represent politics.

Complete the Image

Getting into groups of three, two people start with a frozen handshake. A third person taps someone out to replace them and moves into a new image in relationship to the other partner who is still frozen in their original image. The students continue the process, one by one, by tapping one another out and replacing themselves with an embodiment of a new image.

- Themes: select from an array of themes such as power, race, obstacles, liberation, etc.
- Freeze images and have students "dynamize" their images by adding on repetitive movement and sound into the image bringing them more to life.
- Sample images: handshake; hug; talking while walking in the park; begging for money—all images represent a multiplicity of literal, allegorical, and metaphorical connections to a given theme.

Each of the aforementioned techniques use artistic practice as a means for analyzing an existing reality and imagining a possible future. As students examine their affiliations with the imagery presented through the games, they reflect upon the images' significance and resonance by analyzing societal and personal context. By seeing the problem, one can experience the problem and is more apt to take action in addressing the problem. As Charlene Carruthers (2018) proclaims, "I hope it shakes you, agitates you, and leaves you uncomfortable enough to take revolutionary action for the sake of our collective liberation" (p. XVIII). It is this process of meaning-making for which the basis of action is derived.

Participation, aesthetics, and ethics are building blocks for how

Applied Theatre is evaluated. Boal (2006) states, "We should be clear about the fact that the Aesthetic Process is not the Work of Art. Its importance and its value reside in its stimulation and development of perceptive and creative capacities which may be atrophied in the subject—in developing the capacity, however small it may be, that every subject has for metaphorizing reality. We are all artists, but few of us exercise our aesthetic capacities" (p. 18). The full aesthetic impact of a performance lies not with the product itself, but rather with the generative aliveness of the Applied Theatre process in forging connections among actors, spect-actors, community members, and stakeholders. Therefore, Applied Theatre is active—it is a verb and it is a method through which people experience something together.

In Applied Theatre, students are evaluated in their emergent competency in areas such as improvisation, scripting, playbuilding, collaboration, devised theater, ethical community engagement, and group facilitation. Each of these aspects is demonstrated in response to a given or chosen objective. The nature of the specific project will inform the criteria necessary, however, as a baseline for assessment, the following areas are generally considered:

- "The degree and quality of participation
- The rhythm, form, pace and structuring (aesthetics)
- The risks, trust, sharing and caring of participants (ethics)" (Prendergast & Saxton, 2009, p. 196).

Reflective assignments which engage the student to undertake intrapersonal and interpersonal discovery are an effective means of holistic assessment. Through personal and collective reflection accompanied by mutual constructive criticism, students are able to evaluate their strengths, consider their opportunities for growth, and—most importantly—examine the impact experiential learning has had upon their relationship to the world in which they live.

Applied Theatre motivates people through emotional and embodied response and operationalizes their potential into collective action. It is theater of the people, by the people, and for the people. Applied Theatre integrates fundamental principles of critical inquiry, active participation, capacity building, social and political interrogation, and collective imagination for a vision of a better tomorrow. Such practices enlist society to be re-envisioned, re-invigorated, and re-imagined through performance, activism, and communal action. Racially minoritized students and white students are able to intercede in the aesthetic space to mutually re-shape societal barriers towards liberation. In doing so, minoritized voices assert their interventional power by means of collective making. Applied Theatre supports minoritized bodies to create conditions based in anti-racist, anti-oppressive, and liberatory capacity within and beyond the classroom; so, the power people create is the power people activate.

REFERENCES

Boal, A. (2002). *Games for actors and non-actors. Second edition.* Routledge.

Boal, A. (1979). *Theatre of the oppressed.* Theatre Communications Group.

Boal, A. (2006). *The aesthetics of the oppressed* (A. Jackson, Trans.). London: Routledge.

Carruthers, C. (2018) *Unapologetic: A Black, queer, and feminist mandate for radical movements.* Beacon Press.

Cho, S., Crenshaw, K., & McCall, L. (2013). Toward a field of intersectionality studies: Theory, applications, and praxis. *Signs,38*(4), 785–810. doi:10.1086/669608.

Freire, Paulo. (1998). *Pedagogy of freedom ethics, democracy, and civic courage.* Rowan & Littlefield.

Ganz, M. (2013). *Public narrative worksheet.* Kennedy School of Government. http://marshallganz.usmblogs.com/files/2012/08/Public-Narrative-Worksheet-Fall-2013-.pdf.

hooks, b. (2003). *Teaching community: A pedagogy of hope.* Routledge.

Jeannotte, S. (2003). Singing alone? The contribution of cultural capital to social cohesion and sustainable communities. *The International Journal of Cultural Policy, 9*(1) 35–49. https://www.researchgate.net/publication/228499276_Singing_Alone_The_Contribution_of_Cultural_Capital_to_Social_Cohesion_and_Sustainable_Communities.

Jeung, R., Yellow Horse, A., Popovic, T., & Lim, R. (2021, March 16). *Stop AAPI Hate national report.* Stop AAPI Hate. https://stopaapihate.org/reports/.

Kendi, I. (2019). *How to be an antiracist.* One World.

National Endowment for the Arts. (2007). *The arts and civic engagement: Involved in arts, involved in life.* National Endowment for the Arts. https://www.arts.gov/sites/default/files/CivicEngagement.pdf.

Prashad, V. & Nowak, M. (2017, September 26). Writing while socialist. *Boston Review.* http://bostonreview.net/global-justice/vijay-prashad-mark-nowak-writing-while-socialist.

Prendergast, M., & Saxton, J. (2009). *Applied theatre: International case studies and challenges for practice.* Intellect.

Ritchie, B. (2012). *Arrested justice: Black women, violence, and America's prison nation.* New York University Press.

Rohd, M. (1998). *Theatre for community, conflict and dialogue. The Hope is Vital training manual.* Heinemann.

Tuck, E. (2009). Suspending damage: A letter to communities. *Harvard Educational Review, 79*(3), 409–427.

Samuels, D. (2014). *The culturally inclusive educator. Preparing for a multicultural world.* Teachers College Press.

About the Contributors

N.J. **Akbar** is the associate vice president of diversity, equity and inclusion at Kent State University. As AVP, he serves as the senior deputy to the chief diversity officer responsible for assisting with campus climate, strategic planning, assessment, research and student success for the institution. Additionally, he serves as vice president of the Board of Education in Akron, Ohio. In that role, he authored the resolution declaring racism a public health crisis, which has since been replicated by several districts and co-authored the racial equity policy.

Jennifer D. **Banks** is the mathematics and science coordinator for Washtenaw Intermediate School District. For nearly 20 years, she has served as a teacher and instructional leader. She is passionate about empowering educators, to ensure that all students have equitable access and opportunities to learn and engage in high-quality rigorous mathematics. She has intently worked to expand K–12 educators' understanding of culturally responsive instruction, specifically in the area of mathematics.

Heather **Bennett** assists public school boards and districts with equity focused tools, programming and research. Her scholarship and practice focus on the intersection of education, law, and policy, primarily focusing on the impact of school and housing policies on the educational experiences and opportunities of marginalized students, families, and communities. A former high school social studies teacher, she also obtained her juris doctorate from Penn State, Dickinson School of Law and is licensed to practice law in New Jersey and Pennsylvania.

Ling-Se **Chesnakas** is in her fourteenth year of teaching humanities in the Boston Public Schools. She serves on two advisory boards: the Boston Writing Project and the nonprofit art organization Contemporary Arts International. She has also presented her work with the Right Question Project on using the Question Formulation Technique at various conferences. Her academic accomplishments include a B.A. in English from George Washington University and a M.Ed. from Boston College.

Dominique **Herard** is a first-grade public school teacher in Brookline, Massachusetts. She has taught first grade for ten years and is an educator strongly committed to social justice and educational equity. She is also co-leader of her school's equity team, bringing professional development opportunities to teachers to discuss how racial equity impacts academic and personal growth for both teachers and students. She is the associate director of the Boston Writing Project, a professional development network which allows teachers to teach each other.

Léa **Herbert** is licensed as a National Certified Counselor and a Licensed Clinical Mental Health Counselor. She serves as a member of the AADA-AMCD Partner Task Force Committee and is a National Holmes Scholar and research lead and is also a Social Emotional Learning Cadre Consultant. Her research scholarship focuses on psychotherapy de-stigmatization and psychological wellness, with special emphasis on telehealth, young adult socioemotional health, mental health justice and social media ethics and advocacy.

Patrice W. Glenn **Jones** serves as an assistant professor of English at Embry-Riddle Aeronautical University Worldwide and is the executive director of Online Education and Programs at Alabama State University. She holds a Ph.D. in educational leadership from Florida A&M University, a specialist degree in information science and learning technology from University of Missouri–Columbia, and a master's degree in English from University of North Florida. Her interests include factors that impact Black American student achievement, learning in virtual ecologies, and positive psychology.

Christie **Magoulias** is an associate professor at the University of Illinois at Springfield. She serves as chair of the Department of Educational Leadership. She worked as a 4th grade teacher and instructional specialist in public education. Her career also included professorship in undergraduate and graduate education programs and director of the School of Education at Millikin University. She also serves as the president of the Rochester School District in Rochester, Illinois.

Jennifer L. **Martin** is an assistant professor in the Department of Teacher Education at the University of Illinois at Springfield. She is the editor of *Racial Battle Fatigue: Insights from the Front Lines of Social Justice Advocacy* (Recipient of the 2016 AERA Division B's Outstanding Book Recognition Award). She is the 2019 recipient of the Paula Silver Case Award for Volume Year 2018, *UCEA Journal of Cases in Educational Leadership* (Volume 21) for "The Bathroom Case: Creating a Supportive School Environment for Transgender and Gender Non-conforming Students."

Amanda **Masterpaul** is a lecturer in women's and gender studies and Theatre of the Oppressed practitioner. As an applied theatre artist and educator, Amanda is committed to radical pedagogy, intersectional feminism, and civic artistry. Throughout her career, she has organized alongside community-centered efforts in areas such as gender equity, LGBTQ+ia equality, housing insecurity, and systemic racism.

Tressa D. **Matthews** is the director of academic affairs for a private school in metro Detroit. She has been teaching math to middle and high school students for 18 years. She has a bachelor's in industrial and operations engineering from the University of Michigan. After two years in corporate America, she decided to pursue her passion for secondary mathematics and earned a master's and doctorate in education. Her doctorate research focused on creating supportive classroom environments for African American students to close the graduation gap.

Todd M. **Mealy**, Ph.D., is an adjunct professor in the History Department at Dickinson College and the founder of the Equity Institute for Race Conscious

Pedagogy. For over 20 years, he has taught at high schools in Central Pennsylvania. He is a regular contributor to *Pennsylvania* and has authored seven books, including *Race Conscious Pedagogy: Disrupting Racism at Majority White Schools* (2020) and *This Is the Rat Speaking: Black Power and the Promise of Race Consciousness at Franklin and Marshall College.*

Ted **Nelson**, MSW, earned his master's in social work from Southern University at New Orleans. He has experience in mental and behavioral health counseling, specializing in working with children, youth, and families utilizing executive functional therapy, dialectical behavioral therapy, and cognitive-behavioral therapy. He is a member of the National Association of Black Social Workers and the National Association of Social Workers (NASW).

Connor Towne **O'Neill** is the author of *Down Along with That Devil's Bones: A Reckoning with Monuments, Memory, and the Legacy of White Supremacy.* His writing has appeared in *New York* magazine, *Vulture, Slate,* and elsewhere, and he works as a producer for the NPR podcast *White Lies,* a finalist for the 2020 Pulitzer Prize in Audio Reporting. He teaches at Auburn University and with the Alabama Prison Arts and Education Project.

Tinisha **Parker** spent seven years supporting school counselors in a large district directly as the Director of Advisement and Counseling before transitioning to the Executive Director of Student Services. In this role, she supports school counselors, social workers, and school nurses in addition to several student service programs including homeless, foster care and the career academy programs. She is also the chair of the board for the American School Counselor Association and CEO of Total Perspective Consulting, LLC.

Candace **Pelt**, Ed.D., serves as the assistant superintendent for Central Linn School District in Halsey, Oregon. Previously, she served as Oregon's state director for special education, as an LEA special education and elementary education director, as a school principal, and as a general education teacher at the elementary, middle, and high school levels. Her passion is building educational systems that recognize the assets of all students as the foundation for ensuring an excellent education for all.

Ebony L. **Perro**, Ph.D., is a professor of practice in English at Tulane University, where she teaches first-year writing and honors courses. She earned a Ph.D. in humanities with concentrations in Africana women's studies and English from Clark Atlanta University. Her research and teaching interests include Black girlhood, Black rage, youth activism, and 20th and 21st-century Black women's literature. She is also working on a monograph, *Arcs of Anger: Black Girl Rage in Contemporary Black Women's Literature.*

Lindsey M. **Pike**, MSW, is a Ph.D. scholar and graduate research associate in the Exceptional Student Education Program at the University of Central Florida. She has over seven years of experience working in public schools as both a social worker and a special education teacher. She also served as a youth and family therapist for three years, providing services to children and families with a variety of backgrounds and needs.

Dayle **Rebelsky** is a graduate student at the University of Illinois at Springfield in the Human Development Counseling program. She also serves as a graduate assistant for the Department of Educational Leadership. Her undergraduate work included a psychology major and a sociology minor with a background in research. Her research interests include autism, ADHD, and multiculturalism.

Kevin A. **Rolle** is the chief of staff at Alabama State University. He holds a Ph.D. in education and human resources studies, with a concentration in educational administration and student affairs personnel from Colorado State University, as well as advanced studies in public administration and a master's degree in leisure and recreational studies from Southern University and A&M College. He is a former American Council on Education Fellow whose research interests include executive educational leadership, student success, policy implementation, and process improvement.

Monique S. **Ross**, Ph.D., assistant professor in the Knight Foundation School of Computing and Information Sciences and STEM Transformation Institute at Florida International University. She is a computer science education researcher with a focus on broadening participation in computer science and engineering in women and minorities. She has been awarded the prestigious NSF CAREER award to explore the experiences of Black and Hispanic women in computing.

Marsha L. **Rutledge** is an assistant professor in the Counselor Education program at Longwood University. She is a former Professional School Counselor with 18 years school counseling experience. She is an active member of the Virginia School Counselor Association where she has served in many capacities, including as the chair of the communications and public relations committee. She serves on the diversity, equity, and inclusion committee with the American School Counselor Association and as the chair of the antiracism committee.

Dena D. **Slanda** is a research associate in the College of Community Innovation and Education and serves as the education doctoral program advisor in exceptional student education at the University of Central Florida. She is a co-principal investigator or project coordinator for federal grants for research and personnel/leadership development. She is a published author and has conducted numerous conference presentations focused on culturally proactive pedagogy and practices, equitable educational opportunities, and inclusive practices among other topics.

Aaron **Teo** is a doctoral candidate in the School of Education at the University of Queensland, Australia, and a high school business and legal studies teacher at a Brisbane-based Independent School. He is an executive member of the Business Educators' Association of Queensland and is closely involved with the Queensland Curriculum and Assessment Authority as Legal Studies External Exam Marker and General Business Confirmer. His research focuses on the subjectivities of pre-service and beginning teachers from Asian backgrounds in the Australian context.

Lisette E. **Torres** is a trained scientist and disabled scholar-activist whose expertise includes race, gender, and disability in STEM and higher education; critical theoretical frameworks and qualitative methodologies; workshop and curriculum design; and writing pedagogy. She has a doctorate with a certificate in social justice from the School of Education at Iowa State University and a M.S. in zoology with a certificate in ecology from Miami University. She is also a co-founder and executive board member of the National Coalition for Latinxs with Disabilities (CNLD).

Eric B. **Wells** serves the Oregon Department of Education as the director for IDEA Part B (School Age Special Education). His work focuses on building systems to support the full implementation of IDEA in a manner that promotes equity, inclusion, and results for all students—especially those who experience disability. Academically, he is interested in effective leadership within special education, with his dissertation having focused on the experience of school leaders who promote high levels of achievement for students experiencing disability.

Index